Coming Up Short

COMING UP SHORT

The Challenge of 401(k) Plans

Alicia H. Munnell

Annika Sundén

BROOKINGS INSTITUTION PRESS
Washington, D.C.

Copyright © 2004
THE BROOKINGS INSTITUTION
1775 Massachusetts Avenue, N.W., Washington, D.C. 20036
www.brookings.edu

Library of Congress Cataloging-in-Publication data

Munnell, Alicia Haydock.
    Coming up short : the challenge of 401(k) plans / Alicia H. Munnell and Annika Sundén.
        p.   cm.
Includes bibliographical references and index.
    ISBN 0-8157-5888-X (cloth : alk. paper)
    1. 401(k) plans.   2. Pension trusts—United States.   3. Defined contribution pension plans—United States.   4. Old age pensions—United States.
5. Retirement income—United States—Planning.   I. Sunden, Annika E.   II. Title.
    HD7105.45.U6M86   2004
    331.25'2—dc22   2003026256

9 8 7 6 5 4 3 2 1

The paper used in this publication meets minimum requirements of the American National Standard for Information Sciences—Permanence of Paper for Printed Library Materials: ANSI Z39.48-1992.

Typeset in Adobe Garamond

Composition by Betsy Kulamer
Washington, D.C.

Printed by R. R. Donnelley
Harrisonburg, Virginia

Contents

Acknowledgments

The authors would like to thank the Smith Richardson Foundation for its generous support of the project that led to this book. We suspect that the future of 401(k) plans has become even more important than originally anticipated by either the authors or the foundation. We hope that this book makes the 401(k) a more effective source of retirement income for the nation.

The authors would also like to thank the many undergraduate and graduate research assistants who helped bring this project to completion. Marta Capasso, Sheila Campbell, Madhavi Deschmuk, and Matthew Riordan all made significant contributions to developing the original study. Jamie Lee, Kristen Richard, and Greg Wiles did a wonderful job on revisions under the able leadership of Kevin Meme, whose role far exceeded that of a research assistant. One graduate student in particular deserves special thanks: Mauricio Soto produced the simulations used throughout the study, trained other students in using the Survey of Consumer Finances and the Health and Retirement Study, and served as a sounding board for our ideas throughout the project. He should be considered a coconspirator. We were also lucky to have Steve Sass edit the final draft of the study.

Finally, thanks go to our friends and colleagues who generously gave their time to read and comment on the first draft of this book. Their comments were invaluable. Our readers include Ken Bombara, Jeffrey Brown, Din Cahill, Peter Diamond, Karen Ferguson, William Gale, Peter Orszag, Patrick Purcell, Daniel Halperin, Vincent O'Reilly, Dallas Salisbury, Eric Sondergeld and his colleagues at LIMRA, Sylvester Schieber, and Jack VanDerhei. We are also grateful to our colleagues at the Center for Retirement Research at Boston College—Kevin Cahill, Amy Chasse, Andy Eschtruth, Lisa Gentile, and Elizabeth Lidstone—who have contributed in a myriad of ways.

At Brookings Institution Press, Christopher Kelaher shepherded the book through its routine; Diane Hammond edited the manuscript expertly, while Carlotta Ribar proofed the pages with care, and Sherry Smith provided a timely index.

COMING UP SHORT

1

Introduction

Even before the collapse of Enron, the protracted bear market, and the mutual fund scandals, questions about how to provide people with an adequate retirement income were high on the national policy agenda. The number of Americans over age sixty-five will double by 2030. With a life expectancy at age sixty-five of roughly twenty years, these individuals will spend more time in retirement than individuals before them. To ensure that today's workers will have a secure retirement, we need to understand what sources of income retirees have available now and what they are likely to have in the future.

The public debate about retirement income has focused on the future of Social Security, the basic tier in the U.S. retirement system. The second tier, employer-sponsored pensions, has received considerably less attention. These programs, however, are a crucial source of retirement income for middle-income families. This book explores the fastest-growing type of employer-sponsored pension, namely 401(k) plans. These plans merit serious attention in their own right, as 58 percent of households with pension coverage rely solely on 401(k)s and similar plans to supplement Social Security.[1] Yet the median combined balance of a 401(k) and an individ-

1. According to the Federal Reserve Board's *2001 Survey of Consumer Finances,* 58 percent of households in 2001 covered by a pension had only a defined contri-

1

ual retirement account (IRA) for household heads in their late forties and early fifties is only $37,000. In addition, some troublesome features of 401(k)s and defined contribution plans generally, such as lump-sum distributions upon job change and at retirement, are increasingly common in the rest of the pension system.

The emergence of 401(k) plans is a phenomenon of the last twenty or so years.[2] In 1980 most workers covered by a pension had a defined benefit plan. These plans typically provide employees lifelong monthly retirement benefits based on years of service and final salary. For employees who remain with one firm throughout their working lives, defined benefit plans can offer a predictable and substantial stream of monthly benefits. Mobile employees, however, forfeit some pension income when they change employers.

From the employer's perspective, defined benefit plans help manage the work force by encouraging longer tenure and efficient retirement.[3] Since pension benefits based on final earnings increase rapidly as job tenures lengthen, these plans motivate workers to remain with the firm. Defined benefit plans also encourage workers to retire when their productivity begins to decline.[4] But for employers, these plans also have two disadvantages: exposure to financial market risk and lack of employee turnover even when desired.

For a variety of reasons, the nature of pension coverage has changed. It has become a 401(k) world. The 401(k) plan is essentially a savings account. The employee and, most often, the employer contribute a percentage of earnings into the account. These contributions are invested, generally at the direction of the employee, mostly in mutual funds of stocks and bonds. When the worker retires, the balance in the account determines the retirement benefit, which is almost always paid in a lump sum.

It is easy to understand the popularity of 401(k) plans. They are portable, which means that mobile workers can take their balances with them. Employ-

---

bution plan, 23 percent had both a defined benefit and a defined contribution plan, and 19 percent had only a defined benefit plan. The comparable numbers for individuals in 1998 derived from form 5500, which companies are required to file with the Department of Labor, are 55 percent, 31 percent, and 14 percent. Form 5500 also indicates that 74 percent of those covered by a defined contribution plan were in a 401(k) plan. If this percentage held true in 2001 and applied to households as well as individuals, it would imply that 43 percent (58 × .74) of households with pensions were covered by only a 401(k) plan.

2. The Revenue Act of 1978 included provisions that allowed explicit salary reduction, a key feature of 401(k) plans, but only after the IRS issued clarifying regulations in 1981 did the 401(k) become popular.

3. Lazear (1979, 1983).

4. Considerable work has been done to document the impact of incentives to retire in defined benefit plans: Samwick (1998); Stock and Wise (1990a, 1990b); Kotlikoff and Wise (1987, 1989); Fields and Mitchell (1984).

ees get statements several times a year, and many have daily access to pension benefit data through the World Wide Web, which makes their benefits seem more tangible. As the plans allow employees to choose investments that match their tolerance for risk, it also gives them a sense of control over their retirement funds. Rapidly rising account balances greatly enhanced the popularity of these plans during the stock market boom of the 1990s. With the sharp decline in the stock market that began in 2000, workers may have become somewhat less enthusiastic about investing their own retirement funds.

Employers also like 401(k)s. These plans are a tangible benefit, which employees appreciate. Employers can use 401(k) plans to attract workers who value saving and who, some economists argue, are presumably more conscientious and productive.[5] And employers' contributions are controllable and do not hinge on stock market and interest rate swings. This means that when the stock market plummets, the employee, not the employer, loses money. And when interest rates fall, rather than the employer paying more for an annuity, the employee realizes a lower retirement income. Moreover, 401(k) plans are fully funded by definition, eliminating the work and expense associated with funding requirements and pension insurance. Generally, they are also less costly for the employer to administer than defined benefit plans.[6]

In view of their appeal to both employees and employers, 401(k)s and similar defined contribution plans are now the dominant form of private pensions in the United States. Of those with pension coverage, 58 percent of households now rely exclusively on 401(k) or similar defined contribution plans; another 23 percent have a defined benefit plan in addition to a defined contribution plan; and only 19 percent rely solely on a defined benefit plan. The shift in pension coverage occurred primarily through the stagnation of defined benefit plans and the establishment of 401(k)s; defined benefit plans were rarely converted to 401(k)s. Many defined benefit plans are starting to

---

5. Ippolito (1998).

6. Of course, another factor is that in 401(k) plans the bulk of contributions come from employees rather than from employers, as is the case for defined benefit plans. The question is whether the shift in the party making the contribution actually represents a shift in burden. Economists would argue that employers decide on the total compensation they must pay their employees and divide that amount between cash wages and fringe benefits. Providing a pension benefit thus implies a cut in wages or a reduction in other benefits, and vice versa. If the economists are correct, similarly situated employees covered by 401(k) plans should have higher (pre-contribution) cash wages than those covered by defined benefit plans. In this case, the fact that the employee makes the payment does not imply an increased burden. The other hypothesis is that global competition has put downward pressure on wages in the United States and that employers have used the shift in coverage to 401(k) plans as a mechanism to slow wage growth. No empirical work has been done to sort out this issue. The discussion in this volume is based on the conventional economic view of a trade-off between pensions and cash wages.

look like 401(k)s, however, through conversions to cash balance plans or some other hybrid form. Although 401(k) and similar plans emerged only in 1981, they will determine the economic security of a significant portion of the baby boom generation. To set the stage for the discussion of 401(k) plans, the next two sections put 401(k)s in perspective by reviewing the evolution of private pension plans and the regulations that govern them.

The Origins of Section 401(k)

The Internal Revenue Code (IRC) treats employer-sponsored benefits more favorably than benefits that individual employees purchase on their own.[7] The rationale is that benefits provided by the employer will be broadly distributed, particularly to lower paid employees who are unlikely to respond to tax incentives. This treatment puts employers in a bind. On the one hand, providing the benefit to all employees lowers costs because of favorable tax treatment. On the other hand, universal provision means that benefits go to some employees who do not value them. Therefore, employers have an incentive to fit their compensation program to their employees' needs but to disguise employee choice in order to retain the tax advantage. (Giving employees choice risks running afoul of the doctrine of constructive receipt.)

If employees can opt for cash, the Internal Revenue Service (IRS) could say that they "constructively received" the cash, and the contribution to the plan would then be subject to tax. In the 1950s several employers offered employees a choice between receiving a year-end bonus and having the same amount deposited in a tax-favored plan. The IRS was asked to determine whether such an option affected a plan's tax status. In 1956 the IRS approved a profit-sharing plan that offered choice, thus indicating that elective contributions were not inconsistent with qualified plan status. Later rulings suggest that the IRS did not view constructive receipt as a problem in the 1956 case because the election of cash had to be made during the year before the actual amount of the bonus was known. This view, however, was somewhat at odds with the treatment of other arrangements. So tax experts were not surprised when the IRS, in 1972, proposed regulations to tax those amounts that employees could choose to receive in cash even if they were ultimately contributed to a plan.

Congress appeared supportive of the 1972 regulation. But in passing the Employee Retirement Income Security Act (ERISA) in 1974 it delayed its implementation for previously existing arrangements until January 1977 and

7. The following discussion is based on Halperin (1983); EBRI (2000).

then until January 1978. In considering the Revenue Act of 1978, the House voted to extend the freeze, implicitly allowing elective contributions. The U.S. Treasury Department, however, wanted a more permanent solution.

Section 401(k) of the IRC was the compromise. Section 401(k) says that if plans with elective contributions meet a special nondiscrimination test—so that excessive benefits do not go to the higher paid employees—then constructive receipt does not apply. The need for broad participation explains why matching contributions are a common feature of 401(k) plans. To ensure that the funds are retained until retirement, section 401(k) also prohibits distributions before age fifty-nine-and-a-half or separation from employment (including death and disability), except in the case of hardship.

The law went into effect in January 1980. In 1981 the IRS issued proposed regulations that sanctioned the use of employee salary reduction for retirement plan contributions. And the rest is history.

401(k) Plans in Perspective

Pension plans are large and complex institutions. They arise naturally from real business needs, bump along on their own for a while, falter here and there, and then require some government oversight and involvement to set them right. That certainly was the case with traditional defined benefit plans.

During the last quarter of the nineteenth century, the large, prosperous, and heavily regulated transportation industry, which employed many workers in hazardous jobs, pioneered the establishment of private plans. In 1875 American Express set up the first pension plan to provide disability benefits to workers with twenty years of service. In 1880 the Baltimore and Ohio Railroad, noted for its enlightened labor policies, organized a plan based on employee contributions. In 1900 the Pennsylvania Railroad established a plan financed by the employer, which served as a model for other railways. By the end of the 1920s the railway industry had extended pension coverage to 80 percent of its workers. In addition, most large banks, utility, mining, and petroleum companies, as well as a sprinkling of manufacturers, had formal plans. While large industrial employers were establishing pension plans, a small number of trade unions were instituting their own schemes for retirement benefits. By 1928 about 40 percent of union members belonged to unions that offered some form of old age and disability benefits.

The Great Depression had a profound effect on both the industrial and union plans. Many railways were operating in the red and did not have pension reserves to help pay benefits to their retired employees. Because so many people were involved, Congress passed the Railroad Retirement Act of 1935 to nationalize the much-stressed plans. Employees covered by other industry plans were often not so fortunate. As business activity declined, many companies could not meet both operating expenses and rising pension payments. In response they made substantial cutbacks, ranging from suspending the accumulation of pension credits to trimming or even terminating the benefits of retired employees. Union plans also were affected by high unemployment, which depleted union treasuries.

After the Great Depression, industry and labor had to recreate the pension system. Although World War II consumed many of the nation's resources that might have been directed toward improved provisions for old age, wartime wage controls provided some support for the expansion of private plans. The War Labor Board, which had set legal limitations on cash wages, attempted to relieve the pressure on management and labor by permitting employers to bid for workers by offering attractive fringe benefits. Pension benefits cost firms little in view of the wartime excess profits tax and the ability to deduct pension contributions.[8]

In the immediate postwar period, employees focused on cash wages to recover ground lost during the period of wartime wage stabilization. But in 1949 pension benefits became a major issue of labor negotiation because of increased employer resistance to further wage hikes, a weak economy, and the obvious inadequacy of Social Security, which averaged only $26 a month at the time. Labor's drive for pension benefits was aided when the Supreme Court confirmed the National Labor Relations Board's 1948 ruling that employers had a legal obligation to negotiate the terms of pension plans. The United Steelworkers of America and the United Automobile Workers then launched successful drives for pension benefits, and other unions soon followed.

The main expansion of today's private pension system, then, actually began during the 1950s. Although growth continued in the 1960s, it was due primarily to expansion of employment in firms that already had pension plans as opposed to the establishment of new plans. Pension coverage continued to expand until the end of the 1970s but has been virtually stagnant since then. Currently, less than half of the private sector work force participates in a pension plan (figure 1-1); a somewhat larger percentage has some coverage at some point in their lifetime. It is definitely better to have a pension than not to have one, regardless of the strengths and weaknesses of one type versus another.

As pensions became an important institution, workers began to rely on employer-provided benefits as a major source of retirement income. Govern-

---

8. Munnell (1982); Ghilarducci (1992).

Figure 1-1. *Private Sector Workers Covered by a Pension Plan, 1940–2002*

Percent

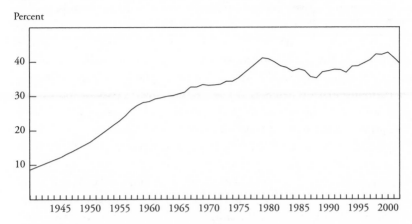

Source: Authors' calculations based on U.S. Bureau of Census, *Current Population Survey* (1978–2002); on Skolnik (1976), p. 4; and on Yohalem (1977), p. 27.

ment also had a stake in the pension system, because the favorable tax treatment accorded these plans reduces federal income tax revenue. Employer contributions to a pension plan are deductible as a business expense when made, investment income earned by pension funds is tax exempt, and the employee is not taxed until receipt of pension benefits.[9] As a result, employees pay significantly less tax on compensation received in the form of deferred pension benefits than in the form of cash wages. The cost of these favorable tax provisions is enormous. After the present value of future tax payments on benefits is deducted, the revenue loss to the Treasury Department is an estimated $172 billion for 2002.[10] This amounted to 20 percent of federal income tax revenues of $858 billion in that year and 42 percent of the $455 billion in payroll taxes collected to support the old age portion of Social Security.

The government's large tax expenditure on the employer-sponsored pension system requires that employees be treated fairly along a number of dimensions. As far back as the 1940s federal regulations insisted that tax-favored plans provide retirement benefits to the rank and file as well as to highly compensated employees. In the 1950s and 1960s it became clear that such plans had other serious problems. Some employers imposed such strin-

9. These provisions, which permit tax deferral on both contributions and the earnings on those contributions, are equivalent to exempting from taxation the earnings on the money that would have been invested after tax, assuming the employee remains in the same tax bracket.

10. http://w3.access.gpo.gov/usbudget/fy2004/pdf/spec.pdf.

gent vesting and participation standards that many workers reached retirement age only to discover that they failed to qualify for a pension because of a layoff or a merger. Even workers who satisfied their plan's requirements had no assurance that accumulated pension assets would be adequate to finance their benefits. A few pension plans were administered in a dishonest, incompetent, or irresponsible way. Managers of other plans engaged in forms of financial manipulation, such as concentrating investments in the stock of business affiliates, which—although not illegal—could jeopardize the value of the portfolio relative to a diversified portfolio.

Because of these unresolved problems, participants were often at the mercy of the sponsors. Employees covered by inadequately funded or mismanaged pension plans bore the risk of losing their pension benefits. The fate of workers in the South Bend, Indiana, automobile plant closed by Studebaker in 1964 is the best known example of substantial benefit loss. Inadequate funding left most of Studebaker's 8,500 employees with either reduced pensions or no pensions at all.[11] Repercussions from the Studebaker and similar incidents contributed to congressional interest in pension reform. After more than ten years of hearings and prolonged debate, Congress passed ERISA. Congress has not passed similar legislation for public employer plans.

ERISA's principal objective was to secure the rights of pension plan participants so that a greater proportion of covered workers would receive their accrued benefits. The legislation introduced participation and vesting standards to make it easier for workers to establish legal claims to benefits. Funding and fiduciary standards included in the law were to ensure that money would be available to pay the legal benefit claims. Despite the funding requirements, the possibility remained that some plans might terminate with inadequate assets. To protect plan participants against this contingency, ERISA also established the Pension Benefit Guaranty Corporation (PBGC), a mandatory insurance program that imposes premiums on defined benefit plans to insure workers against the loss of basic retirement benefits.

Most observers agree that ERISA has succeeded in meeting its stated objective of strengthening workers' claims on benefits. Participation and vesting standards enabled workers to establish a legal right to benefits after a

---

11. The distribution of Studebaker's $24 million of pension fund assets struck much of the public as extremely unfair. Munnell (1982); Sass (1997). The bulk ($21.5 million) went to pay the full benefits to 3,600 workers who were retired or eligible for retirement (age sixty with ten years of service). The remaining $2.5 million went to 4,080 workers who were at least forty years old with ten or more years of service. This payment equaled only 15 percent of the value of this group's accrued benefits. The final group—2,900 workers who were not vested—got nothing.

fixed time period. The implementation of funding and fiduciary standards helped to ensure that money would be available to pay these benefits. As a result of these changes, more workers covered by private sector programs receive benefits, and many get larger benefits than they would have in the absence of ERISA. Some critics contend that ERISA deprived other workers of benefits because small employers were unable or unwilling to meet the new standards and either terminated or did not create a defined benefit plan. Many of these small employers opted for 401(k) or other defined contribution plans to avoid the higher costs associated with a defined benefit plan.

Technically, ERISA's provisions applied to both defined benefit and defined contribution plans. But the main thrust of the legislation was on the defined benefit side. Defined contribution plans existed in the mid-1970s, but in large companies they generally served as supplements to defined benefit plans.[12] In small firms, defined contribution plans in the form of profit sharing or money purchase plans often served as the primary retirement income program.[13] But they covered relatively few workers. And the defined contribution plans that did exist looked different from today's 401(k) plans. Coverage was automatic, and the employer generally made the contributions and selected the investments. Investment options for employees became available only in the 1980s.

The landscape is very different today. As noted above, the 401(k) is now the dominant form of pension plan, and the majority of 401(k) participants have no additional source of retirement income other than Social Security. The defining characteristic of 401(k) plans is that they shift the risks and responsibilities associated with providing retirement income from the employer to the employee. Shifting the risk means that employees both enjoy the gains and suffer the losses of their investment decisions. In terms of responsibilities, the employee decides whether or not to participate, how much to contribute, how to invest the assets, and how to withdraw the

12. For large employers the supplements were either thrift savings plans, to which the employee contributed on an after-tax basis and the employer matched pretax contributions, or deferred profit-sharing plans, in which the contributions varied annually. The profit-sharing plans were prevalent among banks, although Kodak and Xerox were pioneers in this area. One problem with these plans was that the regulations allowed distributions after two years of accumulation. While many plans required or encouraged lower paid employees to put money in, they also allowed them to withdraw their money after two years—at the same time they were putting new money into the plan. Because the lower paid employees were not contributing any additional funds, such plans were in effect limited to higher paid employees. To ensure that the same pattern was not repeated with 401(k) plans, section 401(k) prohibits distributions before age fifty-nine-and-a-half or separation from service, except in the case of hardship.

13. The largest defined benefit plan in the country, TIAA-CREF, also served as the primary plan for people employed in higher education and the nonprofit sector.

money at retirement. In addition, most workers have access to 401(k) funds before retirement, adding another element of individual responsibility.

This shift in risk and responsibilities raises a number of significant issues during both the period when employees accumulate assets in their accounts and the period when they withdraw their funds. This book explores these issues. Its focus is on individuals and how they fare under the new employment-based pension system. By design, little attention is given to the effect of pensions on national saving, how pensions affect aggregate labor supply, or how the U.S. pension system compares to those in other countries.

Organization of the Book

The book is organized around the sequence of decisions that individuals must make with regard to their 401(k) plans: whether or not to participate, how much to contribute, how to invest the funds, what to do with accumulations when changing jobs, and how to deal with the lump-sum payment at retirement.

To set the stage for this analysis, chapter 2 explores the possible ways that the shift in coverage from defined benefit to 401(k) plans could affect future retirement income. The avenues for change include the number of people participating in plans, total pension accumulations, the distribution of risk between employee and employer, and incentives for employees to shift jobs and retire.

Given the popularity and growth of 401(k) plans, one would have thought that their introduction might have boosted pension plan coverage in the United States. But overall pension coverage has remained virtually unchanged.[14] Also unchanged is the potential for significant retirement income. Simple simulations show that potential accumulations under either a hypothetical defined benefit plan or a 401(k) plan are substantial. Similarly, participants in 401(k) plans, like their defined benefit brethren, also face the potential erosion of the purchasing power of their benefits after retirement due to inflation. A number of factors, however, have changed: 401(k) plans eliminate impediments to mobility and incentives to retire early, both positive changes. But they also shift to the employee all the investment risk and reward during the accumulation phase and the mortality and interest rate risk and reward upon retirement. On balance it is hard to tell whether workers as a group are ahead or behind because of the shift from defined benefit to 401(k)

---

14. Although the portion of the work force covered by a pension has remained unchanged, the portion of pension participants with vested benefits has increased significantly.

plans and whether particular groups are affected differently. Answering these questions requires a detailed look at each stage of the 401(k) process.

Chapter 3 looks at participation and contribution issues. Participation in a 401(k) is voluntary, and about 26 percent of those who are eligible choose not to participate.[15] Failure to participate may be rational for people under severe financial pressure. But it may also be due to shortsightedness or a lack of information. Once individuals decide to participate, they need to decide how much to contribute. Less than 10 percent of participants contribute the maximum, despite the obvious tax advantages and the possibility that their employer will make a matching contribution. One question is why contributions remain low, and another is whether the current level of contributions can ensure adequate retirement income. This chapter investigates why so many workers elect not to either participate or contribute the maximum and how various policies could increase participation and contribution rates.

The next two chapters look at investment issues. Chapter 4 addresses how successful 401(k) participants are as investors. The evidence suggests that they do not do a good job. More than half have all their money either in a no-stock or a virtually all-stock portfolio. It could be that these patterns are age appropriate: no stocks for those approaching retirement and all stocks for the young. Participants could also hold other assets outside the plan that balance their overall portfolio. But this asset allocation pattern does raise the question of whether the portfolios of 401(k) participants are adequately diversified, and the evidence is hardly reassuring. Aside from their 401(k) accounts, the average participant has little in the way of assets other than housing. Participants in 401(k) plans almost never rebalance their portfolios, as prudent financial theory suggests, either in response to a run-up in the stock market or to reduce risk as they age. It seems that investing is a complicated proposition for the vast majority of participants. This should not be surprising since the only investment decisions that most people make are in their 401(k) plan. The options for improving investment choices are either to make the investment process easier or to make all participants into investment experts.

Investment allocations look even worse once company stock—the stock of the company the investors work for—enters the picture. Chapter 5 shows

15. The discussion here and in chapter 3 focuses on participation among those eligible to participate. But not all employees are eligible. The law specifically permits an exclusion from consideration of any employees covered by a collective bargaining agreement, providing there is evidence that the retirement benefits resulted from good faith bargaining. Certain nonresident aliens and airline pilots as well as employees not meeting the minimum age and service requirements may also be excluded. VanDerhei and Olsen (2001).

that 17 percent of all 401(k) assets are invested in company stock. Nationwide, roughly 20 million participants hold more than 10 percent of their 401(k) assets in company stock. This pattern appears mostly in large plans; less than 3 percent of 401(k) plans have company stock, but these plans cover 42 percent of participants.[16]

Substantial investment in company stock flies in the face of modern financial theory, since diversifying a portfolio offers large and essentially costless gains. It is even more important to diversify investments away from one's employer. Nevertheless, both employees and employers are enthusiastic actors in the drama. Many employees are drawn to something familiar, something they know, and underestimate the risk of investing in company stock. They tend to place a lot of weight on past performance; if their company's stock has done well in the past, they assume it will do well going forward. And if they see executives getting rich, many want to get in on the action. Employers also tend to push company stock. They contend it aligns the employees' interests with that of the business and makes them more productive. And for reasons discussed in chapter 5, most employers prefer to make 401(k) matching contributions in stock rather than cash. As both employees and employers are enthusiastic about investing in company stock, changing this practice is no small problem. The challenge is to reduce employee holdings of company stock without damaging the usefulness of 401(k) plans.

After focusing on participation, contribution, and investment issues, chapter 6 turns to the question of leakages from 401(k) plans. Participants are often allowed to borrow from their accounts and to withdraw money before retirement to cover housing, medical, and other expenses. Workers also ordinarily have the option of taking a lump-sum distribution when they change jobs. (Increasingly, this has become a design feature of defined benefit plans as well.) To the extent that participants take money out of their 401(k) plan, either through borrowing and not repaying the loan or by spending distributions, they will have less income in retirement.[17]

The evidence suggests that borrowing is not a major concern but that cashing out lump-sum distributions is a serious problem. About 20 percent of the dollars from such distributions are not rolled over into an IRA or another 401(k) plan. In particular, small accumulations held by young people are typically spent. This is also true of lump-sum distributions from defined benefit plans. The result is that these individuals will have signifi-

16. VanDerhei (2002).
17. For individuals who expect their earnings to rise sharply as they age, cashing out might be optimal. But for most participants, cashing out probably represents shortsightedness about their retirement needs.

cantly smaller balances than suggested by the simple simulation discussed in chapter 2. The final way in which people can reduce the effectiveness of 401(k) accumulations is by cutting back their other saving. Here, the evidence suggests that the reductions may be more modest than those that occur in response to a defined benefit plan. Nevertheless, current and potential leakages from 401(k) plans are a significant problem.

Chapter 7 explores the final stage of the 401(k) process: figuring out what to do with accumulated funds at retirement. Unlike traditional defined benefit pensions that have only an annuity option and provide participants with steady benefits for as long as they live, 401(k) plans generally pay out lump sums. Large numbers of the new hybrid defined benefit plans also pay lump sums, raising the same issues. Since 401(k)s are still a relatively recent phenomenon and most participants are still in the work force, little research has been done on the withdrawal phase. However, these plans are maturing and millions of baby boomers are beginning to retire, and how participants use their 401(k) money will become an increasingly important issue.

Lump-sum payments mean that these retirees must decide how much to withdraw each year. In doing so, retirees run two possible risks, either consuming their nest egg too quickly and running out of money before they die or consuming it too slowly and unduly restricting their standard of living in retirement. These risks could be eliminated through the purchase of annuities, but the individual annuity market is tiny. Once people are given a pile of wealth, they want to manage and control it themselves. Nor do they appear to understand the risk of outliving their resources or the higher level of income that annuities offer. Too often they view annuities as a gamble with the insurance company, where the insurance company wins if they die early. Without annuitization, however, the baby-boom generation, which is the first to rely predominately on 401(k) plans to supplement Social Security, is going to have a difficult time in retirement. And the elimination of automatic protection for the surviving spouse suggests that poverty among elderly widows may well increase.

The concluding chapter, chapter 8, explores possible ways to reform 401(k) plans. The evidence from the previous chapters suggests that, although in theory workers could do very well under 401(k) plans, in practice they do not. Balances, even for long-service employees, are substantially less than those produced by even the most sophisticated simulations. The problem is that the entire burden is on employees, and many make mistakes at every step along the way. A significant 26 percent of those who are eligible do not participate; less than 10 percent of those who do participate contribute the maximum; over half do not diversify their investments, and almost none rebalance their portfolios in response to age or market returns; many cash out when they change jobs; and most do not annuitize at retirement. Changes are clearly needed to make 401(k) plans a more successful vehicle for providing retirement income.

One obvious answer that emerges from the study is to take advantage of participants' inertia and set the defaults in 401(k) plans to the desirable outcome. That is, all eligible participants would be automatically enrolled; their contribution would be set at the level of the employer match; their portfolio (say, at age 30) would be 70 percent stocks and 30 percent bonds and automatically rebalanced as they age; investment in company stock would be restricted; lump sums would be automatically rolled over; and retirement payments would be made in the form of a joint-and-survivor-indexed annuity. Of course, individuals could opt out at any stage. But research indicates that people tend to stay where they are put, and these defaults would put them in a much better place.[18]

The chapter also explores the broader question of changing the nature of 401(k) plans to reduce the investment and interest rate risk faced by employees. One option is some version of a cash balance plan modified to pay benefits as annuities rather than lump sums; this option would offer lower risk, albeit with lower returns than 401(k) plans. Finally, the chapter explores the implications of less certain private pension benefits within the context of the declining role of Social Security. It questions whether a new layer of retirement protection—some form of universal pension—might alleviate the pressures on 401(k) plans and provide coverage for those who have no employer-sponsored pension.

18. Choi and others (2001a, 2001b); Madrian and Shea (2002).

2

401(k) Plans and Retirement Income

The growth of 401(k) plans affects future retirement income through a variety of channels, with impacts on coverage, total resources, the distribution of risk between employer and employee, and incentives for workers to shift jobs and to retire. This chapter explores each of these channels, finding that in some cases the story is clear, in other cases it is not. For example, 401(k) plans definitely eliminate the impediments to labor mobility and incentives to retire at a particular age commonly found in traditional defined benefit plans. These plans also expose employees to new participation and contribution decisions and financial risk, which they do not bear in traditional plans. It remains unclear, however, whether people, in the end, will have more or less retirement income. To answer that question, the following chapters examine the participation, contribution, investment, and withdrawal decisions that those covered by 401(k) plans actually make.

401(k) Plans, the Dominant Form of Pension

The nature of employer-sponsored private pension coverage has changed dramatically over the past twenty years. The focus of this book is the sweeping shift in coverage from defined benefit to 401(k) defined contribution plans. It is important to keep in mind, however, that significant changes are currently under way in the defined benefit world, where hybrid plans increasingly report accrued benefits as lump-sum amounts. Many of the issues raised in the context of 401(k) plans, such as the risks associated with lump-sum payments or the absence of early retirement incentives, are now equally applicable to the new hybrid defined benefit plans. See box 2-1.

Twenty years ago, most people with pension coverage had a traditional defined benefit plan that paid benefits at retirement in the form of a lifetime annuity. The payment could be calculated in various ways. The annuity might be a dollar amount a month for each year of service, say $50, so workers with twenty years of service would receive $1,000 a month at age sixty-five. The benefit could also be a percentage of final salary for each year of service, say 1.5 percent, so workers with twenty years of service would receive 30 percent (twenty years at 1.5 percent) of final salary for as long as they lived. The employer finances these benefits by making pretax contributions into a pension fund; employees typically do not contribute. The employer holds the assets in trust, directs the investments, and bears the risk. The Pension Benefit Guaranty Corporation (PBGC), a self-financing agency within the Department of Labor, guarantees (within limits and subject to certain restrictions) the payment of vested benefits in the event of plan termination.

Today the world of pensions looks very different. Most people with pensions have a defined contribution plan, most often a 401(k). In contrast to traditional defined benefit plans, defined contribution plans are like savings accounts. Generally, the employee, and often the employer, contributes a specified percentage of earnings into the account. These contributions are invested, usually at the direction of the employee, mostly in mutual funds consisting of stocks and bonds. Upon retirement, the worker generally receives the balance in the account as a lump sum, albeit with the option to roll it over to an individual retirement account (IRA).

The defining characteristics of a 401(k) plan are that participation in the plan is voluntary and that the employee as well as the employer can make pretax contributions to the plan. These characteristics shift a substantial portion of the burden for providing for retirement to the employee; the employee decides whether or not to participate, how much to contribute, how to invest the assets, and how to use the 401(k) accumulations at retirement. In addition, workers have some access to 401(k) plan funds before retirement, adding another element of individual responsibility.

Figures 2-1 and 2-2 show the growing importance of defined contribution plans generally and of 401(k) plans in particular. By any criterion—assets,

Box 2-1. *Lump-Sum Distributions and the New Hybrid Defined Benefit Plans*

In addition to the shift in pension coverage from defined benefit to 401(k) plans, many employers are converting their traditional defined benefit plans to hybrid plans. The key characteristic of these hybrids is that they define the benefit in terms of a lump sum rather than an annuity payment. The growing importance of hybrids is reflected in a sharp increase in the percentage of defined benefit participants with access to lump-sum payments at retirement, which rose from 23 percent in 1997 to 43 percent in 2000.

Cash balance plans are the most popular hybrid. Bank America created the first cash balance plan in 1985, and a number of other employers followed suit in the late 1990s. As in traditional defined benefit plans, the employer makes the contributions, owns the assets, selects the investments, and bears the risk. The Pension Benefit Guaranty Corporation (PBGC), established by the Employee Retirement Income Security Act of 1974 (ERISA), also insures the benefits. To the employee, however, cash balance plans look much like defined contribution plans. The employer typically contributes 4 or 5 percent of the worker's pay to a "notional" account and provides an interest credit (generally at some specific rate such as that on U.S. Treasury securities) on the balances. Employees receive regular statements and generally withdraw the balance as a lump sum when they retire or terminate employment.[1]

Another type of hybrid is the pension equity plan. They are quite different in that they do not involve accounts. Rather, they define the lump-sum benefit as a percentage of salary times years of service. For example, the benefit might be 8 percent of final salary for each year of service. If employees leave after ten years, they would receive a benefit equal to 80 percent (8 percent × 10 years) of final salary, payable as a lump sum.

Hybrid plans are attractive to employees because they provide the visible and portable benefits of a defined contribution plan while securing the accrual and government insurance of a defined benefit plan. Employers believe that expressing benefits as a lump sum improves communication and the employee's appreciation of the plan. Hybrid plans also eliminate the rather substantial risks involved in employer funding of retirement annuities. And it is easier to convert a defined benefit to a hybrid than to a defined contribution plan.[2]

continued on next page

1. Since hybrid plans are defined benefit plans, by law they must offer an annuity option, but it appears that the majority of workers opt for the lump-sum benefit.

2. For the employer to switch from a traditional defined benefit plan to a hybrid requires only a plan amendment. To switch to a defined contribution plan, the employer must first terminate the defined benefit plan, which could trigger a reversion excise tax of either 20 or 50 percent on the surplus plan balance. See Gale, Papke, and VanDerhei (2003).

Box 2-1. *Lump-Sum Distributions and the New Hybrid Defined Benefit Plans (continued)*

If employer contributions to the plan remain unchanged, the conversion from a traditional defined benefit plan to a hybrid will redistribute benefits among workers. The gainers will be young workers who leave after ten years of service; the losers will be workers who retire after thirty years of service. With contributions constant, the only way to improve the benefits for mobile employees is to reduce benefits for long-service workers.[3]

A 2002 survey of large defined benefit plans (a thousand or more participants) found that 19 percent had a hybrid design.[4] Among the Fortune 100, hybrids are even more popular; thirty-two of the top one hundred firms had a hybrid pension plan in 2002.[5] Assuming only modest growth in hybrid plans, lump-sum payments from employer-sponsored pension plans should exceed annuity payments for men retiring as soon as 2010.[6]

3. Watson Wyatt Worldwide, "The Unfolding of a Predictable Surprise" (www.watsonwyatt.com/research/resrender.asp?id=w-326&page=1).

4. Watson Wyatt Worldwide, "Survey of Actuarial Assumptions and Funding" (www.watsonwyatt.com/research/resrender.asp?id=w-631). Among large employers, hybrids are particularly prevalent in telecommunications, financial services, and utilities. Among the smaller firms, hybrids occur primarily in the health industry. See Clark and Schieber (2002).

5. Watson Wyatt Worldwide (2002). Currently, the Department of Labor's form 5500 data do not provide enough information to identify cash balance plans. But the IRS included additional questions in 1999, so it will soon be possible to determine the extent to which cash balance plans have spread.

6. VanDerhei and Copeland (2001).

benefits, participants, and contributions—defined contribution plans grew enormously as a share of total pensions between 1979 and 1998. Similarly, between 1984 (the first year separate data are available for 401(k) plans) and 1998, all dimensions of 401(k) plans increased dramatically, rising from 25–35 percent of the defined contribution totals to 70–80 percent. Part of the increase can be explained by the fact that any defined contribution plan with a 401(k) feature was reclassified as a 401(k) plan. Thus TIAA-CREF, the largest of the private plans (which used to be counted as a money purchase pension plan), is now counted as a 401(k); this would also be true of any profit-sharing plans that adopted a 401(k) feature. But not all the growth came from reclassification; many employers also established new 401(k)s, as discussed below.

One obvious question when considering the enormous growth of 401(k)

Figure 2-1. *Defined Contribution Plans as a Share of Total Pension Plans, 1979 and 1998*

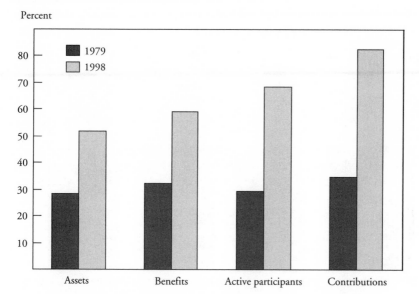

Source: Authors' calculations based on U.S. Department of Labor, Form 5500 data.

plans is how they help in managing a work force.[1] At first glance, defined contribution plans generally, and 401(k) plans in particular, do not appear capable of retaining skilled workers and allowing the retirement of older employees who have become less productive. Once vested, workers do not forfeit any benefits when they change employers. Nor do defined contribution plans contain the incentives to retire at the specific ages that employers embed in traditional defined benefit plans. Why then are employers interested in defined contribution plans if they cannot use them to control the behavior of their work force?

An interesting notion put forth by Richard Ippolito is that the power of pensions may rest in their ability to attract and retain high-quality workers rather than to directly affect employee productivity.[2] Ippolito argues that it

1. Employers want to retain workers because they have invested resources in training them and because hiring is expensive. See Lazear (1985). Since bondage is not an option, employers use a rising wage profile and defined benefit plans to encourage workers to stay. As workers age, however, their generally rising wages often exceed their generally declining productivity. As it is difficult to fire older long-term workers, employers tailor the provisions of their defined benefit plans to encourage retirement at a desired age.

2. Ippolito (1997).

Figure 2-2. *401(k) Plans as a Share of Total Defined Contribution Plans, 1984 and 1998*

Percent

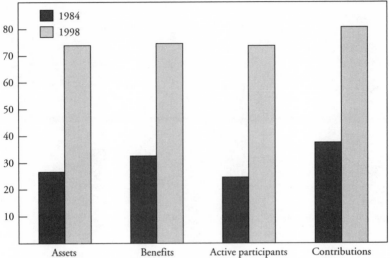

Source: Author's calculations based on Form 5500 data.

is difficult to change employee performance and that it is better to attract the right kind of workers in the first place. And how do employers find good workers? Easy, says Ippolito: Savers are good workers. Why are savers better workers than nonsavers? Because savers have lower discount rates, says Ippolito, and thus place greater value on future outcomes. Low discounters are less likely to play hooky or treat equipment carelessly— they understand that careless actions today will hurt their reputations tomorrow.

Firms that offer pensions are more likely to attract low discounters, as high discounters prefer cash now to pensions later.[3] This type of "sorting" is not perfect; firms will inevitably pick up some high discounters. The challenge is to get the high discounters to leave. Defined contribution plans, and

3. Salop and Salop (1976) introduced the notion of "sorting," or selection effects, to the labor market literature. They describe two kinds of workers: "quitters" and "stayers." In their model, any kind of pension attracts stayers, because quitters attach a low probability to actually receiving a pension. In other words, simply setting up a pension reduces quitting. Several researchers—Allen, Clark, and McDermed (1993); Gustman and Steinmeier (1992, 1993); Ippolito (1998)—find that quit rates are lower at firms with a defined contribution plan than those with no pension.

Figure 2-3. *Households with Pension Coverage, by Type, 1992–2001*

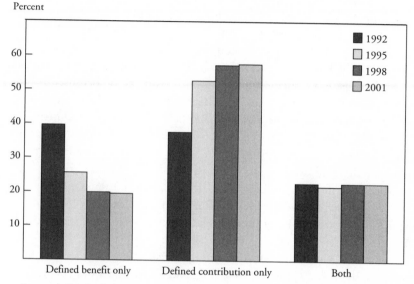

Percent

Source: Authors' calculations based on Board of Governors, *Survey of Consumer Finances* (SCF), 1992, 1995, 1998, and 2001.

particularly 401(k) plans, do this in two ways. First, the lump sum provided by defined contribution plans gives high discounters an incentive to quit and get the money. (Lump-sum payments from the new hybrid defined benefit plans will have the same effect.) Second, the employer match in 401(k) plans allows the firm to pay high savers a greater amount than they pay low savers. In other words, low savers either select themselves out to get the lump sum or choose to pay themselves less. In either case, 401(k) plans allow the employer to get and retain a more productive work force.

Regardless of whether the "sorting" argument holds, recent data show that 401(k)s and other defined contribution plans were clearly the dominant form of pension in the 1990s. Over the period 1992–2001 the share of households with pension coverage that relies solely on a defined contribution plan increased from 37 percent to 58 percent (figure 2-3). At the same time, the share of households with only a defined benefit plan dropped from about 40 percent to 19 percent. About 23 percent of households had dual coverage, and this share held steady through the 1990s. To determine whether this growth of 401(k) plans has been good for workers, it is necessary to consider the impact on coverage, accumulated plan assets, labor mobility, retirement incentives, and the financial risk borne by the employee.

401(k) Plans and Pension Coverage

One avenue through which the explosion of 401(k) plans could affect retirement income is pension coverage. That is, given their popularity and growth, the introduction of 401(k) plans could have resulted in more pension coverage than would have occurred otherwise. Whether or not 401(k) plans boosted coverage is a difficult question to answer, however, because it is not clear what would have happened in the absence of the 401(k) explosion. Would pension coverage have remained constant, increased, or declined?

Those who claim that 401(k) plans have dramatically increased retirement saving assume that the percentage of the work force with pension coverage would have dropped over the last twenty years if 401(k) plans had not happened on the scene. The decline could have occurred in response to the factors normally cited for the decline in defined benefit plans, such as the movement out of manufacturing or increased administrative costs. It is a plausible position. But our view is that pension coverage would have remained relatively constant. That is, we believe that roughly half of the work force or their agents have the income, interest in saving, and knowledge of tax benefits to demand some form of employer-sponsored plan. Over the last twenty years, 401(k) plans best satisfied the need of workers and employers who were looking for a retirement-saving vehicle; if 401(k) plans had not emerged, employers would have remained with defined benefit plans or opted for a more traditional defined contribution plan.

Although determining the counterfactual is necessarily speculative, the fact that pension coverage has remained virtually unchanged over the last twenty years is indisputable. As figure 2-4 shows, the percentage of the private sector work force participating in a pension plan in 2002 was virtually the same as in 1979, regardless of how participation is measured. This supports our notion that pension coverage largely reflects an underlying demand by workers for pension benefits and that the growth of 401(k)s replaced coverage under traditional plans. How did this happen?

A point worth emphasizing is that the conversion of a defined benefit plan to a 401(k) was extremely rare, particularly among large plans. One study carefully followed a sample of 249 defined benefit plans with at least 500 participants over the period 1987 through 1995; of the 249 original plans, 214 remained in 1995.[4] Of the 35 plans that sponsors terminated, 3 were

4. Ippolito (1999). These results are consistent with those of Kruse (1995) and Papke, Petersen, and Poterba (1996), even though both studies adopted different methodologies. The first tracked all pension plans from 1980 to 1986 using data from Form 5500; the second surveyed a sample of 401(k) plans in 1987 to see if they had replaced a defined benefit plan. In

Figure 2-4. *Private Work Force Participation in a Pension Plan, 1979–2002*

Percent

Source: Authors' calculations based on U.S. Bureau of the Census, *Current Population Survey* (CPS), 1979–2002.

replaced by a new defined benefit plan, 14 by no new plan, and only 18 by a defined contribution plan. In other words, most participants in the original sample were still in a defined benefit plan at the end of the study; their employers did not replace their defined benefit plan with a 401(k).

Instead of conversions from defined benefit plans, initial coverage by 401(k)s resulted from the addition of 401(k) provisions to traditional thrift and profit-sharing plans in the early 1980s. This was an obvious move because thrift plans, which generally served as supplements to defined benefit plans, required employees to make after-tax contributions. Since 401(k) plans allowed pretax contributions, introducing a 401(k) provision meant that employees could maintain their contribution level and see an increase in take-home pay. In the case of profit-sharing plans, the shift to 401(k)s and voluntary participation allowed employers to reduce the profits distributed to employees. Table 2-1 indicates the importance of such thrift and profit-sharing conversions: 30 percent of 401(k) participants in 1995 were in plans established before 1980. Since 401(k) plans did not become popular until

---

each case, the researchers found that most new 401(k) plans had not replaced a preexisting defined benefit plan.

Table 2-1. *401(k) Plans and Participants, by Date of Plan Establishment, 1995*

Date plan established	Plans in 1995		Participants in 1995	
	Number	Percent	Number (thousands)	Percent
Pre-1980	24,030	12.0	9,428	30.0
1980–84	18,965	9.4	5,513	17.6
1985–89	59,182	29.5	8,698	27.7
1990–94	69,564	34.6	6,162	19.6
1995	28,243	14.1	1,519	4.8
Date not specified	831	0.4	65	0.2
Total[a]	200,815	100.0	31,385	100.0

Source: U.S. Department of Labor (2001–02).
a. Totals may not add due to rounding.

1981, when the Internal Revenue Service (IRS) issued clarifying regulations, a plan established before 1980 is generally presumed to be a thrift or profit-sharing plan that was converted to a 401(k).

The second step in the growth of 401(k) coverage was a surge in new plan formation in the 1980s. (Figure 2-5 presents initial applications to the IRS for determination letters to start or terminate a plan, which is an imperfect but useful measure of plan formation.) This surge continued through the 1980s, after the emergence of 401(k) plans. The 1980s expansion produced 40 percent of the 401(k) plans in 1995, with 45 percent of the participants (table 2-1).

The third factor in the shift to 401(k) coverage was a virtual halt in the formation of new defined benefit plans and a spike in terminations during the late 1980s. Terminations increased sharply in the late 1980s after the Tax Reform Act of 1986 placed restrictions on small defined benefit plans that benefited only highly paid individuals. Applications dropped after 1990 when the government placed an excise tax on the reversion of money from overfunded plans.[5] These developments cut the number of defined benefit plans by 70 percent (from a peak of 175,143 in 1983 to 56,405 in 1998) and the number of active participants by 25 percent (from 30 million in 1983 to 23 million in 1998).[6]

5. Applications for new plans are measured by initial applications to the IRS for determination letters. Employers are not required to obtain an IRS determination letter to verify their qualified status before they start a plan, but many do. Determination letters are therefore not a precise measure of new plan formation but provide useful information. See McGill and others (1996).
6. These numbers come from the Department of Labor's form 5500. For data on insured participants in single-employer and multiemployer plans, see Pension Benefit Guaranty Corpo-

Figure 2-5. *Net Change in Defined Benefit and Defined Contribution Plans,*
1960–2002

Thousands of applications

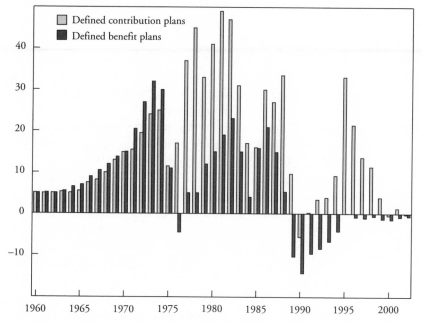

Sources: Warshawsky (1995); U.S. Internal Revenue Service (1988–2002); McGill and others
(1996).

Why did 401(k) plans spread while defined benefit plans languished? A
key factor was clearly the enormous appeal of 401(k) plans to both employees and employers. Employees gained control of their retirement planning,
could make tax-deductible contributions, and saw their accounts grow.
Young mobile workers could easily take their 401(k) accumulations with
them as they moved from job to job. From the employers' perspective,
401(k) plans offered a form of pension that their workers appreciated. Moreover, the employer eliminated the risks involved in funding future retirement
annuities. And the cost of a 401(k) plan was highly predictable, which

---

ration, *2001 Pension Insurance Data Book* (pbgc.gov.master.com/texis/master/search/mysite.
html?q=data). The total number of insured rose from 37.0 million in 1983 to 42.6 million in
1998. An increasing portion of these, however, were separated, vested, and retired participants.
The number of active vested participants covered by the PBGC declined from 26.9 million in
1983 to 22.7 million in 1998. These numbers suggest that an increasing proportion of participants were vested (90 percent in 1983 and 99 percent in 1998).

became increasingly important during the 1980s as the economic environment became more competitive. Moreover, evolving computer and communications technology made it a lot easier to administer a 401(k) plan.[7]

At the same time, employment was shifting to sectors of the labor market in which defined benefit plans were less attractive. Employment was declining in large, unionized, manufacturing firms, which typically offered defined benefit plans, and was growing in high-tech firms and small, nonunionized companies in the services and trade sectors, which typically did not. Defined benefit plans are a sensible arrangement for manufacturing, which has large, well-established firms and long-service employees. They are ill suited to service industries, whose companies come and go and the work force is mobile. Several studies find that changes in industry composition, unionization, and firm size account for about half the decline in defined benefit coverage.[8]

The regulatory environment also caused existing small firms and new companies established in the 1980s and 1990s to opt for a 401(k). ERISA imposed minimum standards for participation, vesting, and funding that were particularly stiff for defined benefit plans. For example, ERISA significantly tightened funding requirements. While defined contribution plans are fully funded by definition, defined benefit plans now required more elaborate estimations of liability based on the age, length of service, and salary of employees many years in the future, which greatly increased the need for actuarial services. The PBGC also imposed premiums on participating plans to finance the insurance of pension benefits.

In addition to ERISA, during the 1980s Congress passed significant legislation affecting defined benefit plans every few years. The increased regulation was aimed at making pensions, which are supported by federal income tax preferences, fairer. But it also made the pension system more complex and more costly to administer. For example, Congress changed the extent to which pensions can be reduced to reflect Social Security benefits, the share of benefits that can go to highly compensated employees, and the extent to which firms can deduct contributions to defined benefit plans for income tax purposes.[9] Congress also repeatedly raised PBGC premiums and imposed an

---

7. Letter from Sylvester Schieber, Watson Wyatt Worldwide, April 11, 2003.

8. See, for example, Andrews (1992); Gustman and Steinmeier (1992); Ippolito (1995).

9. The Omnibus Reconciliation Act of 1987 reduced the full funding limits for defined benefit plans from 100 percent of projected plan liability to the lesser of that value or 150 percent of benefits accrued to date. Basing funding limits on benefits already accrued means that funding contributions no longer include any provision for anticipated pay increases. See McGill and others (1996). The funding restriction means that sponsors cannot get the full tax advantage that comes with the ability to prefund defined benefit plans and exposes the sponsor to higher costs in the future.

excise tax on employers who claimed the excess assets (the assets not needed to satisfy benefit obligations) of terminated defined benefit plans. The cumulative impact of the legislative changes has greatly increased the relative costs of defined benefit plans.[10] The increase has been particularly pronounced for small plans; over the period 1981–96 administrative costs as a percentage of payroll nearly tripled for defined benefit plans, compared to less than doubling of defined contribution plans.

A considerably less important but reinforcing phenomenon was corporate raiders eager to get their hands on "excess" pension assets. For example, in 1975 the German retailer Tengelmann Gruppe took over the Great Atlantic and Pacific Tea Company (A&P) and over the next several years recouped a large part of its investment by in effect terminating the overfunded defined benefit plan and pocketing the excess assets, netting $265 million of the $540 million in the pension fund.[11] In 1985 financier Ronald Perelman took over Revlon, closed down its pension plan, and got control of $100 million in surplus pension assets.[12] Similarly, Charles Hurwitz took over Pacific Lumber, shut down the pension plan, and used $55 million in surplus pension assets to help finance his buyout. After a number of these cases, Congress imposed a 50 percent excise tax on "reversions," and pension terminations at large companies declined sharply.[13]

In short, the dramatic shift in pension coverage from defined benefit to 401(k) plans is due to changing economics, increased regulation of defined

10. The biggest increase in both absolute and relative costs of defined benefit versus defined contribution plans occurred in the late 1980s as plans adjusted to the Retirement Equity Act of 1984 and the Tax Reform Act of 1986. See Hustead (1998). The Retirement Equity Act of 1984 required a joint-and-survivor annuity as the default annuity form, with spousal notification and approval of another election, and reduced the maximum age and service requirements a plan could require. The major changes in the Tax Reform Act of 1986 involved minimum coverage and nondiscrimination tests, the definition of a "highly compensated employee," minimum vesting standards, and new integration rules. These changes increased record-keeping requirements, administrative expenses, and benefit costs.

11. "A Bit of Tengel," *Economist,* April 19, 1980, p. 65; Williams (1988).

12. Ellen E. Schultz, "Pension Termination: '80s Replay," *Wall Street Journal,* June 15, 1999, p. C1.

13. The bull market of the 1990s rekindled employer interest in the reversion of surplus pension reserves. Employers figured out that they could pay an excise tax of 20 percent rather than 50 percent if they put one-quarter of the surplus from the terminated plan into a "replacement plan." In 1999 Dillard's Inc., the acquirer of Mercantile stores, shifted 25 percent of Mercantile's $194 million surplus into Dillard's existing 401(k) plan, where the money can be used to make future matching contributions. See Schultz, "Pension Termination: '80s Replay." The company paid 20 percent on the remaining $145 million and pocketed the rest. Financially troubled firms also found the termination of overfunded plans an appealing way to pay creditors.

benefit plans, the lure of "excess" pension fund assets, the appeal of visible account balances, and the sense of control provided by these plans. The enormous increase in 401(k) plans, however, has not been accompanied by an overall increase in pension coverage. Thus whether individuals are better or worse off depends on whether those with pension coverage will have more or less retirement wealth.

401(k) Plans and Retirement Income

Even if 401(k) plans have not increased coverage, they may have improved retirement prospects if they provide more retirement income for those lucky enough to have a pension. That is, will people with a 401(k) have more retirement income than they would have under a traditional defined benefit plan?

The answer to this question can be approached in a number of ways. A useful starting point is a simple simulation to determine how much pension wealth a retiree would have under a typical defined benefit plan and under a typical 401(k) plan. Pension wealth is defined here as the projected value of benefits over the worker's lifetime, given the probability of being alive to receive them, discounted back to retirement, at either age fifty-five or age sixty-two.

Although defined benefit provisions vary a lot from firm to firm, a typical plan might provide 1.5 percent of final salary for each year of service, have a normal retirement age of sixty-two, and an early retirement age of fifty-five. If workers retire before age sixty-two, benefits are often reduced by 5 percent for each year before sixty-two; that is, if someone retires at sixty, benefits will be 10 percent below their value as calculated by the benefit formula.[14] With these assumptions and an assumed earnings profile, it is possible to calculate projected pension benefits. To translate that flow of benefits into pension wealth requires assumptions about mortality and a discount rate. In the following calculations, future benefits are discounted to the present using a government bond rate.[15]

14. These parameters are consistent with those reported by the U.S. Department of Labor (1999) for medium and large establishments. With respect to early retirement, the benefit will be lower not only because of the actuarial reduction but also because of fewer years of service.

15. We used the ten-year Treasury bond for this calculation because it is consistent with the rate used to produce annuity payments from 401(k) plans. The average real rate on the ten-year bond over its existence (1954–2002) was 2.6 percent. Since we assumed 3 percent inflation, the nominal rate used in the simulations was 5.6 percent. In fact, minimum lump-sum payments from defined benefit plans have been based on the thirty-year Treasury bond. Between 1977 (the first year for the thirty-year bond) and 2002, the average real yield on the ten-year bond

In the case of 401(k) plans, pension wealth at retirement is simply the accumulation in the plan at that time. The median contribution rate for participants in 401(k) plans is 6 percent of earnings, with an effective employer matching contribution of 3 percent.[16] We assume that 401(k) contributions are invested 50 percent in stocks and 50 percent in bonds, with a real return—that is, return in excess of inflation—of 4.6 percent.[17] Inflation is assumed to be 3 percent, so the nominal rate of return is 7.6 percent.

The earnings history is identical in both cases and is based on the general growth of wages in the economy, due to inflation and the increase in real wages, and on the rise and fall in earnings across the typical worker's career. In the earnings history in our simulation, the worker begins participating at age thirty, with a salary of $17,000, and ends with $52,650 at age sixty-two. This pattern of continuous employment and contributions should be viewed as a base case. The impact of job mobility, withdrawals, and investment risk are considered in turn.

Table 2-2 summarizes the results of the simple calculations. Under the assumptions described above, the employee appears to do somewhat better under a typical 401(k) plan than under a traditional defined benefit plan. More sophisticated analyses that incorporate the variability in plan provisions, earnings profiles, and rates of return yield similar results.[18]

The wealth figures can be expressed as replacement rates, which relate the individual's initial annual retirement income to earnings before retirement. The income provided by the 401(k) uses an actuarially fair annuity over currently expected longevity at retirement, funded by ten-year government bonds.[19] At age sixty-two, our hypothetical 401(k) generates a replacement rate of 59 percent compared to a defined benefit rate of 50 percent. The later

was 3.5 percent and for the thirty-year bond, 3.7 percent. So the decision to use a consistent rate for the defined benefit and 401(k) calculations had little impact on the results. Since the government is no longer issuing thirty-year Treasury securities, the IRS now specifies, under section 417 of the Internal Revenue Code, the rates for calculation of lump-sum payments from defined benefit plans.

16. Holden and VanDerhei (2001c).

17. These are the assumptions used by the President's Commission to Strengthen Social Security (2001); the Office of the Actuary of the Social Security Administration made the original recommendation. Equities are assumed to provide a real return of 6.5 percent, corporate bonds 3.5 percent, and Treasury bonds 3 percent. In addition, the commission assumed administrative costs equal to thirty basis points. Critics have argued that these costs could be higher.

18. Even and McPherson (2001); Poterba, Venti, and Wise (1998, 2001); Samwick and Skinner (2001). Even and McPherson caution that 401(k) plans may put low-income workers at a greater risk of low pension wealth.

19. The ten-year Treasury bond had an average annual return of 2.6 percent over the period 1954 (the year the bond was introduced) through 2002. So a nominal rate of 5.6 percent was used to calculate the annuity payment.

Table 2-2. *Simulated Wealth and Replacement Rates, Typical Defined Benefit Plan and 401(k) Plan, Retirement at Age Fifty-Five and Age Sixty-Two*[a]

Plan	Age fifty-five	Age sixty-two
Pension wealth (dollars)		
Defined benefit plan	213,916	303,560
401(k) plan	229,378	353,408
Replacement rate (percent)		
Defined benefit plan	32.5	50.4
401(k) plan	34.8	58.7

Source: Authors' calculations.

a. Calculations are based on a pattern of wage growth over a worker's career that is a composite of two factors. The first is the growth of nominal wages across the economy due to inflation and real wage growth. We use the projections of the Office of the Actuary of the Social Security Administration of 4.1 percent nominal wage growth, with inflation at 3 percent and real wage growth at 1.1 percent. The second factor is the rise and fall of earnings across a worker's career. We use an age-earnings profile based on career earnings profiles for males and females born between 1926 and 1965. In this profile, earnings reach a peak at age 47. After adding the economy-wide factors, real wages peak at age 51 and nominal wages at age 61. To facilitate comparisons with data collected in the 2001 Survey of Consumer Finances, our simulation sets the salary at age 50 to $44,000—the median wage for a 50-year-old covered by a pension plan in the 2001 Survey. This results in a salary of $17,000 at age 30, when the workers in the simulation begin to participate in a plan; and an ending salary of $52,650 at age 62. The contribution rate for the 401(k) is 9 percent a year, with a 7.6 percent nominal rate of return on assets. Defined benefit plan amounts are based on 1.5 percent of the average of the last five salaries for each year of service, with a 5-percent discount for each year of benefit receipt before age 62. We use inflation-adjusted values for pension wealth at age 55 to facilitate comparisons with pension wealth at age 62.

the retirement, the higher the 401(k) replacement rate relative to that in the hypothetical defined benefit plan. The results from the simple simulation are consistent with those from a detailed analysis of 2.5 million participants drawn from a database collected by the Employee Benefit Research Institute (EBRI) and the Investment Company Institute (ICI). The EBRI/ICI analysis does not assume constant contributions, as we do in our simulations, but rather focuses on workers who have spent their entire working lives covered by a 401(k) plan and then incorporates typical behavior. Median replacement rates by income quartile for participants turning sixty-five between 2035 and 2039 are

—51 percent for the first quartile,

—56 percent for the second quartile,

—61 percent for the third quartile, and

—69 percent for the fourth quartile.[20]

20. Holden and VanDerhei (2002). This example refers to continuous coverage under a 401(k) plan. If participants had contributed continuously at a combined employer-employee

Table 2-3. *Replacement Rates under Three Assumptions, Defined Benefit and 401(k) Plans*
Percent

Plan and assumption	Age of joining plan						
	25	30	35	40	45	50	55
Defined benefit							
1.00 salary multiple	39	34	29	23	18	13	8
1.50 salary multiple	58	50	43	35	27	20	12
2.00 salary multiple	77	67	57	47	37	26	16
401(k)							
6.60 nominal return	59	49	40	31	22	15	8
7.60 nominal return	72	59	46	35	24	16	8
8.60 nominal return	89	70	53	39	27	17	9

Source: Authors' calculations based on the simulations summarized in table 2-2.

Despite some variation by income level, the numbers confirm that people covered continuously by a 401(k) plan can accumulate significant retirement wealth, perhaps even more than they would have received from a traditional defined benefit plan.[21]

Estimates of proceeds from any retirement plan are sensitive to the underlying assumptions. In the case of defined benefit plans, the salary multiple in the benefit formula is particularly important. For 401(k) plans, the rate of return is key. The sensitivity to each of these factors is shown in table 2-3. Also evident is the effect of the starting age. If the worker joins before age forty, 401(k) arrangements consistently yield higher replacement rates. At age forty or older, defined benefit plans generally do substantially better.

The outcome is also sensitive to the contribution rate for 401(k) plans, which consists of the employee's contribution and the employer match. In the past, fluctuations in contributions have not been an important issue because the median employee contribution held fairly steady at 6 percent and

---

rate of 9 percent, the relevant replacements rates by quartile would have been 60 percent, 65 percent, 68 percent, and 74 percent, respectively. The replacement rates are higher than shown in our simulation most likely because participants start their contributions earlier and work until age sixty-five, rather than age sixty-two.

21. Samwick and Skinner (2001) also produced simulations that show 401(k) plans provide benefits at retirement that are at least as good and often better than those provided by defined benefit plans.

the employer match at 3 percent. With the onset of the recession in March 2001, however, employers started to cut back. One survey reports that the average (which is different from median) employer match declined from 3.3 percent of earnings in 1999 to 2.8 percent in 2002.[22] And a number of large companies have cut back since then. The Ford Motor Company and DaimlerChrysler suspended their employer match for 2002 as part of a cost-cutting program; Goodyear suspended its match for 2003. In March 2003 the struggling Charles Schwab Corporation announced that it would suspend its employer match.[23] Prudential Securities and Textron followed suit shortly thereafter. In short, the assumption that the median contribution is 9 percent of earnings may be somewhat optimistic.[24]

One additional caveat is warranted. The example assumes that the employee has the same earnings under a 401(k) and under a defined benefit plan. Economists would argue, however, that similarly situated employees covered by 401(k) plans should have higher (precontribution) cash wages than those covered by defined benefit plans. A by-product of the shift from defined benefit to 401(k) is that the bulk of contributions come from employees rather than from employers. But who pays the pension contribution should have no obvious implications on the amount of compensation employers provide. Employers essentially decide on the total compensation they must pay their employees and divide that amount between cash wages and fringe benefits. Contributing to a pension thus implies a cut in wages or a reduction in other benefits, and vice versa.[25] The relevance for the simulations presented above is that the employee covered by the 401(k) plan would

22. Profit Sharing/401(k) Council of America (2003).
23. Mary Williams Walsh and Patrick McGeehan, "Schwab to End Match to 401(k)s," *New York Times,* March 14, 2003.
24. For implications of suspending the employer match, see Munnell and Sundén (2003).
25. The potential trade-off between higher pensions and lower wages may be somewhat more complicated than a simple one-for-one offset. For example, by reducing employee turnover or shirking or by facilitating retirement of less productive workers, the introduction of a deferred compensation arrangement might increase productivity and thus make employers willing to increase total compensation. Alternatively, because of the favorable tax treatment of pensions, the employer has somewhat more money available than if it paid all compensation in cash; the firm could retain this windfall as profit or share some of it with employees, thereby raising total compensation. Even if the trade-off between pensions and wages occurs in the aggregate, it may not happen on a person-for-person basis. For example, raising pensions for minimum wage workers cannot lead to a reduction in wages, because the employer cannot reduce wages below this level. Similarly, plans must cover at least some lower paid employees to qualify for special tax treatment. But those employees may have no interest in saving for retirement, so plan sponsors may have to use some of the tax benefits to increase the total compensation of "reluctant savers."

be expected to have somewhat higher cash wages and therefore greater 401(k) accumulations than shown in table 2-2.[26]

Another way to say something about future benefit levels is to look at assets per participant. Data suggest that defined benefit plans have a lot more put aside for each active participant than 401(k) plans.[27] But nothing is easy in this business! A number of adjustments are required to get a fair comparison. First, it is essential to include IRAs when considering 401(k) plans, since most of the assets in these plans are rollovers from 401(k)s and the earnings on those rollovers. Increasingly, of course, IRA accumulations also include rollovers from cash balance and other hybrid defined benefit plans. This adjustment also requires estimating the number of people with only IRAs and adding them to the total number of 401(k) participants. Similarly, the number of people with a claim on the accumulated assets of defined benefit plans should include "separated" as well as active participants.[28] Finally, and perhaps most important, the accumulations must be adjusted to reflect the fact that defined benefit accumulations reflect projected benefits, whereas 401(k) assets are only accumulations to date.[29] Once the appropriate adjustments are made, assets per participant are roughly the same for 401(k) and defined benefit plans.

The relevant comparison is definitely assets per participant and not contributions. Some researchers compare contribution rates under 401(k) and traditional defined benefit plans and conclude that saving is much higher in 401(k) plans because contributions, as a percentage of wage and salary, are twice as high as contributions going into defined benefit plans. But contributions do not reflect the rate at which benefits are building up under the two plans. What matters in defined benefit plans are changes in accrued vested benefit obligations. Employers contribute to the plan to prefund this commitment. If the stock market goes up, as it did in the 1990s, the plan's assets rise; at the same time, rates of return on investments, and thus discount rates

26. Also see Brown (1980).

27. The data are from the Department of Labor's form 5500.

28. Separated participants are former employees of the sponsoring firm who have accrued benefits under the plan. The PBGC provides annual data on the number of vested separated participants.

29. The Omnibus Reconciliation Act of 1987 reduced the full funding limits for defined benefit plans to the lesser of either 100 percent of projected plan liability or 150 percent of benefits accrued to date. Data from Watson Wyatt Worldwide, "Survey of Actuarial Assumptions and Funding" (www.watsonwyatt.com/research/resrender.asp?id=w-631&page=1), indicate that assets of defined benefit plans averaged 1.33 of accrued liability throughout the 1990s. To put defined benefit and 401(k) assets on the same basis, we divided defined benefit assets by 1.33. (The Taxpayer Relief Act of 1997 gradually raised the current liability funding limit to 160 percent in 1999, and the Economic Growth and Tax Relief Reconciliation Act of 2001 raised the limit to 165 percent in 2002, 170 percent in 2003, and eliminated it thereafter.)

used to calculate the value of future pension obligations, are relatively high. Because pension funds are flush and future benefits are heavily discounted, employers often do not have to make any contribution at all during a bull market. In contrast, stock market fluctuations are unlikely to affect contributions to 401(k) plans.

The general conclusion emerging from the comparisons discussed above is that workers covered continuously by hypothetical traditional defined benefit and 401(k) plans will reach retirement with substantial sums. The accumulations will be considerably smaller in the case of a defined benefit plan if the employee changes employer (even if all employers sponsor identical defined benefit plans). They will also be smaller in a 401(k) plan if employees begin saving for retirement later in life or if they withdraw their contributions.[30] The next sections explore each of these issues.

401(k) Accumulations and Timing of Contributions

Although the simulation assumes that the employee starts contributing at age thirty and contributes at a steady rate until retirement, one recent strain of the literature suggests that many people do not begin saving for retirement until around age fifty. In fact, concern about people getting to fifty years old with inadequate retirement savings was a major rationale for the provisions in the Economic Growth and Tax Relief Reconciliation Act of 2001 that allow 401(k) participants aged fifty or over to make additional contributions.

That people do not save until later in life is reasonable, according to a standard financial planning model based on the life-cycle hypothesis.[31] This hypothesis says that people want to have a relatively stable level of consumption over their lifetime, so they save during their working years and draw down their savings in retirement. But when do they save? Take the example of a married couple who has two children, one born when the couple is age twenty-five, the other when the couple is thirty. The couple plans to purchase a home and send their children to college; they must pay federal and state income taxes and Social Security payroll taxes in addition to preparing for retirement.

The model suggests that the household does some small saving before the birth of its second child but spends these savings on a house down payment

30. Accumulation in a 401(k) will also be smaller if the worker takes a lump-sum distribution when changing jobs. In addition, participation in 401(k) plans is voluntary. About 26 percent of eligible employees choose not to participate, while employees covered by defined benefit plans are automatically included.

31. Gokhale, Kotlikoff, and Warshawsky (2002).

and other household expenses before the second child is born. From age twenty-five to age forty, the couple uses most of its saving to pay down the mortgage. Once the mortgage is under control, the couple starts saving seriously for their children's college education. Between ages forty-five and fifty their children are in college, and the parents draw down their savings to cover tuition payments. Only after the children have completed their college education can the couple start saving substantial amounts for retirement.

Starting retirement saving late in life is only the output from the financial planning model, not necessarily a description of reality. Nevertheless, some studies that look at people's consumption and income over their life suggest that it is a reasonably accurate description of what people actually do. Aside from amounts saved through the purchase of housing, consumption and earnings track each other quite closely before middle age.[32] This pattern implies that saving for retirement occurs only in the last fifteen years or so before retirement.

The argument that people delay retirement plan contributions until their fifties, however, is not consistent with data from the Survey of Consumer Finances (SCF), which show a relatively constant contribution rate after age thirty and roughly the same percentage of eligible workers contributing in all age groups (table 2-4).[33] Thus people do not delay putting money into their 401(k) plan.[34] The question is whether they leave it in.

Table 2-5 suggests that they do not. Median 401(k)/IRA holdings as reported in the 2001 SCF are dramatically lower than those estimated for the hypothetical worker in our simulation. For example, median holdings are $37,000 for an individual aged forty-five to fifty-four, whereas the simulation described above indicates that the steady accumulator with roughly the same salary would have amassed $155,709 by age fifty. A recent study by the Congressional Research Service (CRS) confirms our results on 401(k)/IRA balances.[35]

---

32. Kotlikoff and Summers (1981); Carroll and Summers (1991).

33. The SCF is a triennial survey sponsored by the Federal Reserve Board in cooperation with Statistics of Income of the Department of the Treasury. The SCF collects detailed information on household assets, liabilities, and demographic characteristics, including pension coverage, participation, plan characteristics, and contribution levels. The SCF surveys approximately 4,000 households and oversamples wealthy households to provide reliable estimates of highly concentrated assets.

34. This finding is consistent with those of other studies. See for example Clark and others (2000).

35. Using the Census Bureau's Survey of Income and Program Participation (SIPP), the CRS found that the median holdings of workers ages forty-five to fifty-four was $28,000 in 2000—very close to the SCF figure of $37,000. See Purcell (2003b).

Table 2-4. *Median 401(k) Contribution Rate, by Age, 2001*
Percent

| Age group | Contribution rate[a] | | Share of eligible workers contributing |
	Employee	Employer	
20–29	5.2	3.0	64.3
30–39	6.0	3.0	74.5
40–49	6.0	3.0	76.0
50–59	6.0	3.0	72.6
60–64	5.0	4.3	77.8

Source: Authors' calculations based on the 2001 SCF.

a. The contribution rate is calculated as the median for those making positive contributions. Of those who chose to participate in the plan, roughly 98 percent contribute.

Table 2-5. *401(k)/IRA and Simulated Accumulations, by Age Group, 2001*
Dollars

| Age group | Accumulations | |
	Actual (2001 SCF)	Simulated
35–44	24,000	58,503
45–54	37,000	155,709
55–64	42,000	289,073

Source: Authors' calculations based on the 2001 SCF and simulations summarized in table 2-2.

Are these numbers an accurate representation of what is going on in 401(k) plans? On the one hand, the reported amounts are an overstatement in that they include total IRA balances. The implicit assumption is that all the money in IRAs came from 401(k) rollovers. This clearly is not correct: Some of the money came from direct contributions and from rollovers from defined benefit plans. On the other hand, respondents could be underreporting their assets, but this seems unlikely; participants get regular statements from their 401(k) plans, and people probably check their IRA balances at least once a year.[36] Similarly, it is important to remember that 401(k) plans only became popular in 1981, so people may not have had adequate time to build up their balances. At the same time, as discussed earlier, a significant

36. Another issue is average versus median balance; averages tend to be higher because holdings in defined contribution plans are skewed toward high-income individuals. But even the mean values for people aged forty-five to fifty-four are only $105,300 in the SCF and $60,740 in the SIPP, both below the amount suggested by the simulations. The mean amount in the SCF is higher than in the SIPP because of the SCF's oversampling of wealthy households.

Figure 2-6. *401(k) Account Balances as Share of Earnings,*
by Age and Tenure, 2001

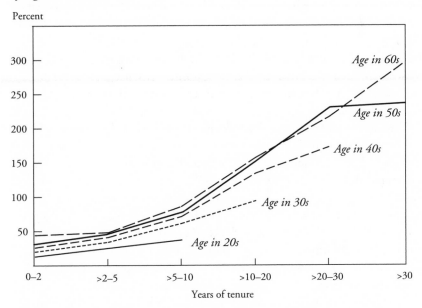

Source: EBRI/ICI Participant-Directed Retirement Plan Data Collection Project; data provided by
Jack VanDerhei.

number of today's 401(k) plans are converted thrift plans and therefore could
contain balances from before 1981.

The most optimistic view of 401(k) holdings comes from a recent study
that relates balances to age and tenure and therefore addresses the issue of
limited contribution periods.[37] The analysis is based on the EBRI/ICI database, which in 2001 consisted of a representative sample of 401(k) plans
(48,786 of them) and their 14.6 million participants. By their very nature,
the data can only show the holdings for participants in their current plan. As
expected, balances as a percentage of earnings increase with age and time in
the plan (figure 2-6). The best possible statistic from this analysis is that people in their sixties who have been in a 401(k) plan for more than thirty years
have balances of about 290 percent of earnings. This sounds like a lot of
money—roughly $145,000 for the worker earning $50,000—but this result
must be interpreted with caution. First, these are average, not median, ratios,
and balances skewed toward higher paid workers overstate the balances for

37. Holden and VanDerhei (2003).

the typical worker. Second, using a rough rule of thumb, an assets-to-earnings percentage of 280 implies a replacement rate of 28 percent.[38] This is less than half the 58 percent produced by the simulations and, even when combined with Social Security, will not produce adequate replacement. Third, many workers will not be able to enjoy more than thirty years of continuous participation in a 401(k) and will end up with significantly lower replacement rates.[39] Thus even the most positive perspective on 401(k) balances suggests that they are modest today and, more important, will be modest in the future.

The finding that the typical 401(k) participant has only modest holdings appears inconsistent with other studies. For example, one study asked whether 401(k) accumulations generate significant income for future retirees and responded with a resounding yes.[40] Another group of researchers reported that the ratio of private pension assets to wages and salaries increased fivefold between 1975 and 1999 in large part due to 401(k) plans and that this "will likely mean large increases in the assets of future retirees."[41] Simulations like these, including our own, do show that 401(k) plan accumulations could be significant, but surveys show that for the typical person they are not.

Perhaps, we should not be expecting dramatically higher 401(k) holdings. A recent look at the ratio of pension assets to wages and salaries for the period for which consistent data are available indicates that they have increased from 90 percent in 1985 to about 140 percent in 2002.[42] This 55 percent increase, albeit over a shorter period, is a far cry from the fivefold

---

38. The replacement rate can be estimated by dividing the 401(k) earnings percentage by ten. This calculation assumes an annuity factor of ten, commonly seen as a good approximation of the compounded effects of mortality and discount rates for individuals near retirement. For example, an individual approaching retirement with 401(k) balance equal to 150 percent salary will have a replacement rate of 15 percent.

39. Holden and VanDerhei (2002).

40. Holden and VanDerhei (2002).

41. Poterba, Venti, and Wise (2001), p. 51.

42. Authors' calculations based on data from the Board of Governors, *Flow of Funds* (2003), and the Bureau of Economic Analysis (2002). Poterba, Venti, and Wise (2001) may exaggerate the growth in pension assets relative to wages and salary because of data problems and the bull market of the 1990s. The data problem is that asset figures before 1985, particularly for IRAs, are not accurate. The Federal Reserve has created a consistent series for defined benefit, defined contribution, and IRA assets from 1985 to the present. These data show that private pension assets rose from 90 percent of private sector wages and salary in 1985 to 143 percent in 2002. These figures should be adjusted for the Thrift Savings Plan, which is included in the private sector data and grew from zero in 1986 to about $100 billion in 2002. With this adjustment, the 2002 figure becomes 140 percent of wages and salaries. Thus over the period 1985–2002 the ratio of private pension assets to wages and salaries increased 55 percent.

Table 2-6. *401(k) Accumulations at Age Sixty-Two, by Starting Age*
Dollars

Age at which contributions begin	9 percent contribution rate	Contribution rate that maintains constant total contributions
30	353,408	353,408
35	277,007	308,845
40	208,232	275,270
45	146,539	244,473
50	93,358	216,763
55	49,542	192,244

Source: Authors' calculations based on simulations summarized in table 2-2.

increase between 1975 and 1999 that has received so much attention. Moreover, such an increase seems fully consistent with the rising percentage of the work force entering their prime savings years (forty-five years and older) and the continued trend toward full funding of defined benefit plans.[43]

But the problem still remains of reconciling low asset holdings with the reported contribution rates to 401(k) plans. Every study, including the data reported in table 2-4, indicates that those who join 401(k) plans make significant contributions across age and income groups. Yet they do not appear to end up with substantial asset accumulation. How does this happen? Apparently the lure of the employer match encourages workers to contribute, while the pressure to spend leads them to take their investments in cash when they change jobs. (The problem is discussed in detail in chapter 6).

To the extent that young people cash in their 401(k) savings, they effectively postpone saving for retirement until they are older. The timing of retirement saving, however, has an enormous impact on how much money people have when they stop working. Table 2-6 shows accumulations at age sixty-two, depending on when the individual starts contributing. At a 9 percent combined employee-employer contribution rate and our standard return on assets, a worker who starts contributing at age thirty will have $353,408 at age sixty-two, the amount in the simulation presented earlier. However, if the employee starts contributing at a later age, the total drops. Part of the loss comes from lower contributions and part from the shorter period of time in which investment earnings accumulate. The importance of investment earnings is illustrated in the second column of table 2-6. This calculation allows the contribution rate to vary, so that the participant can make catch-up con-

43. The percentage of the labor force aged forty-five and older increased from 27.9 percent in 1985 to 35.6 percent in 2001. See U.S. Bureau of the Census (1995, 2002).

tributions in order to keep lifetime contributions the same regardless of when they start. Here the decline in wealth is due entirely to lower investment earnings resulting from the abbreviated accumulation period. Even with the same lifetime contributions, starting at age fifty rather than age thirty reduces the accumulation at age sixty-two from $353,408 to $216,763. For workers with relatively flat age-earnings profiles, or who shift to more conservative investments as they age, the decline would be even greater.

In 401(k) plans, a major risk to future accumulations is thus the failure to save continuously from the beginning of one's working life. Young people appear to put the money into their plan, but when they receive lump-sum payments as they change jobs they also appear to take a significant portion in cash. In terms of dollar amounts, 20 percent of lump-sum distributions are taken as cash; in terms of number of distributions, 55 percent are taken as cash. These transactions usually involve small amounts typically associated with younger workers. This pattern is consistent with the notion that individuals do not start continuous retirement saving until they are older.

Mobile Workers and Traditional Defined Benefit Plans

Although a late start is a major risk to benefits under a 401(k) plan, shifting jobs seriously erodes retirement income in traditional defined benefit plans. Despite a significant growth in hybrids, more than half of defined benefit plans still base benefits on some form of final average earnings.[44] Workers with such plans who change jobs, even among firms with identical plans and immediate vesting, receive significantly lower benefits than workers with continuous coverage under a single plan. The reason job changers have less retirement wealth is because their benefits are based on earnings at the time they terminate employment. Workers who do not change jobs see their earnings rise over their careers, due to inflation and productivity growth. Job changers, however, lose the increase in their retirement benefits generated by this growth in nominal earnings (table 2-7).These differences would be greater if inflation and real wage growth were faster, because final earnings from earlier jobs become increasingly insignificant with rapidly rising wages (figure 2-7).

The only way for mobile employees to avoid such losses under traditional plans would be for the employer to provide benefits based on projected earnings at age sixty-two rather than on earnings at the time the employee leaves

---

44. Watson Wyatt Worldwide, "Survey of Actuarial Assumptions and Funding" (www.watsonwyatt.com/research/resrender.asp?id=w-631).

Table 2-7. *Wealth under a Defined Benefit Plan, Three Job Change Scenarios*
Dollars

Age	No job change	Job change at age 45	Job change at age 40 and age 50
35	20,421	20,421	20,421
45	91,187	81,547	70,552
50	147,268	116,611	102,804
55	213,916	163,822	143,942
62	303,560	237,926	213,190

Source: Authors' calculations based on simulations summarized in table 2-2.

Figure 2-7. *Defined Benefit Replacement Rates, Three Job Change Scenarios and Three Inflation Rate Scenarios*

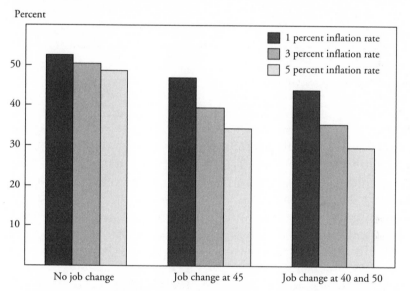

Source: Authors' calculations based on the simulations summarized in table 2-2.

the job. Improving benefits for terminated employees, however, would greatly increase employer costs or lower benefits for the remaining employees. The current practice of providing lower benefits to mobile employees also reduces turnover and retains skilled workers, which, after all, was one of the motivations for establishing traditional defined benefit plans. Hence indexing the benefits for terminated employees has never been politically acceptable. But the new cash balance plans accomplish precisely this goal through more steady benefit accruals. The result is improved benefits for mobile employees at the expense of long-term workers.

Figure 2-8. *Median Years of Tenure with Current Employer for Workers over Age Twenty-Five, 1983–2002*

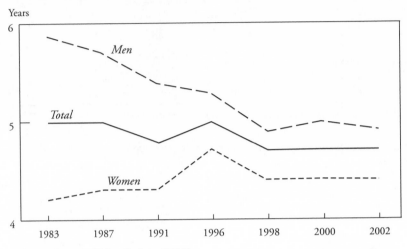

Source: Bureau of Labor Statistics (2003).

Because mobile workers lose a significant portion of their benefits under traditional defined benefit plans, the simple simulations presented earlier, which show the retirement wealth of employees with continuous coverage under a traditional defined benefit plan, significantly overstate the benefits that average workers get in the defined benefit world.

Commentators often suggest increased mobility of U.S. workers is one factor that explains the shift in coverage from defined benefit plans to 401(k)s. The U.S. work force is extremely mobile. For workers twenty-five years and older, median tenure with current employers is less than five years (figure 2-8). Among those ages forty-five through forty-nine, less than half have been with their employer for more than ten years (figure 2-9).[45] Whether mobility has increased over time is an unsettled and controversial question. Though anecdotes of large layoffs in downtimes and job-hopping workers in boom times are rife, the statistics look remarkably stable. Determining trends in labor mobility, however, is more complicated than looking at graphs; it involves sorting out cyclical factors and changes in the age and sex composition of the labor force. For example, greater participation by women lowers average job tenure, as women enter and exit the labor force to raise children. But as more women build careers, tenures increase. The age

45. Authors' calculations based on Current Population Survey, 1983–2000.

Figure 2-9. *Employed Workers Aged Forty-Five through Forty-Nine with More than Ten Years of Tenure, 1983–2002*

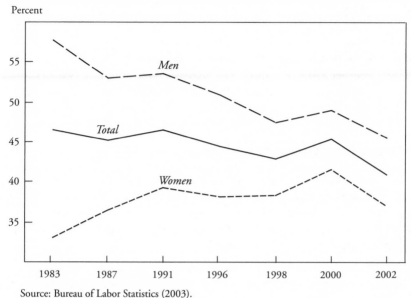

Percent

Source: Bureau of Labor Statistics (2003).

distribution of the labor force is also important, since older workers are more likely to be in longer tenure jobs.

Economists who have studied trends in mobility have split into two camps, one that supports the popular view of increased mobility and another that disputes it. Using the Current Population Survey (CPS) data, the first group of researchers finds a moderate decline in job stability from the 1980s into the early 1990s, though women experienced increased stability.[46] This group also detects a decline in job stability for older workers, especially men, which points to a decline in career jobs. Other researchers, using data from the CPS and the Panel Study of Income Dynamics (PSID), find a decline in the share of workers with ten or more years of tenure with the same employer.[47] With most of the change occurring among older workers toward the end of the period, their results are consistent with popular opinion.

The skeptics employ different data sets and different measures to challenge the conventional wisdom. Using the PSID and monthly data from the Survey of Income and Program Participation, researchers find no change in short-term turnover for male workers between the 1980s and 1990s.[48] Using

46. Neumark, Polsky, and Hansen (1999).
47. Jaeger and Stevens (1999).
48. Gottschalk and Moffitt (1999).

the March CPS (a more extensive survey than the standard CPS used in the studies mentioned above), another researcher finds that the rate at which employees separated from their jobs actually decreased slightly between 1976 and 2000.[49] A third group among the skeptics finds that long-term employment remains common, though the distribution of those jobs appears to be changing as women compete with men for the long-term jobs.[50]

Thus whether labor mobility has increased over the last two decades remains an open question. That the U.S. labor market is highly mobile, however, is not in doubt.

401(k)s and the Timing of Retirement

The simulations presented above assume that employees covered by a traditional defined benefit plan and those covered by a 401(k) plan retire at the same age. This is probably not correct; the shift to 401(k) plans will almost certainly affect retirement patterns. The reason is that provisions in many traditional defined benefit plans offer significant incentives to retire early, but 401(k) plans are neutral with respect to retirement age.

Traditional defined benefit plans are structured to encourage workers not only to remain with the firm until retirement but also to retire by a particular age. They do that by providing a significant pension benefit at the age of early retirement—a benefit with far less than the full actuarial reduction for the longer period of time that the worker will receive a pension.[51] Workers can claim this pension with less than a full actuarial reduction only if they stay to the age of early retirement, often fifty-five; the benefits of those who leave earlier are determined under the regular benefit formula. So the value of a worker's benefits rises gradually until age fifty-four and then jumps suddenly at age fifty-five. At that age, the increased value of pension wealth, and the income it provides, becomes a significant incentive to retire.[52] The sub-

49. Stewart (2002).

50. Farber (1996, 1997).

51. A fair actuarial adjustment for early retirement is approximately 7 percent for each year before the normal retirement age. Many traditional plans, however, reduce the annual benefit by only 5 percent for each year before the normal retirement age.

52. An intuitive explanation of the early retirement incentive is offered by Halperin and Schnall (2000). Assume that the firm imposes no reduction for retiring before age sixty-two. Then, although working past the early retirement age allows the person to earn additional benefits for additional years of service, it also reduces the value of benefits earned up to that age. The dollar value of these benefits remains unchanged, but they will be received for fewer years. This decline in value of retirement benefits from continued employment was even more severe before legislation prohibited the practice of ceasing benefit accruals after the normal retirement age.

sidy implicit in the less-than-actuarial reduction then gradually declines and disappears entirely at the normal retirement age.[53] The disappearance of the subsidy provides a powerful incentive to retire before the plan's normal retirement age (see box 2-2).[54]

Defined contribution plans operate differently. A worker's accumulated pension wealth changes each year by contributions to the account and the earnings on accumulated assets, but it is unaffected by the worker's retirement decision. Pension wealth continues to rise even if contributions are zero (assuming that earnings on assets are positive), and retirement incentives are simply not present. The only aspect of pension wealth in a defined contribution or 401(k) plan that might affect retirement age is the constraint, imposed by the government, that funds cannot be withdrawn without a penalty until the worker reaches age fifty-nine-and-a-half.[55] Otherwise, 401(k) plans should not encourage retirement at any particular age.

Two pieces of evidence suggest that the shift from defined benefit to 401(k) plans will change retirement patterns. The first is a couple of empirical studies showing that the financial incentives in defined benefit plans cause employees to retire earlier than employees in defined contribution plans.[56] According to one study, defined benefit participants retire almost two years sooner. Based on this estimate, changes in pension type between 1983 and 1993 raised the median retirement age over that period by roughly three months. The other study finds that workers covered by a defined benefit plan retire fifteen months earlier than those covered by a 401(k) plan.[57]

The second piece of evidence is more suggestive than scientific. American men have retired at younger and younger ages over the course of the last cen-

53. Often working beyond the normal retirement age results in negative pension accruals. The law requires that the wage increases of those who work beyond the normal retirement age be reflected in higher retirement benefits. But it does not prevent firms from capping the years of service used to calculate benefits; nor does it require firms to provide actuarial adjustments for the fact that participants will receive benefits for fewer years. See McGill and others (1996).

54. Considerable research has been done on the incentives embedded in defined benefit plans. An early study by Kotlikoff and Wise (1989) documents the incentives in a single plan for a Fortune 500 company and in a nationally representative cross section of plans. Stock and Wise (1990a, 1990b), Lumsdaine, Stock, and Wise (1992), and Samwick (1998) have done similar studies. Researchers have taken different approaches to characterizing the incentives in the plans. Stock and Wise developed an "option value" measure to reflect the utility gains or losses from postponing retirement, while Coile and Gruber (2000) introduce a somewhat simpler concept of "peak value" of pension wealth accruals.

55. Withdrawals without penalty can begin at age fifty-five as part of an early retirement arrangement. Moreover, withdrawals based on life expectancy or in the form of an annuity can begin at any age without penalty.

56. Friedberg and Webb (2000).

57. Munnell, Cahill, and Jivan (2003).

Box 2-2. *Hybrid Defined Benefit Plans and Early Retirement Incentives*

The elimination of early retirement subsidies may be an important motive behind the conversion from traditional defined benefit plans to hybrids, both cash balance and pension equity plans.[1] The figure shows the present value of accrued pension benefits as a multiple of annual pay under a traditional plan and a hybrid plan. Hybrid accumulations rise at a steady pace with no jump in benefits at an early retirement age and no decline thereafter. Thus they provide no incentive to leave. The elimination of the early retirement incentives is in part probably a response by employers to changing labor market conditions. The 1990s saw low unemployment rates and relatively small numbers of workers entering the market. Employers may no longer want pension plans that encourage workers to leave in their fifties, when they are still productive and still useful to the company.

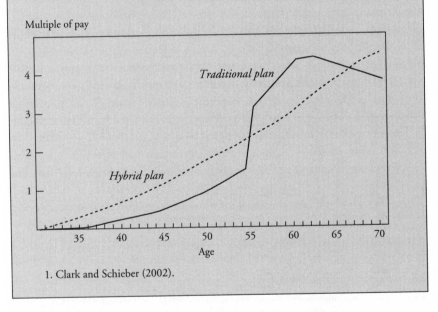

Multiple of pay

1. Clark and Schieber (2002).

tury. Since 1985, however, the downward trend in retirement age appears to have stabilized. The question is, Why? One explanation is that the environment has changed, with one important change in the environment being the shift from defined benefit to defined contribution plans.[58] In short, all else

58. Burtless and Quinn (2001). Other potential explanations include the fact that Social Security was no longer growing more generous, the Social Security earnings test was relaxed, and by 1986 mandatory retirement was virtually eliminated for the vast majority of workers.

equal, eliminating the incentives to retire early commonly found in defined benefit plans should lead to later retirement. This impact on retirement calls into question the results of the simulations presented earlier, which assume that the typical worker covered by a defined benefit plan and the typical worker covered by a 401(k) plan retire at the same age. All else equal, the 401(k) worker is likely to retire later and thus end up with more retirement wealth.

Financial Risk

When defined benefit and 401(k) plans are compared, rarely is all else equal. A key way in which the two plans differ is the allocation of financial risk. One type of financial risk is the possibility that the real rate of return will fall below historic norms during the accumulation phase. That is, if the stock market falls, the sponsor of a defined benefit plan must cover promised benefits. In a 401(k) plan, the participant suffers the loss. Another type of financial risk occurs at retirement. In a traditional defined benefit plan, benefits are paid automatically as an annuity and are guaranteed for as long as the employee lives. The only way that a 401(k) participant or a particpant in a new hybrid plan can insure against outliving resources is to purchase an annuity, and the price of that annuity will largely depend on the interest rate at which the insurance company can invest its funds. In the case of a traditional defined benefit plan, the employer bears this risk.

The first source of financial risk occurs before retirement. Figure 2-10 shows the real (inflation-adjusted) returns on stocks and bonds during the last hundred years. Over this period the average real return on stocks was 6.9 percent and on bonds 1.6 percent. The variability, as measured by the standard deviation, was much higher for stocks than bonds: 18.8 percent and 3.8 percent. This means that stock returns varied from negative numbers in 1920 and 1980 to returns in excess of 12 percent in the mid-1930s, the 1960s, and the 1990s. In contrast to these enormous fluctuations, the simulations in this chapter assume that the worker earns a steady rate of return of 7.6 percent (4.6 percent real plus 3 percent inflation) based on a portfolio equally divided between stocks and bonds. This produces an accumulation of $353,408 at age sixty-two for our hypothetical worker; if returns were higher the accumulation would be greater, if lower the accumulation would be smaller. Thus the outcome in a 401(k) plan, or any defined contribution plan, depends on what investments the participant selects and how those investments perform over time. (The impact of investment decisions on retirement wealth is discussed in detail in chapters 4 and 5.)

Figure 2-10. *Real Stock and Bond Returns, 1910–2002*[a]

Percent

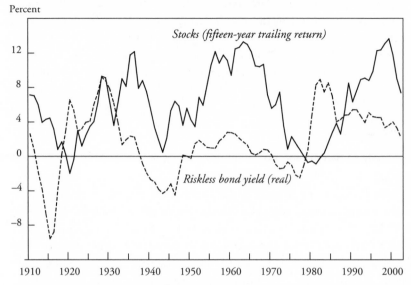

Source: Burtless (2002). Burtless's calculations use data from Standard and Poor's composite stock price index, Federal Reserve Bank of St. Louis, and U.S. Bureau of Labor Statistics.

a. To eliminate some of the fluctuations in annual rates of return, Burtless reports the annual rate of return on a dollar invested in the stock market fifteen years before the indicated years.

The second source of financial risk occurs if the participant wishes to purchase an annuity to avoid outliving his or her accumulated wealth. The price of the annuity depends on a host of factors: the age of the worker, marketing and other expenses incurred by the insurance company, the amount of adverse selection (that is, the extent to which only people who expect to live for a long time purchase annuities), and the interest rate. If interest rates are high, the insurance company can expect to make substantial earnings on the participant's initial payment and therefore can provide a high monthly amount to the purchaser. If interest rates are low at the time the annuity is purchased, the monthly payment will also be low. (Annuitization is discussed in chapter 7.)

A recent study shows how these two types of financial risk can affect the pension benefits received by a participant in a 401(k) plan.[59] The exercise involves a number of assumptions. Workers are assumed to enter the work force at age twenty-two beginning in 1871, to work forty years, to retire at age sixty-two beginning in 1911, and to live another eighteen years. Each

59. Burtless (2000).

Figure 2-11. *Replacement Rates, Two Investment Strategies, 1910–2002*

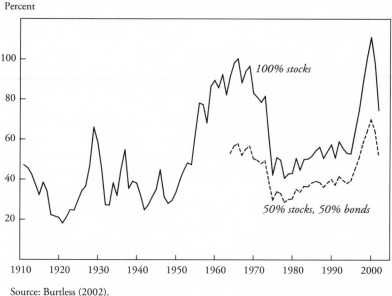

Percent

Source: Burtless (2002).

year they contribute 6 percent of their income to their defined contribution plan; they invest either all in stocks or half in stocks and half in bonds; and at retirement they buy an annuity. Real wage growth in the economy is 2 percent a year. Figure 2-11 shows the benefits received as a percentage of earnings before retirement. Remember, these workers differ only in that they face different stock and bond returns over their lifetimes.

Under the strategy of investing all their contributions in stocks, workers retiring in 1920 would have received a replacement rate of 20 percent; in 1960, 85 percent; in 1980, 40 percent; in 2000, 110 percent; and in 2002, 49 percent. These differences in replacements rates are due solely to the fluctuations in stock returns and in the interest rates that insurance companies use to determine annuity payments. Figure 2-11 also shows the replacement rates for workers who split their portfolio evenly between stocks and bonds. Replacement rates for them are approximately two-thirds of that gained by those who invested only in stocks. While the fluctuations are somewhat less, they remain quite pronounced. When the employee bears the investment risk, pension income will depend crucially on the investments selected and the performance of those investments.

Many contend that shifting the financial risk to the employee is a major attraction of 401(k) plans to employers. The argument requires a little thought, however, since the employer could always have shifted that risk by relying on defined contribution rather than defined benefit plans. Yet during the pre-ERISA period, employers chose to adopt defined benefit plans as their primary pensions. Why did their willingness to bear risk change? Perhaps it did not. Maybe employers were never willing to bear the full financial risk, and before ERISA they shifted some of the risk to employees by only partially funding their benefit commitments or funding them with company stock. If things turned out badly, employees would end up with less than their promised benefits. After ERISA, partial funding was far less available as a risk-sharing mechanism. Employers were required to fund their pensions more fully, investment in company stock was limited, and employers were required to pay premiums to the PBGC and were also required to back any shortfall with their own net worth.[60] As a result, employers had to bear much more of the risk. They found this unacceptable and shied away from establishing new defined benefit plans. The advent of 401(k) plans simply made the change to defined contribution plans easier. Today, the majority of households with pensions are covered by plans in which they bear the full financial risk.

Highlighting the risk in defined contribution plans does not mean that traditional defined benefit plans are risk free. Before 1974 employees covered by inadequately funded or mismanaged defined benefit plans bore the risk of losing their benefits if their plan terminated. Now employee pensions are insured by the PBGC.[61] For pension plans terminating in 2003, the maximum amount guaranteed by the PBGC is $3,665 a month for a worker retiring at age sixty-five, less for workers who claim benefits before age sixty-five. When a plan terminates without sufficient assets, the PBGC assumes the assets of the plan and the responsibility for paying guaranteed benefits. The PBGC can hold the sponsoring company liable for the underfunding, although the PBGC may not always be able to collect. Any insured benefits not covered by the plan's assets and the net worth of the company are covered by PBGC revenues from premiums assessed on employers. Workers whose vested pensions do not exceed the maximum covered by the PBGC—and this includes most workers—are protected against the loss of benefits under a defined benefit plan. Higher earners, however, may lose substantial pension income.

Although the PBGC protects benefits already earned, workers still face the possibility of abrupt changes in expected retirement benefits. This happens

60. Beginning in 1988 employers with underfunded plans were required to pay higher PBGC premiums than those whose plans were fully funded.
61. Munnell (1982).

whenever a company shuts down a plan and does not replace it. Less dramatic but still significant changes to expected pension benefits can occur when an employer transforms a traditional defined benefit plan to a cash balance or some other type of hybrid plan. The prospect of substantially smaller future accruals is particularly hard on employees in their fifties, who have little time to revamp their retirement savings plan.

Conclusion

This chapter addresses the question of whether employees are better or worse off as a result of the shift from defined benefit plans to 401(k) plans. The answer appears to be as follows. The percentage of the work force covered by pensions is no greater today than it was before the shift: roughly half of those aged twenty-five through sixty-four are covered by a pension plan at any moment in time. So the question becomes whether those lucky enough to have a pension are faring better or worse. Simple simulations suggest that workers have the potential to do better under a 401(k) plan than under a typical defined benefit plan. Steady participation should provide a sixty-two-year-old worker (earning $52,650 today) with pension wealth equal to about $355,000—6.7 times final earnings. This amount combined with Social Security would provide an adequate replacement of preretirement earnings.

This simple conclusion has to be modified in a number of ways, since different types of coverage bring different types of risk. Those covered under a defined benefit plan will have lower benefits to the extent that they change employers, even if all their employers sponsor an identical plan. The problem arises because benefits are based on earnings at termination rather than on earnings at age sixty-two. Similarly, many workers retire before the normal retirement age, because of the incentives embedded in most defined benefit plans, and end up with lower pension benefits.

On the 401(k) side, one major risk is that people do not save at a high enough rate over their lifetime, forgoing significant interest earnings on their contributions and ending up with much smaller accumulations at retirement. It appears that the contribution rate is relatively stable across age groups, so that people are not postponing contributions into 401(k) plans. On the other hand, accumulations in 401(k) accounts are significantly less than the simulations suggest if a total of $355,000 is to be reached. Even employees in their sixties with more than thirty years of participation have assets equal to 2.9 times their earnings rather than the 6.7 factor suggested by the simulations.

On balance, it appears that the temptation to use the money in 401(k) accounts results in people having less retirement income than they would if they were covered by a traditional defined benefit plan that pays an annuity. Of course, workers whose employers have converted to cash balance or pension equity plans face the same temptation. The shortfalls will be much more severe for low-income workers, since a disproportionate share of the lower paid workers either choose not to participate or participate at low levels. (This issue is explored in more depth in chapter 3.)

Another major risk—one that has become particularly evident during the recent stock market downturn—is that the employee bears the investment risk in a 401(k) plan. Many participants near retirement have seen their accumulated assets decline by as much as 50 percent since the onset of the bear market in 2000. Less talked about but equally important is the interest rate, which affects how much income the accumulated assets can produce in retirement. The combination of smaller account balances from a dismal stock market and meager earnings in a low-interest-rate environment presents what may be a worst-case scenario for participants nearing retirement today.

3

Participation and Contributions in 401(k) Plans

One of the defining characteristics of 401(k) plans is that participation is voluntary and that the employee as well as the employer can chose to make pretax contributions to the plan. In the defined benefit world—even in hybrid plans that look much like defined contribution plans—participation is automatic for all eligible workers, and the employer contributes and selects the investments. In 401(k) plans, on the other hand, the employee decides whether or not to participate, how much to contribute, and how to invest the assets.

The conclusion that emerged in the previous chapter was that how much retirement income workers will have depends crucially on whether they save in their 401(k) plans continuously throughout their working lives. The goal with regard to 401(k) plans is to ensure that eligible workers participate and that they contribute the amount needed to maintain their standard of living in retirement. This chapter takes a closer look at these participation and contribution decisions in 401(k) plans. (The following two chapters discuss investment decisions in 401(k) plans.)

Procrastination and inertia emerge as important explanations both for lack of participation in 401(k) plans and for the fact that those who do participate rarely change their contributions. For many workers the 401(k) plan presents one of the few financial decisions they ever have to make for themselves. Pension plans are complicated, and for many participants the decisions just seem overwhelming. The two final sections of the chapter discuss some policy options that may help workers to participate by capitalizing on the inertia in employees' behavior. (See appendix to this book for details on the regulatory framework covering participation and contributions in 401(k) plans.)

How Much Should People Save for Retirement?

Retirement benefits should enable individuals to maintain their standard of living in retirement. To set the stage for the discussion of 401(k) participation and contribution decisions it is useful to first look at how much people should save for retirement overall. For several reasons, the cash income needed to maintain living standards is likely to be lower in retirement. Retirees no longer need to save for retirement, and they pay lower taxes. Work-related expenses, such as clothing and transportation, are either no longer necessary or are much reduced. Furthermore, many households have paid off their mortgages, and they can consume some of their assets. Therefore, financial advisers often recommend that households require 65–85 percent of their preretirement income to maintain their well-being in retirement.

For workers in the low and middle portion of the income distribution, Social Security today provides considerable replacement income. A worker with a history of average earnings who retires at age sixty-five receives around 41 percent of preretirement earnings. Low-income workers receive a replacement rate of about 56 percent. The problem is that these replacement rates are scheduled to decline even under current law. The increase in the normal retirement age from sixty-five to sixty-seven is equivalent to an across-the-board benefit cut. Medicare part B premiums, which are deducted automatically, are scheduled to rise from 7 percent to 10 percent of Social Security benefits. And a greater portion of benefits will be taxable under the personal income tax. Any additional cuts to eliminate the program's financing gap will reduce replacement rates further. Finally, most people retire before age sixty-five, so their benefits are actuarially reduced. By 2030 the net Social Security replacement rate for a sixty-five-year-old with average earnings is likely to be about 27 percent and for the sixty-two-year-old about 21 percent.[1] Thus people will need to replace about 40–55 percent of their preretirement earnings from pension benefits and other saving to maintain their well-being in retirement.

1. Munnell (2003).

Are people saving enough to reach the suggested replacement rates? One way researchers have looked at this issue is to examine what happens to consumption at retirement. Although consumption is expected to be lower in retirement due to declining expenses, several studies indicate that consumption falls even more than anticipated.[2] Furthermore, the drop in consumption is larger for households that have less generous pension and Social Security benefits. These results imply that households' savings may be inadequate to reach target replacement rates. However, another study finds that the fall in consumption could be explained by the reduction in work-related and other expenses and, therefore, does not imply that people reach retirement with too little saving.[3] Researchers who examined savings targets based on the ratio of a household's wealth to its earnings find that, even though saving may be adequate for a majority of households, families in the bottom quartile of the wealth-to-earnings ratio are not saving enough.[4]

Taken together the various studies suggest that, although retirement saving may be adequate for some households, others clearly run the risk of ending up with too little retirement income today. The voluntary nature of 401(k) plans and the reduction in Social Security replacement rates increase the risk that in the future an even larger share of workers will lack sufficient retirement income.

Determination of Participation

The introduction of 401(k) plans has changed workers' responsibility in planning for retirement. In the defined benefit world, a worker in a company with a pension plan automatically participates in the pension plan, and the employer makes the contributions. Although many firms have converted their traditional defined benefit plans to hybrid plans that look more like defined contribution plans, participation and contributions are still automatic.

In the 401(k) world, things are different. The plans are voluntary in the sense that workers decide whether to participate and how much to contribute. These decisions are crucial for how much retirement savings a worker will have at retirement. The intent, of course, is that workers will participate and will make significant contributions. But far from all do. Data from the Current Population Survey (CPS) show that, in 1988, 43 percent of eligible

2. Bernheim, Skinner, and Weinberg (2001); Banks, Blundell, and Tanner (1998).

3. Hurd and Rohwedder (2003).

4. The model includes several important factors excluded from earlier studies, such as the use of housing equity or part-time work to finance consumption in retirement. See Engen, Gale, and Uccello (1999).

Table 3-1. *Eligibility and Participation in 401(k) Plans,*
by Earnings and Age, 2001
Percent

Earnings and age	Eligibility, all workers aged 20–64	Participation, eligible workers	Participation, all workers
Earnings (dollars)	52.1	74.1	38.6
Less than 20,000	27.5	49.9	13.7
20,000–39,999	56.9	70.5	40.1
40,000–59,999	70.1	78.7	55.2
60,000–79,999	76.3	83.2	63.5
80,000–99,999	77.4	87.6	67.8
100,000 and more	75.4	88.7	67.1
Age			
20–29	43.9	65.7	28.8
30–39	54.7	76.0	41.6
40–49	57.0	77.6	44.2
50–59	52.3	74.1	38.8
60–64	39.9	79.8	31.8

Source: Authors' calculations based on Board of Governors, *Survey of Consumer Finances* (SCF) (2001).

workers did not participate. By 1993 the situation had improved, but still 35 percent did not participate. According to the Survey of Consumer Finances (SCF), nonparticipation continued to decline during the 1990s. By 1998 nonparticipation was 25 percent. The most recent data from the 2001 Survey of Consumer Finances, however, show that the downward trend has stopped; in 2001, 26 percent of workers who were offered plans did not participate. Why do workers stay out of 401(k) plans? The answer is that the decision to participate is influenced both by individual characteristics and by plan design.

Income, Age, and Other Individual Characteristics

In one survey, many workers who had elected not to participate in a 401(k) plan explained that they "couldn't spare the money."[5] This statement suggests that low-income workers may be less likely to participate, and the evidence bears this out (table 3-1). Among workers with earnings between $20,000

5. Hinz and Turner (1998). Economists argue that the introduction of a pension benefit implies a reduction in cash wages because firms are not going to increase total compensation. For households with very low incomes, such a reduction would bring consumption close to the poverty level. For those households it probably makes more sense to increase current take-home pay rather than reducing it. It would therefore be better to improve retirement benefits through some redistributive policy rather than through tax-favored employer-sponsored pensions. See Halperin and Munnell (2004).

Table 3-2. *Participation of Eligible Workers in 401(k) Plans,*
by Earnings and Age, 2001
Thousands of dollars

Age	<20.0	20.0–39.9	40.0–59.9	60.0–89.9	80.0–99.9	>100.0
20–29	36.9	65.9	72.9	86.7	*	*
30–39	49.9	69.8	78.5	87.0	81.8	91.4
40–49	55.0	73.2	80.7	80.0	92.6	96.2
50–59	68.4	70.6	73.5	72.7	95.6	87.2
60–64	*	73.2	76.5	*	*	*

Source: Authors' calculations based on the 2001 SCF.
*Fewer than five observations.

and $40,000, only about half are eligible to join the plan; among those eligible, 70 percent participate. Among workers earning more than $40,000, two out of three are eligible and 80 percent or more participate. Thus the voluntary nature of 401(k) plans implies that low-income workers are at risk of failing to accumulate enough retirement wealth.

The previous chapter indicates that retirement wealth depends crucially on the age at which workers start making contributions. The earlier that workers start participating, the better off they will be in retirement. Table 3-1 indicates, however, that workers ages twenty through twenty-nine are less likely to participate than older workers.

Table 3-2 shows how earnings and age together affect the participation decision. Fewer than half of workers aged twenty to forty with earnings below $20,000 choose to participate in a 401(k) plan. Even for workers with salaries close to average ($20,000–$40,000), participation rates are low. It is not until workers approach age fifty that participation rates are similar to those for high-income workers. The simulation model presented in the previous chapter shows that a worker who postpones participation until age fifty will have only 26 percent of the retirement wealth of a similar worker who participated since age thirty.

In addition to earnings and age, other individual characteristics also influence workers' decisions. Several studies using data on households and firms examined how the various characteristics taken together affect the decision to participate.[6] The findings from these studies not only confirm the importance of earnings and age but also show that workers' financial knowledge

6. The studies that examine the factors that affect participation and contribution in 401(k) plans fall into two groups: those based on the Current Population Survey 1988 and 1993 Employee Benefit Supplements and those based on plan data. In addition, a study by Munnell, Sundén, and Taylor (2002) used the 1998 Survey of Consumer Finances.

affects their decision to participate. Workers commonly complain that pension plans are complicated and difficult to understand. Not surprisingly, researchers find that education and financial knowledge increase participation rates. The more schooling workers have, all else equal, the more likely they are to participate.

Researchers also find that many workers are overconfident about how much money they will have for retirement and therefore fail to save. In the 2002 Employee Benefit Research Institute's Retirement Confidence Survey, 47 percent of respondents said that they think that they will have enough money for retirement. Half of this group, however, had not yet started to save! Such overconfidence could stem from short planning horizons—a failure to even think about retirement. People who have long planning horizons and think about the next five years or more when they make financial decisions are far more likely to participate in 401(k) plans than workers who plan for only the next few years.[7] A survey by the Vanguard Group reports similar findings.[8] Workers who consider themselves "successful planners" have higher participation rates than workers who consider themselves "live-for-today" types.[9] People who like to save also tend to save more in all forms. One measure of workers' taste for saving is the amount of savings they have in addition to their 401(k) plan. The higher the workers' nonpension wealth, the more likely they are to participate in a 401(k) plan.

Plan Design

The features of the 401(k) plan have a significant impact on the participation decision. In particular, the presence of an employer matching contribution is important. Employers are not obligated to make contributions to 401(k) plans, but the vast majority of participants (91 percent, according to data from the Employee Benefit Research Institute/Investment Company Institute [EBRI/ICI] 401(k) database) belong to plans that offer a match.[10] In a survey of eligible workers who chose not to participate, 80 percent reported that they would likely enroll in the plan if offered a match or a better match.[11] Results from statistical analyses that relate the participation decision to an individual's characteristics and to plan design consistently show that the presence of an employer match makes it much more likely that employees

---

7. Munnell, Sundén, and Taylor (2002).

8. Vanguard Center for Retirement Research (2001).

9. Miller (2002).

10. The EBRI/ICI Participant-Directed Retirement Plan Data Collection Project includes administrative records for 11.8 million 401(k) plan participants.

11. Investment Company Institute (2000).

will participate.[12] Interestingly, while the presence of an employer match affects the decision to participate, the level of the match seems to be less important. The ability to borrow money from the plan or to make hardship withdrawals also makes workers more likely to participate in a 401(k).[13] If workers lose access to their funds until retirement, those who are liquidity constrained are less likely to participate. One concern, however, is that workers participate in the plan to take advantage of the employer match but then borrow or withdraw the funds before retirement.

Pension Coverage of Nonparticipants

401(k) plans were first introduced as supplements to defined benefit plans. Although reliance solely on 401(k) plans has increased significantly, many workers are still employed by firms that offer both a defined benefit plan and a 401(k) plan. Automatic coverage under a defined benefit plan, however, cannot explain the limited participation in 401(k) plans. Only 37 percent of nonparticipants are covered by a defined benefit plan, and the majority of these workers are high earners.[14] This means that most low-income workers who choose not to participate—85 percent of nonparticipants earning less than $20,000 and 60 percent of those earning between $20,000 and $40,000—are without pension coverage.

Workers' Contributions

The decision to participate is the first in a set of decisions that workers must make about their 401(k) plans. After deciding to participate, a worker has to decide how much to contribute to the plan. As discussed in chapter 2, how much workers contribute is crucial for how much retirement wealth they will have. The data presented in table 3-3 reveal that, once a worker has decided to participate, the percentage of earnings contributed is fairly similar across earnings and age categories.[15]

In addition to the employee contribution, the employer generally makes a matching contribution. The employer match has two components: the per-

---

12. For example, see Papke (1995); Papke and Poterba (1995); Even and MacPherson (2001); Clarke and Schieber (1998); and Choi and others (2001b).

13. Hungerford (1999).

14. Authors' calculations, based on 2001 Survey of Consumer Finances.

15. As noted in chapter 2, the median employer contribution held fairly steady at 3 percent during the 1990s. However, with the onset of the recession in March 2001, some employers, such as Ford, DaimlerChrysler, Goodyear, and Charles Schwab, started to cut back. Mary Williams Walsh and Patrick McGeehan, "Schwab to End Match to 401(k)s," *New York Times,* March 14, 2003.

Table 3-3. *Median Employee and Employer Contributions,*
Workers Participating in 401(k) Plans, 2001
Percent

Earnings and age	Employee contribution (median)	Employer contribution (median)
Earnings (dollars)	6.0	3.0
Less than 20,000	5.0	3.0
20,000–39,999	5.0	3.0
40,000–59,999	6.0	3.0
60,000–79,999	6.0	3.0
80,000–99,999	6.0	4.0
100,000 and more	7.9	3.0
Age		
20–29	5.2	3.0
30–39	6.0	3.0
40–49	6.0	3.0
50–59	6.0	3.0
60–64	5.0	4.3

Source: Authors' calculations based on the 2001 SCF.

centage of contributions that the employer will match (the match rate) and the percentage of the employee's earnings on which matches will be provided (the match level). According to the EBRI/ICI 401(k) data, the most common match is 50 percent of the employee's contribution (the match rate) up to 6 percent of earnings (the match level). The effective rate of this is 3 percent of earnings. Figure 3-1 shows the distribution of effective match rates.

Plan design, and in particular the match rate and the match level, are important determinants of how much participants contribute. Although it is clear that the match itself increases participation rates, it is less clear how the match level affects contributions. Suppose that a firm that previously did not match contributions decides to match 50 percent of the employees' contribution up to 6 percent of earnings. Some employees might lower their contribution rates, because they need to contribute less to reach the same overall contribution level. Other employees might increase their contributions up to 6 percent, because they receive an extra fifty cents for each dollar they contribute. Hence the theoretical outcome is ambiguous. Researchers find both positive and negative effects on worker contributions when match rates change. However, several studies show that contributions tend to cluster around the match level.[16] That is, if the employer matches up to 6 percent of

16. Kusko, Poterba, and Wilcox (1998); Choi and others (2001a).

Figure 3-1. *Distribution of Effective Match Rates among Plans Offering Matching Contributions, 1999*

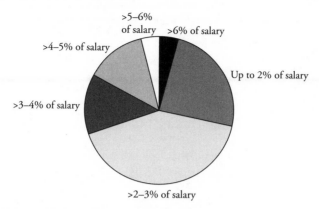

Source: Holden and VanDerhei (2001c).

earnings, employees are likely to contribute 6 percent to take full advantage of the match.

The ability to access the 401(k) account before retirement increases contributions. One study finds that the ability to borrow, holding all other factors constant, increases contribution rates by 2.6 percentage points.[17] Once again, it is worrisome if workers participate and contribute only so they can use the funds for a purpose other than retirement. The same study finds, however, that a worker's planning horizon is important to how much is contributed. Participants who only consider the next year or so in their financial decisions contribute significantly less to their 401(k) plans than workers with long horizons.

To ensure that high-income workers do not benefit unduly from the tax preferences accorded employer-sponsored pensions, Congress limited how much can be contributed to 401(k) plans. The Economic Growth and Tax Relief Reconciliation Act of 2001 (EGTRRA) raised the contribution limits.[18] One of the main arguments in favor of raising the employee contribution limits is that it would increase retirement savings. This argument implies that many workers were restricted by the limits before the increase. This is not the case. In fact less than 10 percent of workers were restricted by the 2001 limit of $10,500. The data also show that contributing the maximum is strongly related to earnings. A small percentage of low earners contribute the

17. Munnell, Sundén, and Taylor (2002).
18. See appendix for a discussion of contribution limits.

Table 3-4. *Participants Making Maximum Employee Contributions,*
by Earnings and Age
Percent

Earnings and age	Participants
Earnings (dollars)	
Less than 20,000	0.1
20,000–39,999	0.5
40,000–59,999	2.5
60,000–79,999	12.6
80,000–99,999	17.2
100,000 and more	53.0
All	8.4
Age	
20–29	2.6
30–39	8.4
40–49	8.8
50–59	12.4
60–64	12.6

Source: Authors' calculations based on the 2001 SCF.

maximum, while the percentage rises sharply for participants earning $60,000 or more (table 3-4).[19]

In summary, the participation and contribution decisions are strongly related to income and age. If income and age were the sole determinants, however, little could be done to improve retirement saving. But participation and contributions are also related to workers' planning horizons, the existence of a match rate, and the ability to borrow funds. These are factors that can be affected by policy. For example, individuals' horizons can be extended by information about the importance of planning, and employers can improve the appeal of their plans by providing matching contributions and the ability to borrow. The next two sections examine various policies that help increase participation and contributions among eligible workers.

19. These findings are consistent with a study by the U.S. General Accounting Office (2001), based on the 1998 Survey of Consumer Finances, that finds that 8 percent of participants would benefit from an increase in the contribution limits. Studies based on tax data find that approximately 5 percent of participants make maximum contributions. See Richardson and Joulfaian (2001). The share contributing the maximum is higher in the SCF than in tax data because the SCF oversamples high-wealth households and therefore provides a better description of the upper tail of the distribution.

Building on Procrastination and Inertia

The discussion so far indicates that, although simulations suggest that 401(k) plan accumulations can be significant, surveys show that they typically are not and that it is mostly young and low-income workers who choose not to participate in 401(k) plans. This group could benefit greatly by participating. They have a long time until retirement and can take advantage of the compounding of interest. They have few other assets, and participating in the 401(k) would provide retirement security that this group would otherwise not have. Given the scheduled reductions in Social Security replacement rates and the nation's increased reliance on 401(k) plans, this lack of participation is creating a serious retirement income problem.

Many workers who do not participate in 401(k) plans report that they cannot put away any money. As seen from the discussion above, many of these workers also have a short planning horizon. In addition, researchers contend that making decisions about retirement is one area in which workers are likely to procrastinate.[20] In fact, a common response of workers as to why they are not participating is, "I never got around to it."[21] One reason workers may not "get around to it" is that making decisions about a 401(k) plan is complicated. For many workers, and especially young workers, it is the first financial decision they have to make. In addition to deciding to participate workers must figure out how much to contribute and how to invest the money. Since plans often offer a myriad of options, the decisions can seem overwhelming. As a result, workers may put off the decision or simply feel that the cost of figuring it all out is greater than the benefit of participating.

Information on the importance of saving for retirement may help workers to decide to participate. But if procrastination and inertia are important, even workers who know they should participate may not. A solution that addresses both problems is to enroll all workers automatically and to let those who do not want to participate opt out. In 1998 and 2000 the Internal Revenue Service (IRS) issued regulations that allow employers to enroll employees automatically in 401(k) plans. Firms are willing to implement automatic enrollment because it makes it easier for them to pass nondiscrimination testing. Benefits consultants estimate that 14 percent of 401(k) sponsors had adopted automatic enrollment by 2002, up from 7 percent in 1999.[22] The advantage for workers is that they do not have to take any steps to enroll,

---

20. O'Donoghue and Rabin (1999).

21. Hinz and Turner (1998).

22. Hewitt Associates (2001). A survey of companies shows that 28 percent of companies were considering automatic enrollment. See Madrian and Shea (2002).

Table 3-5. *Effects of Automatic Enrollment on Participation,*
by Earnings and Age
Percent

Earnings and age	Participation rate, old cohort, no automatic enrollment	Participation rate, new cohort, automatic enrollment
Earnings (dollars)		
Less than 20,000	20.0	79.5
20,000–29,999	31.7	82.8
30,000–39,999	50.1	88.9
40,000–49,999	61.6	91.8
50,000–59,999	70.2	92.8
60,000–69,999	79.2	94.7
70,000–79,999	76.3	91.5
80,000 and more	76.3	94.2
All	48.7	85.9
Age		
20–29	36.7	82.7
30–39	47.9	86.3
40–49	54.9	90.1
50–59	64.3	90.0
60–64	60.6	86.0

Source: Madrian and Shea (2002).

which eliminates both the procrastination problem and the cost of "figuring it out."

Several studies show that automatic enrollment significantly increases participation.[23] Table 3-5 presents the response in a firm that introduced automatic enrollment for new employees in 1998.[24] The overall participation rate jumped from 49 percent to 86 percent. The changes were even larger for low-income workers. Only 32 percent of employees earning between $20,000 and $29,999 had participated before automatic enrollment; after automatic enrollment the participation rate was 83 percent, just 3 percentage points less than the rate for all employees.

For automatic enrollment to increase retirement saving, workers must stay in the plan. If workers who do not enroll on their own before automatic enrollment simply opt out after automatic enrollment, the policy would have no effect on retirement savings. But few workers at the firms that implement automatic enrollment opt out. In fact, the share that leaves is remarkably similar to the share that drops out of plans without automatic enrollment.

23. Madrian and Shea (2002); Choi and others (2001a, 2001b).
24. Madrian and Shea (2002).

One explanation for the low opt-out rates is inertia. Another explanation could be that once employees are in the plan they realize the benefits of savings. In either event, automatic enrollment has a powerful effect in increasing retirement saving, particularly for low-income workers.

The firms that introduced automatic enrollment in the studies mentioned above set the employee contribution rate to 2–3 percent of earnings, although most matched contributions up to 6 percent.[25] (Before the introduction of automatic enrollment, most workers who participated in the plan contributed at the 6 percent level.) Employees who wanted to contribute more than the default rate had to tell the firm to change their contributions. Most of the automatically enrolled workers remained at the default rate, even though it meant that they did not take advantage of the full match. After three years, almost half of the automatically enrolled workers still contributed at the default rate. Those who increased their contribution rates were mostly high-income workers. This experience with automatic enrollment demonstrates the power of inertia in the contribution decision and points to the importance of designing default options.[26]

In short, automatic enrollment has a dramatic effect on employee participation rates, with the largest increases among groups that benefit the most: low-income workers. Average savings in plans with automatic enrollment are lower because workers tend to stay with the low default contribution rates. The savings for workers at the low end of the wage distribution, however, are higher than what they would have been if they had to actively elect to join the plan.

Education and Participation

The previous section indicates that automatic enrollment substantially increases participation. Even workers who say that they cannot afford to save remain in the plan after being enrolled. Much of the explanation for low participation rates among young and low-income workers rests on factors such as short planning horizons and lack of financial knowledge. These characteristics make participation and contribution decisions overwhelming, and young and low-income workers often simply put off making a decision. All these factors can be affected by financial education.

---

25. A survey conducted by the Profit Sharing/401(k) Council of America (2001) shows that, overall, 76 percent of the firms that introduced automatic enrollment chose a contribution level of 2–3 percent.

26. Another example of employee inertia emerged from an experiment that shows that employers could increase contribution rates by letting employees precommit part of future salary increases to their 401(k) plans. See Benartzi and Thaler (2001).

Employers often offer financial education to encourage the rank and file to participate so that the firm's 401(k) plan passes nondiscrimination testing. (See appendix for nondiscrimination provisions.) Plan administrators also offer education, although this may be designed more to increase the asset base than to help with nondiscrimination testing. According to a survey from the mid-1990s almost 90 percent of all large firms offered some kind of financial education, most having added the programs after 1990.[27] Teaching workers the importance of retirement saving and the advantages of participating in a pension plan has had some positive effects, although the magnitude is difficult to measure.[28]

Various researchers have assessed the effects of employer-based informational programs on participation and contributions. One study confirms that employees who used the informational materials had higher participation rates than employees who did not.[29] A survey of employers likewise finds that workers who participate in retirement planning seminars have higher participation rates and that the largest gains are among nonhighly compensated employees.[30]Another study finds that employees who use the education materials are more likely to participate in the plan.[31] On the other hand, the effect on contribution levels is small.

Not all employees attend financial education seminars or read the materials. This is of concern if those who do not take part are also nonsavers. A recent study, however, shows that peer effects can be an important determinant of participation rates in 401(k) plans. That is, even if some workers do not participate in financial education, the fact that their colleagues do and communicate the information could have a positive effect on nonattendees' participation. The researchers demonstrate this effect by offering a group of employees a monetary reward to attend an educational seminar. The reward tripled attendance, and 401(k) participation increased significantly among those who attended. Participation in the 401(k) plan also increased among employees who had not attended the seminar but who worked in the same departments as those who did, demonstrating the peer effect on participation decisions.[32]

---

27. Bayer, Bernheim, and Scholz (1996).

28. To fully evaluate the effects of employer education it is necessary to compare the benefits of increased participation with the costs of providing education. Currently, no study has undertaken a cost-benefit analysis of employer education.

29. Bernheim and Garrett (1996).

30. Bayer, Bernheim, and Scholz (1996).

31. Clark and Schieber (1998).

32. Duflo and Saez (2002).

Conclusion

This chapter considers the participation and contribution decisions in 401(k) plans. In contrast to traditional defined benefit plans, employees must decide whether or not to participate and how much to contribute. The voluntary nature of 401(k) plans puts the risk and responsibility on the worker to plan for retirement. To provide the 40–55 percent or more of preretirement earnings that retirees will need in the future to supplement Social Security, it is important that eligible workers participate and contribute as much as possible toward their saving target.

Participating in and contributing to a 401(k) plan involves complicated transactions, which can be overwhelming. Many workers, especially the young and the low paid, have little experience in making financial decisions. As a result, many of these workers simply decide not to participate or put off the decision to participate. Workers also say that they cannot afford to save. The net result is that only 74 percent of eligible workers actually participate in 401(k) plans. Most participants are in plans in which employers match contributions, and employee contributions tend to cluster at the match level.

The question is how to increase participation and contribution rates for young and low-income workers. The answer appears to be automatic enrollment. Beginning in 1998 the IRS allowed firms to automatically enroll all workers who were eligible to participate in the plan. Those who did not want to participate could opt out. This change in the default option dramatically increased participation rates, especially among low-income earners. Even after three or four years, the vast majority were still participating.

The dramatic increase in participation resulting from automatic enrollment shows the importance of procrastination and inertia, behavior that is readily affected by setting the default to the desired outcome, in this case participation. Even workers who stated that they could not afford to save remained in the plan. This indicates that, once workers experience the advantage of saving, they will continue to save.

4

Investment Decisions in 401(k) Plans

The explosive growth of 401(k) plans has left employees with tough investment decisions. A lot is at stake; poor investment choices will leave households with unacceptably low retirement consumption. This chapter explores the options facing 401(k) participants and how participants select their investments. The evidence suggests that most people do not do a very good job. The question is whether it would be better to turn employees into sophisticated investors or to make 401(k) investing simpler. The next chapter turns to the special issues raised by employee investments in company stock.

Investment Options

Unlike traditional defined benefit plans and the new hybrid plans, in which the employer guarantees a certain monthly benefit, retirement income in 401(k) plans depends on the success of the participant's investment choices. Moreover, most participants' financial security in retirement rests on these choices because the 401(k) often represents the bulk of the family's financial assets. In 2001, for example, households approaching retirement (ages fifty-five to sixty-four) had a median wealth of $181,500. Housing, pensions, and nonfinancial assets account for 78 percent of the total, leaving

Table 4-1. *Median and Mean 401(k)/IRA Assets, Households, by Age Group, 2001*

Dollars

Age group	Median	Mean
20-29	4,000	10,100
30-39	16,000	36,200
40-49	35,000	92,100
50-59	50,000	158,500
60-64	59,000	198,600
65-69	78,000	194,500
All (20-69)	27,600	100,400

Source: Authors' calculations, based on Board of Governors, *Survey of Consumer Finances* (SCF), 2001.

the household approaching retirement with less than $40,000 in financial assets.[1] Thus for middle-income families, the allocation of their 401(k) assets determines their financial posture.

For higher income families who do have some outside investments, the importance of their 401(k) investment decisions depends on what they do with the rest of their portfolio.[2] That is, to determine whether participants make sensible 401(k) investment decisions requires knowing how they invest their outside assets as well. Several studies that looked at these outside investments find that investment allocations inside and outside retirement accounts are similar.[3] Participants who hold mostly interest-earning assets in their 401(k) plans also hold mostly interest-earning assets outside of their 401(k) plans, and the same is true for stocks. Thus for high-income as well as middle-income households, what happens in their 401(k) plan is a pretty good indication of how secure they will be in retirement.

Before looking at how people make investment decisions, it is useful to have a sense of how much money they have in their accounts. Again, the data include individual retirement accounts (IRAs) because, at least until recently, these balances are mostly rollovers from 401(k)s.[4] Median 401(k)/IRA assets for households in 2001 were $27,600, and the mean was $100,400 (table

1. Aizcorbe and others (2003). For further information, see discussion of table 7-6 in chapter 7.

2. More than 60 percent of households with 401(k) plans have some investments outside the plan. That is, they own mutual funds, bonds, directly held stock, savings bonds, or certificates of deposit in addition to their 401(k) plan.

3. Bodie and Crane (1997); Sundén and Surette (1998); Ucello (2000); Weisbenner (1999).

4. Estimates are that 22 percent of the annual flow into IRA accounts can be attributed to rollovers and 76 percent to investment returns primarily on rollover amounts; only about 2 percent of the inflow comes from tax deductible contributions. See Copeland (2001).

Table 4-2. *Annual Returns on Financial Instruments and Inflation Rate,*
1926–2001

Percent

Financial instrument	Rate of return	Standard deviation
Stocks[a]	10.2	20.5
Long-term corporate bonds	5.9	8.7
Intermediate government bonds	5.4	5.8
U.S. Treasury bills	3.8	3.2
Inflation	3.0	4.4

Source: Ibbotson (2003). Based on copyrighted works by Ibbotson and Sinquefield. All rights reserved. Used with permission.

a. Stocks refer to the returns on large company stocks. Over the same period, the return and standard deviation on small company stocks was somewhat higher: 12.5 percent return, with a standard deviation of 33.2 percent.

4-1). The mean is higher than the median because the dollars are skewed toward the large accounts. In both cases, however, these are modest balances. Note that in 2003 a $100,000 life annuity purchased by a male aged sixty-five yields about $670 a month.

In making 401(k) investment decisions, the initial challenge is how to balance risk and return—that is, how much to invest in stock and how much in bonds or some form of fixed income security. The next step is how to adjust those initial allocations in response to age and changes in the market. Setting the initial allocations was once pretty easy because the options were few: It simply required getting the proportions right. That is, people could choose among a bond fund, a stock fund, and perhaps a money market fund (table 4-2). Investors could figure out how much risk they could withstand and vary their equity and other holdings accordingly.

Today, sponsors of 401(k) plans have dramatically increased the number of options available to participants. For example, in plans managed by Fidelity Investments, which represent $400 billion in assets (or 18 percent of the holdings of defined contribution plans), the number of investment options has more than doubled over the period 1995–2000. Plans with 10,000 participants or more now offer an average of thirty-eight investment options, up from fourteen in 1995; even plans with 5,000–10,000 participants average twenty-two options, up from nine in 1995. But this is not a phenomenon limited to a few large plans. Roughly half of participants in the Fidelity sample are in plans that provide more than sixteen options. These include money market funds; guaranteed investment contracts; short-term, intermediate, and long-term bonds; high-yield bonds; large-cap and small cap domestic equities; global equities; and equities from emerging markets.

Fidelity plans may be at the high end in terms of options, but they are representative of the trend toward more choice.

Many of the investment options are made through mutual funds. Despite recent scandals of abusive trading practices, mutual funds are the logical investment for 401(k) plans. As a result, the mutual fund industry has grown enormously with the expansion of 401(k) plans. These funds offer diversified investments at lower costs than the employer would incur if required to hire outside investment managers to satisfy fiduciary standards. Mutual funds also offer the employee self-directed investment with some protection against unsuitable investments.[5]

The important issue is whether an increasing number of investment options helps or hinders plan participants.[6] Psychologists and economists generally believe that more choice is better. Psychologists argue that having personal choice increases motivation, sense of control, performance, and general satisfaction. In typical experiments, psychology researchers give individuals a choice among half a dozen activities in one case and in the other tell them specifically what to do; they then compare participants' motivation. Time and again the studies show that giving choice increases motivation and improves the performance on a variety of tasks. Economists also claim that more choice is better, as it allows individuals to balance marginal cost and marginal utility and move to an optimal position.

Recent research from both corners challenges this accepted wisdom. One fascinating study by two psychologists notes that most choice studies involve a relatively small number of options.[7] They were interested in finding out what happens as the range of choice expands significantly and the difference among the choices becomes smaller. They conducted three experiments. In the first, they set up tasting booths for jam in a gourmet supermarket on two consecutive Saturdays. On the first Saturday they offered twenty-four flavors of Wilkins and Sons jams, and on the second Saturday they offered six flavors. Customers were permitted to taste as many as they wanted and were

---

5. A mutual fund is an account run by an investment company that raises cash from investors through sale of shares and invests that cash in stocks, bonds, or money market instruments. The company makes its money by charging investors a fee to manage the underlying assets. Open-end funds, which are required to buy back outstanding shares at any time at a price that reflects the value of the underlying securities, are the most popular and what most people think of when they use the term *mutual fund*. In contrast, closed-end funds issue a fixed number of shares, and once the shares are issued they are not redeemed by the funds but rather are bought and sold by investors on the open market. As a result, the value of closed-end mutual fund shares depends on the supply and demand for these securities rather than solely on the value of the underlying investments.

6. Loewenstein (1999).

7. Iyengar and Lepper (2000).

given coupons for one dollar off the purchase of any jam. Predictably, the booth with twenty-four flavors attracted more shoppers: 60 percent of passing shoppers stopped at the booth with twenty-four jams but only 40 percent when only six were on display. However, only 3 percent of those visiting the twenty-four-choice booth bought jam, compared to 30 percent of those visiting the six-choice booth. More choice attracted shoppers but made it difficult for them to make the decision to buy.

The results from the two other experiments are equally telling. Students in an introductory social psychology class were told they could write a two-page essay for extra credit. One group of students was given six possible essay topics; the other group was given thirty. The question was how many students would do the assignment and how the quality would vary between the limited-option and extensive-option groups. A statistically significant larger percentage of the limited-option group wrote an essay, and the quality of their essays was somewhat better than the essays written by the other group. In other words, limited choice led to better performance. The final experiment involved the sampling of chocolates. One group selected from a limited array of chocolates, one from an extensive array, and the control group sampled a chocolate chosen for them. The goal was to measure their satisfaction with the process, their enjoyment of the chocolate, and their purchasing behavior. People reported enjoying the process of choosing a chocolate more from a display of thirty than from a display of six. Despite their greater initial enjoyment, however, participants in the extensive-display group were more dissatisfied and regretful of their choices than the others, and they were subsequently less likely to select chocolates rather than cash for their participation in the project.

The three experiments suggest that people in extensive-choice situations enjoy the process but that they find making choices difficult. They seem to become more unsure of the right option as the possibilities expand. If excessive choice creates difficulties with jams and chocolates, it could be quite discouraging in situations in which the costs of making a "wrong" decision are much more significant, such as investing one's 401(k) money.

Two behavioral economists explored how investors view the opportunity to put together their own portfolios from an array of investment options.[8] That is, do employees prefer the portfolios they construct themselves to the average or median portfolio of their co-workers? The economists conducted two experiments. First, they collected portfolio and demographic data for staff employees of the University of California at Los Angeles who participated in the university's 403(b) pension plan (the nonprofit sector's version of a 401(k)

8. Benartzi and Thaler (2002).

plan). They used this information to estimate the retirement income that participants could expect to receive based both on their own selections and on the mean and median portfolios chosen by all participants. The researchers then asked the participants to rank the attractiveness of three unlabeled retirement income streams emanating from the alternative portfolios. The participants ranked the median portfolio significantly higher and the mean portfolio somewhat higher than their own choice. That is, employees appeared to gain little from the freedom to put together their own portfolio.

In the second exercise, ProManage (an investment management firm) designed an individualized portfolio for each employee of a company. Employees who wanted to select their own portfolio could opt out of the ProManage allocation, and 36 percent, attracted by an extensive menu of choices, chose to do so. The researchers then asked this group to rank their own portfolio, the average portfolio, and the ProManage portfolio according to risk and return. Employees viewed the average portfolio as attractive as their own and the ProManage portfolio as significantly more attractive than their own. In other words, employees were no better off by being able to select their own portfolios.

The question is, Why? One explanation is that people do not do a good job of matching their investments with their taste for risk.[9] A possible solution, of course, is to help people get a better-fitting portfolio. This solution is difficult to execute, however, because people's risk preferences are hard to elicit. Using additional experiments, the same researchers offered participants choices ranging from high risk to low risk, but participants tended to pick the middle option, revealing inconsistent preferences. For example, people offered choices A, B, and C tended to prefer B to C. However, those offered B, C, and D argued that C was more attractive than B.

Thus recent evidence from both the psychological and economics literature suggests that people do not end up any better off with a vast array of choices, and in fact a large number of choices can be demotivating.[10]

Investment Patterns and Performance

With all the options at their disposal, how do people invest their 401(k) plan contributions? Two types of information are available about investment decisions. One is aggregate holdings in defined benefit and defined contribution plans reported in the Federal Reserve Board's *Flow of Funds Accounts*. The

9. Benartzi and Thaler (2002).
10. See also Loewenstein (1999).

Table 4-3. *Private Pension Assets, 2001*

Type of plan	Billions of dollars	Percent of total
Defined benefit	1,811.4	27.7
Defined contribution[a]	2,335.7	35.7
IRAs	2,399.0	36.6
Total	6,546.1	100.0

Source: Board of Governors, *Flow of Funds Accounts* (2002).
a. Includes about $200 billion of assets held in the Federal Thrift Savings Plan.

Table 4-4. *Distribution of Private Pension Assets by Financial Instrument, 2001*
Percent

Financial instrument	Defined benefit	Defined contribution
Equities	47.4	44.8
Mutual funds	5.9	22.8
Bonds	27.7	9.3
Cash	7.6	5.1
Guaranteed investment contracts	4.8	11.9
Other	6.5	6.2
Total	100.0[a]	100.0[a]

Source: *Flow of Funds* (2002).
a. Totals may not add due to rounding.

other type is plan and survey data that show the allocation of contributions and accumulated assets for individual 401(k) participants.

Overall Investment Patterns

Financial assets in private sector defined benefit and defined contribution plans (including IRAs) totaled $6.5 trillion at the end of 2001 (table 4-3). Table 4-4 shows a breakdown by type of investment for both defined benefit and defined contribution plans. Several points are worth noting. One is the amount of equity holdings in each. Defined benefit plans hold about 47 percent of their assets in equities, defined contribution plans hold 45 percent.[11] Furthermore, mutual funds—an important component of the assets of

11. Since most 401(k) participants invest through mutual funds, the high percentage for equities for defined contribution plans (that is, direct equity holdings as opposed to equities held through mutual funds) is surprising. The explanation is that equities here include pools of stocks that companies set up themselves for their 401(k) plans; only mutual funds bought off the shelf are included in the mutual fund line. The other large category of direct equity investment arises from a relatively small percentage of 401(k) participants who invest directly through brokerage accounts.

Table 4-5. *Distribution of Mutual Fund Assets, by Type of Asset, 2001*
Percent

Type of asset	Defined contribution plans	IRAs
Domestic equity	68	60
Foreign equity	7	8
Hybrid[a]	9	8
Bond	7	10
Money market	8	14
Total	100[b]	100[b]

Source: Investment Company Institute (2002).
a. Hybrid funds invest in a mix of equity and fixed income securities.
b. More or less, due to rounding.

defined contribution plans—also reflect equity holdings. Roughly 80 percent of the assets in mutual funds in defined contribution plans are equities (table 4-5). Applying that percentage to both the defined benefit and defined contribution mutual fund numbers yields total equity holdings of 52 percent in defined benefit plans and 63 percent in defined contribution plans. One rule of thumb offered by financial planners is that equities as a percentage of total assets be equal to one hundred minus the person's age. The reported holdings would be consistent with an average age of forty-eight for defined benefit plans and of thirty-seven for defined contribution plans, which is probably fairly close to accurate. Thus in the aggregate, at least, both defined benefit and defined contribution holdings look fairly sensible.

Only limited information is available on asset allocation in IRAs (table 4-6). The data show the type of institution holding the account, as opposed to the type of asset in the account.[12] Mutual fund investments constitute the largest component, and about 80 percent of mutual fund assets are in stock. But no information is available on the composition of IRA assets held by other institutions, which hold the majority of the assets.

Investment Performance

For the period of available data—1985 through 2001 (which includes the enormous run-up in the stock market)—one would have thought that defined contribution plans, with their higher share in equities, would have done better than defined benefit plans. Although annual returns earned by the two types of plan followed each other closely, the average return for defined benefit plans slightly exceeded that for defined contribution plans

12. Board of Governors (2002).

Table 4-6. *Asset Holdings in IRAs, by Institution, 2001*[a]
Percent

Institution	Share of total
Mutual funds	40.3
Life insurance companies	10.3
Money market mutual funds	6.7
Commercial banking	6.7
Saving institutions	2.3
Credit unions	1.7
Other self-directed accounts	32.1
Total	100.0[b]

Source: *Flow of Funds* (2002).
a. Total assets were $2,399 billion.
b. More or less, due to rounding.

(figure 4-1). One expert suggests that during the late 1990s defined benefit plans invested to a larger extent in technology and international stocks with higher return and higher volatility, while the mutual funds in defined contribution plans offered a broader portfolio of traditional stocks with lower returns and lower risk.[13] If this explanation is true, and the asset allocation remained unchanged, defined benefit plans should be a bigger loser in a declining stock market. In any event, the message from the rate of return data is that individual investors in 401(k) plans do not appear to have done any better and may not have done as well as sponsors of defined benefit plans.

Another possible explanation for the lower return in defined contribution plans is investment fees, which typically account for 75–90 percent of total expenses associated with managing 401(k) plans.[14] These fees (which compensate providers of, say, mutual funds for selecting the stocks and undertaking the research that leads to buy and sell decisions) are usually assessed as a percentage of invested assets and are paid by the employee through direct deductions from investment returns. The fees vary by type of investment.[15]

MUTUAL FUNDS. These funds involve two main types of fee. Sales charges take the form of either a front-end load, imposed when the shares are purchased, or a back-end load, imposed when they are sold. A front-end load

13. Julia Coronado, Federal Reserve Board, interview by author.
14. PWBA (1998).
15. Indiana Manufacturers Association, "Pension Welfare and Benefits Administration: A Look at 401K Plan Fees" (www.imaweb.com/discprograms/Financial%20Products/401k_basic_ifo.htm).

Figure 4-1. *Rate of Return of Defined Benefit and Defined Contribution Assets,*
1986–2000

Percent

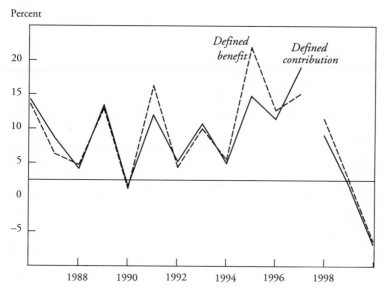

Percent

Plan	Geometric mean	Standard deviation
Defined benefit	7.9	7.1
Defined contribution	7.1	6.5

Source: Authors' calculations, based on Employee Benefit Research Institute (various years).

reduces the amount of the initial investment. A back-end load, whose amount usually depends on how long the shares have been held, reduces the proceeds from the sale. Rule 12(b)(1) fees are annual fees paid out of fund assets to cover commissions to salespersons and brokers, advertising costs, and other services. These fees range between 0.25 percent and 1.0 percent of assets. Front-end and back-end loads are much higher.

COLLECTIVE INVESTMENT FUNDS. These are trusts managed by a bank or trust company that pools investments from 401(k) plans and other similar investors. Each investor owns a percentage of the total assets of the trust. These arrangements do not involve front-end or back-end fees but do impose annual management fees.

GROUP VARIABLE ANNUITIES. Group variable annuities involve employer contracts with insurance companies to provide a range of investment alternatives. The variable annuity contract may "wrap" around a number of mutual funds. As a result, the insurance company charges a wrap fee in addition to the expense charge for each of the mutual funds.[16]

POOLED GUARANTEED INVESTMENT CONTRACTS. These contracts pool a number of fixed-income contracts offered by an insurance company or bank and involve an annual fee.

The level of fees matters enormously. Over time even a small increase in fees will substantially reduce accumulations at retirement. Consider the case of an individual with a starting balance of $50,000 and an annual return of 8 percent. If fees amount to 0.5 percent of assets, the individual will end up with $437,748; if fees are 1.5 percent, the ending balance is $330,718, or about 25 percent less. Fees for mutual funds vary substantially depending on whether the investments are actively managed or follow an index. For example, an actively managed Global Fund costs 1.86 percent of assets annually; the fee for a Standard and Poor index fund is 0.65 percent.[17]

Only one study compares the total costs of a defined benefit and a defined contribution plan, including investment fees.[18] The Illinois Municipal Retirement Fund (IMRF), then being operated as a defined benefit plan, held $14 billion in 1999 and paid total administrative and investment expenses of about $65 million. (Since IMRF is a public pension plan it does not have to pay Pension Benefit Guaranty Corporation premiums, a major expense for private sector defined benefit plans.) IMRF decided to explore the possibility of converting to a defined contribution plan and commissioned a study of the costs and benefits of conversion. The estimated cost of operating IMFR as a defined contribution plan was $315 million, assuming that a third-party administrator charged 1.25 percent of assets to administer the plan and that investment fees for mutual funds were 1 percent of assets. In fact the investment fees alone of $140 million (1 percent × $14 billion) for the defined contribution plan greatly exceeded the total investment and administrative expenses for the defined benefit plan.

The Shape of the Portfolio

So far the discussion has focused only on totals and averages, but these numbers tell us little about how individuals might invest. After all, if a plan has a

---

16. Many group annuity contracts use separate accounts of an insurance company, which are institutionally priced and do not have a wrap fee.

17. Christine Dugas, "Fees Weigh on 401(k) Returns," *USA Today,* September 5, 2002.

18. Illinois Municipal Retirement Fund (1999).

hundred participants and half invest all their assets in stock and the other half all their assets in bonds, the aggregate data suggest that participants are well diversified when in fact they are not. Therefore, it is useful to look at contribution and investment data from particular 401(k) plans to see whether individual participants have balanced portfolios or whether the balance simply reflects offsetting behavior.

Modern portfolio theory provides the foundation for the conventional wisdom that investors should diversify their asset holdings over a variety of securities.[19] It rests on the idea that the returns of all financial assets do not move in lockstep. Instead, the peculiar risks that each security bears—firm, industry, market, inflation, and so on—combine to determine the return on an asset. By building a portfolio of securities that have differing risk characteristics, an investor can create a more efficient portfolio, one expected to achieve a given level of expected return while minimizing risk.

Each asset can be characterized by the return it is expected to earn and its variance, the risk that it may earn less than expected or even fall in value. Assets with greater market risk will tend to have higher expected returns so as to give investors a reason to purchase them. If an investor holds just one asset—for example, shares of ABC Company—then the value of his entire portfolio will rise and fall with ABC's fortunes. Imagine another company, XYZ, with the same expected return but facing different risks. If investors split their portfolios between the two companies, they are able to remove some risk while maintaining the same expected return. This occurs because the two stocks do not move perfectly together; if one falters, the other may still gain. By adding more stocks to the portfolio, the investor may reduce the risk even further while still achieving some target expected return.

To find the best portfolio for a person, economists start by considering all combinations of assets and then selecting those portfolios that have the lowest possible risk for any given return. These portfolios are efficient because it is not possible to achieve a higher return without taking on additional risk. In figure 4-2 return is plotted on the vertical axis, and risk, measured by the standard deviation, is plotted on the horizontal axis. The efficient frontier is shown as the curved line. As investors move further to the right on the effi-

---

19. Markowitz (1991). The Markowitz model, which compares the trade-off between risk and return in the relatively short run, treats short-term cash equivalents, such as money market funds and U.S. Treasury bills, as completely safe investments. In a recent book, Campbell and Viceira (2002) argue that these investments are not that safe for investors with a longer horizon. Long-term investors face the risk of having to reinvest these funds at lower real rates of return in the future. A persistent variation in the real interest rate amplifies the volatility of returns when short-term investments are reinvested over the long run. As a result, short-term fixed-income investments such as Treasury bills can become riskier than bonds over a period of years.

Figure 4-2. *An Efficient Portfolio Frontier through Diversification*

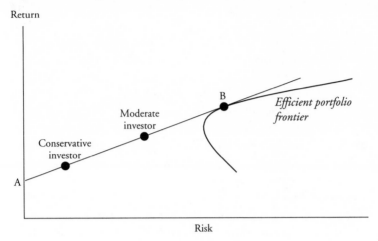

Source: Markowitz (1991).

cient frontier, they increase both their risks and their return. But all the port-folios on the frontier involve some risk, so it is important to also consider a risk-free investment, such as U.S. Treasury bills. Those options that combine Treasury bills with an efficient risky portfolio are all the points between A and B on the straight line in figure 4-2. As investors move from A to B, they move more of their portfolio from the risk-free asset into the optimal mix of risky assets. At point B the investor's entire portfolio is in the optimal mix of risky assets. Where investors land on line A-B depends on their desire for return and their tolerance for risk.

Detailed information on the asset allocation of individual participants shows that more than half of all participants have either most of their accounts invested in stock or nothing at all invested in stock (table 4-7).[20] So although the aggregate data suggest that participants make sensible invest-ment decisions on average, the individual data reveal that a majority of par-ticipants hold either no stock or almost all stock. Given their choices, most participants face the risk of ending up with inadequate retirement income or exposing themselves to large swings in the value of their retirement assets. Of course, critics contend that assessing individuals' 401(k) holdings without knowing their entire asset holdings is of limited value. They argue that most people who save through a 401(k) plan also have Social Security, human cap-

20. Holden and VanDerhei (2001a). The 2000 EBRI/ICI database contains 11.8 million active 401(k) participants. This accounts for 11 percent of all 401(k) plans, 28 percent of all participants, and 33 percent of the assets held in 401(k) plans.

Table 4-7. *Distribution of Equity Funds, 401(k) Participants,*
by Earnings, 2000
Percent

Earnings (dollars)	No equity	Less than 20 percent equity	20–80 percent equity	More than 80 percent equity
20,000–40,000	29.6	8.8	40.1	21.5
40,000–60,000	26.6	8.6	40.8	24.0
60,000–80,000	17.8	9.0	45.8	27.3
80,000–100,000	14.5	8.3	45.9	31.3
More than 100,000	14.8	8.4	44.1	32.7
All earnings[a]	27.8	6.2	36.4	29.5

Source: Holden and VanDerhei (2001a).
a. Includes earnings of less than $20,000 (not shown).

ital, defined benefit pension wealth, housing, and taxable savings. But as discussed at the beginning of the chapter, for most people taxable savings are minuscule, and their 401(k) plan is their major financial asset. Thus the investment allocation within their 401(k) plan is important.

But not all participants are equal. Earnings are an important determinant for how participants choose to allocate their assets. In particular, low-wage participants are more likely to hold no equities and invest their entire 401(k) accounts in interest-earning assets, such as guaranteed investment contracts issued by insurance companies and money market funds. That means that they are more likely to see a return of about 2.4 percent (adjusted for inflation) instead of the historical 7.2 percent return on stocks.[21] That difference in return has an enormous impact on accumulations thirty years down the road. Investing $1,000 for thirty years produces $2,098 (in today's dollars) from a no-stock portfolio, $4,141 from a portfolio that is half stocks and half bonds, and $8,050 from an all-stock portfolio.

Of course, the higher returns associated with stocks also bring more volatility, and one might argue that low-wage workers cannot accept that additional risk. That is, lower paid workers face a lot of earnings risk, such as the risk of becoming unemployed, and they need to offset that risk by investing most of their retirement saving in relatively safe assets. Others contend

21. Although the real return on stocks averaged 7.2 percent over the period 1926–2001, investors cannot count on receiving such a return going forward. See Diamond (1999). Wolman and Colamosca (2002), p. 20, sound an even more cautionary note: "In its most serious and somber moments, Wall Street tells the American family that it can rely on an inflation-adjusted rate of return of 7 percent on its money with a long-term stock savings plan. Reality, on the other hand, suggests that a return of 2 percent is a far more realistic outlook for a period that extends well past the first decade of the twenty-first century."

that the uncertainty in earnings for most people is unrelated to the performance of the stock market, so it does not make sense for low-income workers to shun stocks and forgo the higher returns.[22] Further, unless low-income workers make stock investments, at least when they are young, their savings are unlikely to provide adequate replacement when they retire.

The discussion so far focuses on those who do not diversify; a related question is how those who do diversify allocate their 401(k) assets. As noted earlier, participants have a myriad of choices, and having many choices can be overwhelming. The psychology literature suggests that when individuals are overwhelmed they often fall back on simple rules of thumb. Some researchers claim that 401(k) participants, when faced with several investment choices, tend to follow a 1/n heuristic.[23] That is, participants divide their contributions equally among all investment options. If the plan offers only a few choices, this strategy may result in a diversified portfolio. On the other hand, if plans offer many equity funds, participants tend to invest too large a share in stocks.

Several researchers have observed a variant of the 1/n heuristic when the firm offers company stock. For example, one study examined investment patterns in a large 401(k) plan that offered four investment alternatives: an equity income fund, a Standard and Poor 500 index fund, a guaranteed income fund, and company stock. Participants appear to make their company stock investment first and then allocate their remaining assets equally among the three funds.[24] In another study, researchers found that when firms do not offer company stock, 401(k) participants split their assets roughly equally between equities and fixed-income investments. When firms do offer company stock, participants invest an average of 42 percent in company stock and split the rest between noncompany equities and fixed-income securities.[25] Other researchers challenge the 1/n heuristic, claiming that workers rarely divide their allocation between all possible options but rather select a few funds.[26] Within those options, however, participants may still opt for an equal allocation.

In short, the available evidence suggests that a majority of participants follow simple allocation strategies, either by investing everything in one fund or

22. Ameriks and Zeldes (2001).

23. Benartzi and Thaler (2001). A study of investment behavior in 401(k) plans could not reject the hypothesis that investors follow a 1/n investment allocation. See Liang and Weisbenner (2002).

24. Agnew (2001).

25. Benartzi and Thaler (2001).

26. Holden and VanDerhei (2001b).

by dividing their assets equally among all funds, resulting in either a too-aggressive or a too-conservative portfolio. Both strategies may have large negative effects on the accumulation of retirement wealth. Participants who hold mostly stock as they approach retirement run the risk that a market downturn at retirement will significantly reduce retirement wealth. The onset of the bear market in 2000 made this evident. Many workers may have to postpone retirement and may still end up with significantly lower retirement income than they had expected a few years earlier.[27] Others will not have the option of continued employment because of health or of age discrimination and will experience a significant drop in their standard of living. A too-conservative strategy, on the other hand, could also have negative effects on retirement income because it fails to take advantage of the historically higher returns on equities.

Researchers have worried that women in particular might invest too conservatively. In general, studies of risk aversion show that women are more risk averse than men.[28] Greater risk aversion would lead to less investment in equities and more in interest-earning securities. Indeed, studies that focus on asset allocation of participants in particular 401(k) plans find that women tend to invest their retirement funds in less risky vehicles than men.[29] In contrast, another study based on plan data that estimates investment behavior for men and women separately finds that women are not more conservative investors than men, after controlling for earnings, age, and other important determinants of investor behavior.[30]

The problem with looking at investment allocations in individual plans is that little is known about the participant other than sex and earnings. For example, the researcher does not have information about age, marital status, other assets, home ownership, debt, retirement assets of the person's spouse, and so on. When a similar analysis is done using a representative sample of the population, such as the Survey of Consumer Finances, which includes extensive demographic and economic information, it turns out that gender alone does not determine investment choice.[31] Rather, investment decisions seem to be driven more by a combination of gender and marital status. Single women and married men are most likely to invest primarily in stocks; married women are more likely than single women to choose mostly interest-

---

27. For a discussion of older workers' response to the stock market decline, see Eschtruth and Gemus (2001).

28. For example, Barsky and others (1997).

29. Bajtelsmit and VanDerhei (1997); Hinz, McCarthy, and Turner (1997).

30. Clark and others (2000).

31. Sundén and Surette (1998).

Table 4-8. *Allocation of 401(k) Accounts, Men and Women*
Percent

	Share of participants	
Allocation	Men	Women
Mostly stock[a]	53.1	53.5
Mostly interest earning	11.7	12.0
Diversified	35.2	34.4

Source: Authors' calculations based on the 2001 SCF.
Note: Respondents were given three choices: mostly stock, mostly interest-earning assets, and split between stocks and interest-earning assets.

earning assets. In other words, no strong evidence indicates that women as a group are more conservative investors than men. Indeed, table 4-8 suggests that men and women overall invest their 401(k) accounts in a similar fashion.

Given their allocation decisions, how have 401(k) participants fared over the last few years? A study by the Employee Benefit Research Institute (EBRI) and the Investment Company Institute (ICI) looked at average account balances for a group of 5.3 million participants who held account balances at year-end 1999–2002. It is comforting that mean 401(k) holdings for household heads reported from EBRI/ICI are very close to the average in the 2001 Survey of Consumer Finances (table 4-9).

The change in account balance from year to year depends on three factors: new contributions to the plan, investment returns, and withdrawals. The importance of these factors is evident in table 4-10. Since new contributions dominate for young people, their account balances increased despite the downturn in the stock market. On the other hand, investment returns are important for those in their fifties with substantial accumulations. This group saw their balances decline by about 15 percent over the three-year

Table 4-9. *Mean 401(k) Holdings, SCF and EBRI/ICI, 2001*

Ages	SCF	EBRI/ICI
20–29	$7,228	$14,409
30–39	$28,818	$37,596
40–49	$66,664	$66,299
50–59	$94,490	$97,030
60–69	$148,777	$118,522
All	$58,287	$62,646

Source: Employee Benefit Research Institute (2003); Investment Company Institution (2003); and authors' calculations based on the 2001 SCF.

Table 4-10. *Mean 401(k) Assets, by Age Group, 1999–2002*
Dollars

Age group[a]	1999	2000	2001	2002	Percent change, 1999–2002
20–29	9,571	12,074	14,409	15,035	57.1
30–39	35,112	36,559	37,596	35,282	0.5
40–49	66,702	66,854	66,299	61,033	–8.5
50–59	103,626	100,241	97,030	88,332	–14.8
60–69	134,964	125,601	118,522	106,689	–21.0
All (20–69)	64,074	61,125	62,646	57,668	–10.00

Source: Employee Benefit Research Institute (2003); Investment Company Institute (2003).
a. Age in 1999.

period. The drop in average account balances would have been even larger if participants had not continued to contribute over this period. (Note that the figures in table 4-10 are lower than those in table 4-1 because they do not include balances in IRAs.)

Adjusting Investments over Time

The discussion so far looks at asset allocation at one moment in time, but another important aspect of financial decisions is how people adjust their portfolios over long periods of time. These adjustments can be in response to advancing age or to returns on assets.

Effect of Aging

Most financial planners advise their clients to shift away from stocks and toward bonds as they get older. For example, Jane Bryant Quinn, a columnist for *Newsweek,* tells investors that "younger people should tip toward higher returns because they have time for their stocks to recover from any drop." Similarly, Burton Malkiel, the author of *A Random Walk Down Wall Street,* recommends "more common stocks for individuals earlier in the life cycle and more bonds for those nearest retirement." The authors of *The Wall Street Journal Guide to Planning Your Financial Future* say, "When you're investing for retirement, it usually makes sense to shift your strategy as you get closer to actually leaving the work force—from concentrating primarily on growth to thinking about producing income."[32] As noted above, a typical rule of thumb is that the percentage of people's portfolios held in equities should equal a hundred minus their age, so a thirty-year-old would hold 70 percent

32. Quinn (1997), p. 271; Malkiel (1991), p. 350; Morris, Siegel, and Morris (1998), p. 97.

Table 4-11. *Asset Allocation Recommendations, Five Financial Service Firms, by Years until Retirement*[a]
Percent

| | Years until retirement[a] | | | |
Firm	0–5	6–10	11–15	16 and over
T. Rowe Price				
Stocks	40	60	80	80
Bonds	40	30	20	20
Cash	20	10	0	0
Fidelity				
Stocks	50	60	70	70
Bonds	40	30	25	25
Cash	10	10	5	5
Vanguard				
Stocks	50	60	60	80
Bonds	50	40	40	20
Cash	0	0	0	0
TIAA-CREF				
Stocks	30	45	65	65
Bonds	50	45	35	35
Cash	20	10	0	0
Putnam				
Stocks	30	60	60	75
Bonds	50	30	30	25
Cash	20	10	10	0

Source: T. Rowe Price (www.troweprice.com); Fidelity (www.fidelity.com); Vanguard (www.vanguard.com); TIAA-CREF (www.tiaa-cref.com); Putnam (www.putnam.com).

a. Recommendations are for a person with moderate risk tolerance.

in stocks and a seventy-year-old would hold 30 percent. All of the financial services firms have "calculators" on their websites, where participants can enter their risk tolerance and their years to retirement and receive a suggested allocation among stocks, bonds, and cash. Those with more than ten years to retirement are advised to hold 70–80 percent in stock, while those with less than five years are advised to hold 30–40 percent (table 4-11).

Financial planners give different reasons for this advice: that stocks provide better returns than bonds and are a good hedge against inflation and that a longer time period to invest allows individuals to weather the downturns in the market. The first point reflects the historical fact that stocks yielded a real, inflation-adjusted return between 1926 and 2001 of 7.2 percent, while bonds returned 2.4 percent.[33] But this by itself says nothing about how stock holdings should vary over time. The second point says that investing in equities is less risky over the longer term because it gives the investor more time for prices to return to their long-run averages once they fall out of line.

The question of whether stocks return to their long-run averages is con-troversial.[34] If they do not, a longer time horizon does not reduce the risk associated with equity investment. However, even if stocks do not display "mean reversion," a case can be made for shifting from stocks to bonds based on the pattern of earnings over time. Households hold two types of wealth, financial wealth and earnings wealth (the amount of wages and salary that they can earn each year into the future). Future earnings are by no means cer-tain, but the uncertainty for most people is unrelated to the performance of the stock market.[35] In fact for most households bonds and future earnings have the most similar risk characteristics. As people get closer to retirement, two things happen. First, they have fewer salary payments left to receive so that the value of their labor wealth goes down. Second, as the years pass the household accumulates more stocks and bonds, so their financial wealth goes up. The best way for most people to stabilize the risk in their portfolio over time is to increase bond holdings as a share of their total portfolio as the number of periods to earn labor income declines.

When economists first looked at whether people actually did reduce their equity holdings as they age, they generally concluded that people followed the advice of financial planners. For example, one study of participants in TIAA-CREF in 1995 found that equity holdings declined as age increased.[36] The same pattern is evident in table 4-12, which shows more recent data on the asset allocation of a representative sample of 11.8 million participants in

33. In fact stocks are not a good hedge against inflation in the usual sense of the word, because real equity returns decline as inflation increases both on a year-to-year basis and over longer horizons. The only way equities can serve as a hedge is that the higher average return off-sets some of the erosive effect of inflation. See Brown, Mitchell, and Poterba (2001).

34. Whether stocks display mean reversion or negative long-run serial correlation remains controversial among economists. Studies by Fama and French (1998) and Poterba and Sum-mers (1988) report negative serial correlation, but they have been challenged by researchers on several grounds. Campbell, Lo, and MacKinlay (1997) summarize the literature and conclude, "Overall, there is little evidence for mean-reversion in long-horizon returns, though this may be more a symptom of small sample sizes rather than conclusive evidence against mean-reversion—we simply cannot tell."

35. Jagannathan and Kocherlakota (1996).

36. Bodie and Crane (1997). TIAA-CREF is the largest pension provider in the United States, managing more than $300 billion in assets for 2 million participants. These participants are mainly employees of colleges and universities and of nonprofit organizations.

Table 4-12. *Average Asset Allocation, by Age Group, 2000*
Percent

Age group	Equity funds	Company stock	Balanced funds[a]	Bond funds	Money funds/guaranteed investment contracts	Other[b]
20–29	61.4	15.4	8.6	4.3	8.3	1.7
30–39	60.2	18.4	8.0	3.8	7.9	1.6
40–49	54.8	19.7	8.0	4.2	11.3	2.0
50–59	49.2	19.1	8.0	5.3	15.9	2.5
60–69	39.8	16.3	8.0	7.7	24.7	3.5
All (20–69)	51.3	18.6	8.0	5.1	14.6	2.3

Source: Employee Benefit Research Institute (2001); Investment Company Institute (2001).
a. Includes a mix of stocks and bonds.
b. Includes other stable value funds.

401(k) plans.[37] Considering equity funds and company stock together, average equity holdings decline from 77 percent for participants in their twenties to 56 percent for participants in their sixties.

Whether the future behavior of young people will look like the current behavior of old people remains to be seen. It could be that behavior changes with different cohorts and that people born more recently choose to hold more equity than those born in earlier years. For example, older people who have some first-hand memory of the Great Depression may be more reluctant to take on the risk associated with equity investment. If so, people born before 1935 may have always had lower equity shares than those born later, and the lower shares of currently older individuals represent differences across people of different birth years rather than show what people in general do as they age.

The only way to see whether people actually reduce their equity holdings as they age is to follow a group of people over time. Two economists did just that.[38] They put together quarterly data from 1987 through 1999 for both the allocation of assets and the flow of contributions for about 4,000 TIAA-CREF participants. In one way, this is a good sample for testing whether people reduce equity holdings as they age because for many participants TIAA-CREF is their only retirement plan and represents a substantial portion of their wealth. On the other hand, the sample is not representative of the population, because TIAA-CREF participants are usually better educated than the population as a whole. Therefore, even if TIAA-CREF participants did a good job in reallocating, it does not mean that the whole population was doing a good job.

37. Holden and VanDerhei (2001a).
38. Ameriks and Zeldes (2001).

The TIAA-CREF data show that, over the nine-year period, equity holdings increased for almost all participants who were in the accumulation phase of life. The main reason for the overall increase (which was 9.2 percent) was the high return on equities during the 1990s. Actions taken by individuals to offset this increase reduced allocations by only 1.1 percent. Consider this outcome in the context of the standard rule that equities as a percentage of total assets should equal one hundred minus one's age. This rule implies that individuals should reduce their equity share by 1 percentage point a year, or 9 percentage points over the nine-year period. But since the market increased the equity share by 9.2 percent, individuals should have reduced their share by 18.2 percentage points. Instead, they reduced the share by only 1 percentage point. This says that participants were not following the standard advice to lower their equity share as they aged. The only evidence that equity holdings might decline with age came from the decumulators—those over age fifty who were drawing down their assets. For these individuals, withdrawals and transfers reduced their equity holdings by 13 percentage points. The main conclusion, however, is that people do not reduce their equity holdings as they age. Of course, this study was done in a high-return environment; people might be more likely to reallocate if equity returns were flat.

Response to Investment Returns

Age is not the only reason that people should adjust their portfolios over time. The other reason is investment returns. People select a target allocation depending on returns among stocks, bonds, and money market instruments. Over time, their account balances reflect both their initial choices and returns on assets. If participants never change their investment allocation, even in normal times they will see the ratio of stocks to bonds increase since equities on average have a higher rate of return. This phenomenon was exacerbated during the 1990s, when stocks rose at more than 20 percent a year. Without some reallocation, the bull market would have greatly increased equity holdings as a share of most people's portfolio. The question is whether 401(k) participants rebalanced in the face of the unprecedented run-up in stock values.

No study has addressed this question directly, but comparing the performance of defined contribution and defined benefit plans during the 1990s bull market provides some interesting insights. As shown in figure 4-3, in the late 1980s and early 1990s, both types of plan held roughly 40 percent of their total assets in equities, either directly or through mutual funds. As the market began its swift rise in the mid-1990s, the share of equities in defined contribution plans rose significantly more than those in defined benefit plans. The notion is that the professionals who manage defined benefit plans

Figure 4-3. *Equities as Share of Total Assets, Defined Contribution and Defined Benefit Plans, 1985–2001*

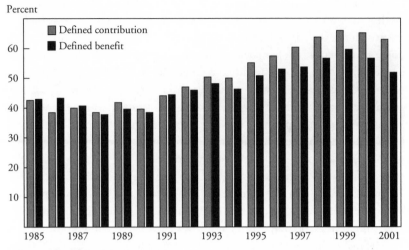

Percent

Source: *Flow of Funds* (various years).

sought to maintain a balance between stocks and interest-earning assets, while individual 401(k) participants did little to rebalance their portfolios.[39] Thus the changes in the composition of aggregate assets during the boom market appear consistent with the finding that individuals do little to rebalance their portfolios as they age. In both cases, individual investors demonstrate an enormous amount of inertia.

Effect of Inertia

It is evident that people do not change their portfolios in response to either age or return on investments. But do 401(k) participants play the market? During the 1990s run-up in the stock market, some evidence indicates that investors engaged in excessive trading and suffered lower returns as a result.[40] Even though these studies investigate a narrow sample of investors who owned discount brokerage accounts—a group that is likely to have an appetite for trading—researchers wondered initially whether workers with 401(k) plans also traded too much. The answer is no: 401(k) participants seldom make changes to asset allocations for any reason. Some recent studies document this inertia directly.

39. Defined benefit plans may also be required to hold interest-bearing assets for those participants who already have retired and are in the payout stage.
40. Barber and Odean (2000, 2001).

In the study of TIAA-CREF participants, the vast majority of households made no or few changes to their portfolio allocations.[41] In terms of flows, 47 percent of participants made no changes, and another 21 percent made only one change over the nine-year period. In terms of assets, 73 percent made no changes, and another 14 percent made only one change. Another study, which examined trading behavior in one large 401(k) plan between August 1994 and August 1998, also finds that trading was infrequent.[42] Of participants, 88 percent never changed allocations, and 6 percent made only one change. The observed trading pattern translates into one change in allocation every 3.85 years. The little trading that did occur tended to be concentrated among high-income and older workers. In other words, 401(k) participants display enormous inertia in regard to changing investments.

Effect of Automatic Enrollment

The significant effect of inertia on asset allocation is consistent with the experiences with automatic enrollment discussed in the previous chapter. In these 401(k) plans, workers were enrolled automatically as soon as they were eligible to participate; employees who did not want to participate could opt out. At enrollment, a participant's contribution level and investment allocation was set to the default option selected by the firm. If employees wanted to increase contributions or change the asset allocation, they had to take the initiative to do so. A majority of plans with automatic enrollment (68 percent) picked a low-risk, low-return default, such as a stable-value fund or a money market fund.

Studies of employee response to automatic enrollment find that a large share of participants kept their account invested in the low-risk, low-return default option.[43] Moreover, the share of participants that allocated their accounts to the money market fund was significantly higher than it had been before the plan adopted automatic enrollment. In other words, participants who might have made a different asset allocation choice in the absence of automatic enrollment remained in the default option under automatic enrollment. Employees in the lower end and in the middle of the wage distribution were particularly likely to stay with the default investment allocation.

People stay with the default for two possible reasons. First, the 401(k)

---

41. Ameriks and Zeldes (2001).

42. Agnew, Balduzzi, and Sundén (2003).

43. About 80 percent initially accepted the default saving rate and investment options they were assigned. After three years in the plan, half of participants subject to automatic enrollment continued to invest their contributions in the default portfolio. Madrian and Shea (2002); Choi and others (2001a, 2001b).

allocation for young participants is often their first financial decision and for many other workers it may be one of the few financial decisions they make. As we have seen, investment concepts are complicated, and few workers have sufficient financial experience, training, or time to figure out the best investment allocation.[44] Given the complexity, workers are likely to procrastinate in terms of making a change.[45] Second, many employees stay with the default option because they interpret it as financial advice from the firm.[46] Even for workers who change their allocations, the default option seems important; participants who changed their allocations had a larger share of their portfolios in the default option than workers who joined the plan before automatic enrollment. They used the default option as a standard against which they evaluated other choices for the portfolio allocation.

The reliance on the default option is just another example of inertia in the investment behavior of 401(k) participants. They do not adjust their portfolios as they age or as returns alter their mix. This inertia has to be considered together with the data showing that people do not make good initial decisions about their 401(k) investments; more than half of participants are either all in stocks or hold no stocks at all. Poor initial investment choices combined with inertia means that people are not doing a good job investing their 401(k) money.

Improving Investment Decisions

Two initiatives are under way to improve the investment decisions of 401(k) participants. One initiative involves federal legislation to make it easier for professional money managers to offer advice to 401(k) participants. Another initiative is the creation of life-style funds that would simplify the investment options faced by the typical 401(k) participant.

The Employee Retirement Income Security Act of 1974 (ERISA) discourages plan sponsors and investment companies from giving "advice" to plan participants, allowing employers and others to provide employees only with "education" about the investment process and about the particular investment choices available. ERISA treats the provision of investment advice as a fiduciary function, so an employer who arranges for financial professionals to deliver individualized investment advice will be deemed an ERISA fiduciary, with the risk of being sued if investments turn out badly. Insurance compa-

44. Bernheim and Garrett (1996).
45. O'Donoghue and Rabin (1999).
46. Choi and others (2001a).

nies and investment managers lobbied Congress to make it easier for them to advise 401(k) participants. In response, two bills have been introduced in Congress that would essentially protect employers from being designated fiduciaries if they give financial services companies the right to advise their employees on an individual basis. The two bills differ in the way they treat conflicts of interest.

At first blush, it may seem strange to question the desirability of investment advice. But the proposed legislation does raise a fundamental issue about how difficult we want the investment decisions faced by the typical employee to be. Investing 401(k) money may simply be too hard for the typical employee, and perhaps the goal should be to make investment easier rather than turn employees into investment experts.

One approach to simplifying the investment process would be to provide tiers of options. Employees enrolling in a 401(k) plan could be told that one of three investment packages—low risk, medium risk, and high risk—meets the needs of most people. Employees would simply answer a few questions to determine their risk tolerance and then select an investment package.[47]

A growing number of investment companies either offer or are considering offering life-cycle or life-stage funds that set an initial allocation to match the participant's risk tolerance and then automatically reduce equity investments as the investor ages. For example, Fidelity has a set of Freedom Funds, each having a target year for retirement: 2010, 2020, 2030. Similarly, Barclay's Global Investors offers LifePath Funds. In each case, as the target year approaches, the company shifts the fund's asset allocation away from equities and into bonds and money market instruments.

Offering employees these funds seems particularly important in view of plan participants' failure to diversify and their inertia with regard to changing investments over time. These funds not only help participants pick sensible initial allocations but also offer automatic periodic rebalancing to restore the participant's target allocation. These packages would need to have Labor Department approval (of course, with no guarantee of return), and employers who offer these packages would need to be freed of liability if the results were unfavorable.

How these options are offered is extremely important, because as discussed earlier, most people tend to pick the middle option. Suppose a plan offers three model portfolios with 0, 40, and 80 percent equity, labeled con-

---

47. The process may be more complicated in that experts say that individuals tend to overstate their tolerance for risk; they generally want to appear more aggressive than they really are. Thus care would be required to elicit the participant's true attitude toward risk.

servative, moderate, and aggressive. In this case, choosing the middle option implies an equity allocation of 40 percent. However, if the equity allocation is 40, 70, and 100 percent, choosing the middle option implies an equity allocation of 70 percent.

The more sophisticated investor or someone who wants to participate more actively could ask for a second level of options with an array of funds from one, two, or even three providers. The truly daring could push even further for a brokerage account of some sort.

This tiered series of options with the simple investment packages sends a message that people do not have to become investment experts—they can coach their kid's soccer team, play tennis, or read a book instead. Enacting legislation that enables outside managers to enter the workplace to offer advice sends a different message. It says that investing 401(k) funds is a difficult task and that one had better study up.

Conclusion

Making decisions about the investment allocation in a 401(k) plan is difficult. Plans increasingly offer more options: Roughly half of 401(k) participants can choose among more than sixteen investment alternatives. Economists and psychologists agree that some choice is good since it increases motivation, sense of control, performance, and satisfaction. But they also agree that too much choice is overwhelming. The fear of making the wrong decision increases with the number of choices and often paralyzes people. Many workers also lack knowledge to make complicated financial decisions. The result appears to be that participants in general follow simple investment strategies and end up with either too much or too little stock in their portfolios. And once they have made a decision on how to allocate their funds they rarely change. Because retirement income depends crucially on how the 401(k) account is invested, this means that many participants are at risk for ending up with unacceptably low retirement income.

One way to help participants is by having employers offer financial advice. Another is to offer simple options. Perhaps the best solution is a combination of the two. But as things stand now, 401(k) participants are not doing a good job investing their money.

5

The Special Case
of Company Stock

Chapter 4 focuses on the traditional investment decisions of diversification among stocks, bonds, and cash and the question of rebalancing over time to offset market returns and to reduce risk with age. This chapter shifts the focus to a unique investment problem of 401(k) plans, namely, excessive holdings of company stock. This issue does not arise with defined benefit plans because the Employee Retirement Income Security Act of 1974 (ERISA) permits no more than 10 percent of assets be held in company stock. No such restriction applies to 401(k) plans; and 8 million participants, approximately 20 percent of 401(k) participants, hold more than 20 percent of their 401(k) assets in company stock. This chapter assesses the adverse impact on financial security of holding excessive company stock. It then explores why so many participants not only fail to diversify but also hold an asset closely correlated with their earnings, and why their employers seem so keen on encouraging this behavior. Finally, it investigates why federal law restricts company stock for defined benefit plans but not for 401(k) plans and explores some legislative proposals for improving the situation.

The Problem with Company Stock

Allowing excessive investment in company stock is dramatically at odds with modern financial theory, which says that diversifying a portfolio offers large gains at little cost.[1] Investment theory identifies two main types of risk: market risk and firm risk. All securities are subject to market risk, which reflects interest rates, the business cycle, and the general state of the economy. An economic downturn will hurt the performance of almost all companies and result in poor stockholder returns virtually across the board. Market risk is not easily eliminated. Firm risk reflects the factors that affect the profits and losses of a specific company and, in contrast to market risk, can be eliminated through portfolio diversification. By buying more than one stock, investors dramatically reduce the total risk associated with their portfolios and maintain the same expected return. For example, a portfolio of twenty to thirty stocks can eliminate almost 60 percent of total risk.[2]

It is even more important for employees to diversify their investments away from their employer. Concentrating their 401(k) investments in company stock means that employees hold their financial assets in a single stock, which is more risky than a diversified portfolio. Moreover, they concentrate their financial bets on a security directly correlated with their own human capital and earnings, which in nearly all cases is their primary source of income.

The broad benefits of diversification may not be obvious since more than a few individuals have done spectacularly well by investing in a single stock. But the key point is that no one knows in advance how any individual stock will perform. Given this uncertainty, the most efficient method of investing—regardless of one's tolerance for risk—is to diversify. The notion of striking it rich by choosing the right company may have a powerful emotional appeal, but it is not the most effective way to achieve even an aggressive investment goal. For example, venture capitalists—who clearly seek above-average returns and have a high tolerance for risk—assemble a portfolio of promising start-ups with the likelihood that one or two will emerge as highly successful companies. Such a strategy will always provide a higher expected return or lower overall risk than an investment in any one venture.

Congress has recognized the advantages of diversification by passing legislation that regulates private pension plans. ERISA requires that fiduciaries (plan sponsors, plan administrators, and advisers) operate the plan in the best

1. Markowitz (1991).
2. Bodie and Merton (2000).

interests of the participants and beneficiaries and discharge their duties for the "exclusive purpose" of providing benefits to participants and beneficiaries. They must act with "the care, skill, and diligence" that a "prudent person" acting in a similar capacity would use and must "diversify" the plan's investments to reduce the chance of loss. In addition to this general guidance, ERISA requires that the fiduciaries of defined benefit plans invest no more than 10 percent of the pension fund's assets in the stock and real property of the sponsoring company.[3]

Although ERISA is quite forceful with regard to diversification for defined benefit plans, it provides defined contribution plans considerable latitude for investment in company stock. ERISA exempts most defined contribution plans—including profit-sharing plans, 401(k)s, and employee stock ownership plans (ESOPs) (see box 5-1)—from both the general diversification provisions with regard to investment in company stock and the explicit 10 percent cap.

According to those involved with the process, early proposals for ERISA had a 10 percent cap for both defined benefit and defined contribution plans. Companies sponsoring profit-sharing plans heavily invested in company stock, however, blocked a cap on defined contribution plans.[4] The differential treatment of defined benefit and defined contribution plans with regard to diversification reflects the fact that the government pursued two goals: one to increase saving for retirement and the other to expand employee economic and political participation in their firm through profit sharing and ESOPs. It was possible to pursue the two goals simultaneously because, in many cases—particularly with large employers—they involved different vehicles. Defined benefit pension plans provided for retirement income while defined contribution plans, especially profit-sharing plans and ESOPs, enabled employees to participate in the employer's profits and acquire company stock.[5]

3. Congress imposed a second limitation on defined benefit plans' holdings of employer stock in 1987. Section 407(f) of ERISA provides that, in addition to the 10 percent limit, the amount of employer stock held by the plan cannot exceed 25 percent of the company's total outstanding stock. In addition, at least 50 percent of the stock of a plan sponsor must be held by independent parties.

4. According to Michael Gordon, pension counsel to Senator Jacob Javits, who was instrumental in the passage of ERISA, Sears Roebuck early on lobbied against a limit on company stock. Later, Southland Corporation (the owners of 7-Eleven Stores), which held a lot of real property used by the company in its defined contribution plan, also mounted a strong—and ultimately successful—lobbying campaign. See PWBA (1997).

5. Another reason for government concern about diversification in defined benefit plans, but not in defined contribution plans, is that it provided insurance for defined benefit promises through the Pension Benefit Guaranty Corporation and wanted those promises backed by a diversified portfolio. The government provided no comparable insurance for defined contribution plans.

Box 5-1. *ESOPs*

ESOPs are defined contribution plans designed specifically to turn employees into owners. Because of the special tax favors that ESOPs enjoy, hybrid 401(k)-ESOP plans, called KSOPs, are also increasingly common. In 2002 roughly 11,000 ESOPs covered 8.8 million people.[1] Some are stand-alone plans while others are part of a larger defined contribution plan. Most ESOPs are operated by privately held companies and serve as a valuable mechanism for capital formation and succession. Less than 5 percent of ESOPs are sponsored by public companies. But since these plans are sponsored by large firms, they cover most of the participants.[2]

ESOPs are especially attractive to employers because they can borrow against (leverage) plan assets. A leveraged ESOP could, for example, borrow $1,000 from a financial institution and use the money to buy a block of preferred stock from the company. The company adds the $1,000 to its working capital and invests it any way it wants. Each year, the company pays a dividend of, say, $100 on the $1,000 investment to the ESOP, and the ESOP uses the money to pay the interest and principal it owes to the lender. As the ESOP pays down its debt, it distributes some of the newly acquired stock to plan participants. A leveraged ESOP is an advantageous way for the employer to raise funds, as the company gets a tax deduction for the full $100 it pays to the ESOP, even though part of this payment is used to repay principal. Thus the ability of ESOPs to leverage their investments to acquire company stock reduces the total taxes paid by the company.[3]

1. National Center for Employee Ownership, "A Statistical Profile of Employee Ownership" (www.nceo.org/library/boxer.corziner.bill.html).
2. National Center for Employee Ownership, "2001 Pension Insurance Data Book" (pbgc.gov.masteer.com/texis/master/search/mysite.html?q=data).
3. Smiley and Brown (2001).

Today, the lines between retirement saving and company stock ownership have blurred. Defined contribution plans—particularly 401(k) plans—have replaced defined benefit plans as the core of the private retirement system. At the same time, because the government actively encourages company stock investments in defined contribution ESOPs and profit-sharing and stock bonus plans, many firms have created plans that combine 401(k) and ESOP characteristics. The result is that many workers have the bulk of their retirement saving invested in company stock, which is inconsistent with the diversification tenets of modern financial theory.

The Economic Growth and Taxpayer Relief Reconciliation Act of 2001 further expanded the tax benefits associated with ESOPs. Under the 2001 legislation, employers can also take a tax deduction for dividends paid to participant accounts that are reinvested in the plan. Earlier tax law allowed deductions only for dividends payable on unallocated stock held by the ESOP.[4] If a firm has a 401(k) with significant holdings of company stock that regularly pays dividends, the new legislation provides an incentive for the firm to designate a portion of the plan that includes the company stock as an ESOP.[5]

The prevalence of ESOPs, profit-sharing, and stock-bonus plans complicates the analysis of company stock holdings in 401(k) plans. For example, Procter and Gamble (P&G) is frequently listed as the U.S. corporation with the highest percentage of company stock in its 401(k) plan, at 95 percent.[6] In fact, P&G's plan is an ESOP that has profit-sharing and 401(k) features. The company contributes common stock to the profit-sharing component and preferred stock to the ESOP. The relatively new 401(k) portion of the plan allows employees to make tax-deductible contributions and to diversify their holdings, but this accounts for only 5 percent of total plan assets.[7] Nevertheless, P&G's sole retirement program—a combination 401(k), profit sharing, and ESOP—with its overall lack of diversification, raises all the issues discussed above.

4. Deductions now include dividends paid on qualifying employer securities held by an ESOP that, at the election of participants or beneficiaries, are paid in one of three ways: paid directly in cash, paid to the plan and distributed in cash no later than ninety days after the close of the plan year in which the dividends are paid to the plan, or paid to the plan and reinvested in qualifying employer securities.

5. Employee Benefit Research Institute (2002).

6. Purcell (2002a).

7. Jacobius (2001).

Share of Company Stock in 401(k) Plans

In 2001 about 17 percent of 401(k) assets were invested in company stock.[6] This share is down slightly from 19 percent in 2000, possibly reflecting a continuing bear market and a flurry of bankruptcies and revelations of cor-

6. Holden and VanDerhei (2003). The number comes from a sample of 48,786 401(k) plans, which in 2001 included 14.6 million active participants and $632.7 billion of assets. The authors estimate that their sample accounts for 21 percent of all plans, 33 percent of 401(k) participants, and about 36 percent of 401(k) assets.

Table 5-1. *Company Stock, by Size of Plan, 2001*
Percent

Number of participants	Share of plans offering company stock[a]	Company stock as share of total assets
5,000 or more	51.9	37.6
1,000–4,999	40.3	9.2
200–999	15.4	3.5
50–199	4.3	1.1
1–49	4.9	0.3

Source: Profit Sharing/401k Council of America (2002).
a. These companies offer company stock for the employer match.

porate fraud. An aggregate number, however, does not tell the full story. Most 401(k) plans do not offer company stock as an investment option. The practice is concentrated in large firms (table 5-1).[7] Because company stock is concentrated in these large plans, the small percentage of plans that did offer company stock in 2001 included 42 percent of 401(k) participants (roughly 18 million workers) and 59 percent of total account balances.[8]

Not only is company stock ownership concentrated among large firms, but also many well-known companies sponsor 401(k) plans that are almost entirely invested in company stock. Table 5-2 shows the companies among Standard and Poor's top 100 with the highest percentage of company stock in their 401(k) plans. Procter and Gamble ranks first among the top 20, which includes Coca-Cola, General Electric, and other familiar names.[9] To put these holdings in perspective, Enron's employees, at their peak, held 60 percent of their 401(k) assets in company stock.

Some argue that company stock in 401(k) plans is not a serious issue because these plans are generally supplementary to substantial defined benefit plans. Several points seem relevant here. First, some of the companies whose 401(k) plans have the greatest concentrations of company stock do not have a defined benefit plan. An analysis by the Congressional Research Service shows that the concentration of company stock is actually greater for firms without a defined benefit plan.[10] Second, defined benefit plans do provide excellent benefits for the long-service employee, but mobile employees

7. Several studies report company stock as a percentage of total assets. The share depends on whether the sample is nationally representative or limited to large firms. National representative samples consistently report 17–19 percent, while large firms report 36–39 percent.
8. VanDerhei (2002).
9. Institute of Management and Administration (2001).
10. Purcell (2003a). The Congressional Research Service sample includes the defined contribution plans of 262 firms that were in either the Fortune 500 or Standard and Poor's 500 and that filed a form 10-K electronically with the Securities and Exchange Commission plus 16

Table 5-2. *Standard and Poor's Top 100 with Largest Holdings of Company Stock in 401(k) Plans and Defined Benefit Coverage, 2001*

Company	Company stock as percent of 401(k) assets	Defined benefit plan?
Procter & Gamble	94.7	No
Pfizer	85.5	Yes
Anheuser-Busch	81.6	Yes
Coca-Cola	81.5	Yes
General Electric	77.4	Yes
Texas Instruments	75.7	Yes
Williams	75.0	Yes
McDonald's	74.3	No
Home Depot	72.0	No
Campbell Soup	61.8	Yes

Source: Institute of Management and Administration (2001); pension data from Department of Labor, Form 5500, 1998.

receive substantially less and will need their 401(k) balances for retirement.[11] Third, even with a defined benefit plan significant concentrations of company stock are not prudent, and one can ask whether it makes sense for tax-subsidized plans to sanction imprudent investments. Thus large holdings of company stock are indeed a serious issue.

Company stock can end up in a 401(k) plan in one of two ways. The firm can offer company stock as an investment option for the employee or it can require that any employer-matching contribution be invested in company stock. Surveys suggest that about 45 percent of firms that offer company stock as an investment option make their matching contributions exclusively in company stock; 55 percent do not.[12] Individual holdings appear to be strongly influenced by whether or not the employer directs its match into company stock. As shown in table 5-3, employees who are free to choose invest 22 percent of their contributions in company stock. In contrast, employees whose employer directs the match to company stock end up with 53 percent (33 percent from their own contributions and 20 percent from the employer match).

---

firms selected randomly from the EDGAR database. The results show that of the 278 companies 73 (average employment of 61,241) had only a defined contribution plan, while 205 (average employment of 41,034) had both a defined benefit and a defined contribution plan. Company stock as a percentage of defined contribution assets was 51.6 percent for the defined-contribution-only companies and 36.3 percent for companies with both a defined contribution and a defined benefit plan.

11. Indeed, in testimony before the Internal Revenue Service, the chief actuary of Watson Wyatt Worldwide reported that, in the defined benefit plans that his company administers, 80 percent of the benefits go to one-sixth of participants.

12. Hewitt Associates (2001).

Table 5-3. *Employer Contributions and Company Stock Holdings, 2000*
Percent

Plan type	Share of assets in company stock
All 401(k) plans	19
401(k) plans with company stock	30[a]
Employee directs all contributions	22
Employer directs match to company stock	53[b]

Source: Holden and VanDerhei (2003).

a. For plans that offer both company stock and guaranteed investment contracts, 27.7 percent of assets are in company stock; for plans that offer company stock but no guaranteed investment contracts, the figure is 31.8 percent.

b. 33 percent by employee, 20 percent by employer.

The average percentage held in company stock also masks considerable variation among individuals. About 35 percent of participants in plans offering company stock hold none at all, while 17 percent are almost entirely invested in company stock (table 5-4).[13] Since some legislative proposals call for a cap of 20 percent, it is interesting to note that 46 percent of participants in plans offering company stock hold more than 20 percent of their 401(k) assets in that form.

One aspect of company stock is how much goes into the plan. The other aspect is restrictions placed on participants' ability to sell that stock in order to diversify their holdings. According to one survey, 81 percent of plans impose restrictions, 4 percent impose partial restrictions, and 15 percent do not impose restrictions.[14] For example, Coca-Cola does not allow participants to sell their stock until they reach the age of fifty-three. Procter and Gamble, Qwest Communications, and others have similar age requirements.[15] The picture may be changing, however. A recent survey by Fidelity Investments of the plans it administers reports that 36 percent of the plans, covering 21 percent of participants, had either removed restrictions on the sale of company stock in the previous year or were considering such a change.

Reasons for Investing in Company Stock

The most likely explanations for employee investment in company stock are that most people are not sophisticated investors, that employees have irrational hopes of striking it rich, and that employers encourage such investments.

13. VanDerhei (2002).
14. Hewitt Associates (2001).
15. Ellen E. Schultz and Theo Francis, "Fair Shares? Why Company Stock Is a Burden for Many—And Less So for a Few," *Wall Street Journal,* November 27, 2001, p. A1.

Table 5-4. *Participant Holdings of Company Stock, 2000*
Percent

Company stock as share of 401(k) assets	Share of participants with specified holdings[a]
0	34.5
>0 to 20	19.3
>20 to 40	13.5
>40 to 60	9.7
>60 to 80	5.7
>80 to 100	17.3

Source: VanDerhei (2002).

a. *Participants* refers to those in plans in which the sponsor offers company stock.

Lack of Investment Skills

In surveys of plan participants over the period 1991–2002, John Hancock Financial Services found that less than one-quarter of respondents characterized themselves as knowledgeable investors.[16] Even those who thought they were knowledgeable showed considerable confusion. The general lack of financial sophistication was reflected in respondents' perceptions about various aspects of risk and return. For example, 40 percent of all respondents thought that money market funds included stocks and 47 percent thought they included bonds. Similarly, even though participants in the survey invested in an array of assets, 40 percent did not respond to a question about future returns for stocks, bonds, or money market funds, and those who did had extremely optimistic projections for the next twenty years.[17] And when asked to rank various assets in terms of risk, the respondents considered company stock less risky than a diversified stock fund (figure 5-1). In other words, 401(k) participants as a group appear not to appreciate the risks associated with investing a significant portion of their portfolio in the stock of their employer.

Investors are also passive in their approach to investments as evidenced by the investment behavior of employees automatically enrolled in 401(k) plans.[18] Of these participants, 80 percent initially accepted the default saving rate and investment options that they were assigned. And after three years in the plan, half of the participants subject to automatic enrollment continued to contribute at the default rate and to invest their contributions in the

16. John Hancock Financial Services (2002).

17. The survey was administered to a random sample of 801 individuals between the ages of twenty-five and sixty-five. The average age was forty-three; over half (53 percent) were male; the median salary was $50,600; median 401(k) balances were $28,900.

18. Choi and others (2001a, 2001b).

Figure 5-1. *401(k) Participants' Perspectives of Risks, Various Investments, 2002*

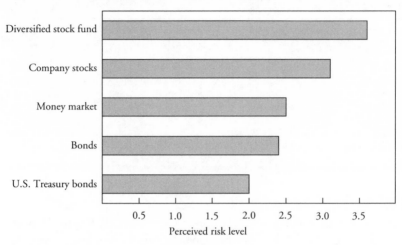

Perceived risk level

Source: John Hancock Financial Services (2002).

default portfolio. Given this tendency, participants are likely to acquiesce when someone puts their 401(k) assets in company stock or tells them that investing in company stock is a good idea.

Participants also appear to be strongly influenced by the employer match, an endorsement effect that induces less than rational investment behavior. Several recent studies confirm that employees of firms that have a match in company stock put more, not less, of their own contributions in company stock.[19] Employees appear to take stock matches as an endorsement that company stock is a good investment. In follow-up questionnaires, two groups were asked separate questions regarding their investments. The first was asked how they would respond if their employer provided a match in international equity. The second was asked how they would respond if their employer provided a match in a diversified stock fund. Both groups indicated that they would buy more of the "endorsed" option. In contrast, rational investors would reduce their holdings of the employer-match option since that is the only way to maintain their original overall asset allocation.[20]

Another type of poor decisionmaking is the inappropriate projection of past performance. Participants tend to assume that their company's stock will do well in the future if it has done well in the past.[21] In one study, employees

19. Clark and others (2000); Benartzi (2001); Liang and Weisbenner (2002).
20. Benartzi (2001).
21. The tendency for people to extrapolate past performances is consistent with representativeness theory discussed by Tversky and Kahneman (1974).

of firms in the sample with the worst performance over the last ten years allocated just 10.4 percent of their contributions to company stock, while employees whose firm experienced the best performance allocated 39.7 percent.[22] Rational investors know that public information, such as past performance, is factored into the price of the stock and that future performance should be about average for a security with similar risk characteristics. Employees who buy company stock after it has appreciated do not in fact fare well going forward. In the study just cited, employees who had invested the most in company stock earned 6.8 percent less in the following year than those who had purchased the least.[23]

Researchers who analyze purchases of company stock rather than asset holdings also find that employee purchases are inversely related to the number of investment options.[24] In their sample, if the plan offers two investment options, participants invest 59 percent in company stock; if the plan offers three options, participants invest 36 percent; four options 26 percent, and so on. That is, employees appear to follow a 1/n naive diversification rule (see chapter 4).

Irrational Hopes

In addition to a general lack of investment skill, many employees seem intoxicated by the possibility of striking it rich and thus develop an irrational faith in the success of their employer. The bull market of the 1990s probably exacerbated the phenomenon. Employees who saw management profiting enormously from their efforts wanted to do the same. One anecdote that reflects this behavior is the near feeding frenzy that accompanied AT&T's initial public offering of its wireless company.[25] Keep in mind that this offering came after the company had already cut 25,000 jobs and more cuts were predicted. Nevertheless, employees were willing to risk their life savings to participate. One employee borrowed $42,600 from his retirement plan and $11,800 from his credit union—more than his annual salary—to buy 2,000

22. Benartzi (2001). Benartzi analyzed contribution behavior at 136 companies in the Standard and Poor's 500 in 1993. Sengmuller (2001) performed a similar analysis for 239 S&P firms for the period 1994–98. He also found that past returns were a strong predictor of the purchase of company stock, although the effect was somewhat smaller than for 1993.

23. This lower return also suggests that employees were not privy to any insider information.

24. Liang and Weisbenner (2002). Data for this study came from form 11-K, which most firms offering company stock are required to file with the Securities and Exchange Commission. The sample includes 994 firms over the period 1991–2000, with the greatest number of observations for 1997 and 1998.

25. R. Blumenstein, "High-Wire Act: As AT&T Unit Sets an IPO, Employees Scramble to Cash In," *Wall Street Journal,* April 26, 2000, p. A1.

shares. "I am putting in everything I have," he said, "I don't want to miss out." Another emptied her Christmas Club and borrowed from friends to buy 200 shares. She explained, "I want as much wireless as I can get my hands on." A brother of another employee advised his sister, "I would risk everything. Sure you can focus on the What ifs. What if you lose your money? But what if you doubled or tripled your money?" AT&T Wireless Services' stock price fell by more than 80 percent from its opening in April 2000 to July 2002.

Employees often seem to think that they have a better sense of the firm's financial future than outside investors. The evidence, however, suggests the contrary. Employees too often are simply swept away by the hope that their employer's stock will skyrocket and they will get rich. One analyst characterizes this motive for buying company stock as "swinging for the fences."[26]

Employer Pressure

The employee, with limited investment skills and often irrational hopes of striking it rich, is not the only problem. There is also the employer extolling the virtue of its stock. As Enron was imploding in late 2001, the Gillette Company in Boston was asked about its practice of directing company stock into its 401(k). Stephen Brayton, a Gillette spokesman responded, "We believe 401(k) [plans] are a long-term investment, and we believe that Gillette stock is an excellent long-term investment."[27] Brayton added, "Making the company contribution in Gillette stock is a great way for employees to share financially in the long-term growth of the company." Gillette is not alone, of course. Employers in general actively encourage employees to buy company stock. Like Gillette, they argue that it is a good investment and a way to demonstrate loyalty to the company.

Reasons Employers Provide Company Stock

Employers clearly value making their 401(k) match in company stock and offering employees company stock as an investment option. The question is, Why? Employers imply that it is cheaper to make contributions in stock than in cash, and they argue that holding company stock aligns the interests of employees with those of the firm. Although rarely mentioned by employers, putting company stock in the hands of loyal employees also serves as a useful mechanism for fending off hostile takeovers.

26. Meulbroek (2002)
27. Ellen E. Schultz, "Should Pension Law Do More to Protect Retirement Savings?" *Wall Street Journal*, January 14, 2002, p. C1.

Cost

In the wake of the Enron disaster, several proposals emerged to limit the holdings of company stock in 401(k) plans. The response from employers was immediate and negative; they wanted employees to hold company stock. "Putting firm caps on the amount of [company] stock in retirement accounts could well hurt—not help—retirement security by leading employers to cut that amount they contribute toward their employees' retirement," said James Delaplane, vice president for retirement policy at the American Benefits Council, which represents large employers.[28] The ERISA Industry Committee (ERIC), a nonprofit association reflecting the views of the sponsors of the nation's largest retirement, health, and welfare plans, expressed a similar sentiment: "If employers are prohibited from requiring their contributions to defined contribution plans to be invested in employer stock, they are likely to curtail their contributions, thereby reducing employees' retirement saving."[29]

In what sense are contributions in stock less costly than cash contributions? In terms of simple arithmetic, they have an identical impact on the wealth of the initial shareholders. If the firm buys stock on the open market to put into the plan, it reduces its cash holdings to the same extent as making a cash contribution. If the firm issues new stock, it does not have to deplete its cash, but earnings per share will be lower because they have to be distributed over more shares.

A cash contribution to a 401(k) plan and a contribution of newly issued stock have an identical impact on the wealth of the initial shareholders. Firm A and Firm B start off with identical values; each has 100 shares of stock outstanding at a price of $10 a share for a total value of $1,000. Firm A pays $91 in cash to the 401(k) plan; this reduces the value of the firm by an equivalent amount to $909. Firm B issues 10 shares of stock to the 401(k) plan. With 110 shares outstanding the price per share drops from $10.00 to $9.10 ($1,000/110), since the value of the firm is unchanged. At the new share price, the 401(k) participants hold 10 shares of stock with a total value of $91, the same as participants in Firm A received in cash contributions. At the same time, the value of the initial shareholders' wealth in Firm B drops to $909, the same as in Firm A. In short, regardless of whether a 401(k) match is provided in cash or stock, it has an equal impact on the wealth of the initial shareholders.

---

28. Ellen E. Schultz and Theo Francis, "Hot Tax Break: 401(k)s—Why Firms Stuff Plans with Stock," *Wall Street Journal*, January 31, 2002, p. C1.

29. ERIC (2002).

This exercise ignores taxes, but companies may receive a tax benefit from matching in company stock.[30] Although dividends paid on company stock are not usually tax deductible, dividends paid on stock contributed to a leveraged ESOP or KSOP may be deductible. Thus the firm can take a deduction when it initially contributes the stock to the plan just as it would for a cash contribution. And it can take future deductions on all dividends paid on that stock. Since in theory the value of the stock is the present value of future dividends, the firm gets to use the dividends for a deduction twice, once at the initial contribution and again when the dividends are actually paid. Some empirical support exists for the tax-advantage argument in that firms providing all the match in company stock were more likely to pay dividends and have a higher dividend yield.[31]

Whatever the reason, employers strongly prefer to make stock contributions to 401(k) plans.[32] In their view, a dollar of cash is actually worth more than a dollar, since cash is costly to raise and often comes with strings attached. The transaction costs associated with issuing new stock to raise cash or floating new debt can be substantial.[33] The alternative of borrowing from financial institutions is difficult because banks fluctuate in their willingness to lend and generally impose stringent loan agreement covenants containing performance requirements on the borrower. Companies that turn to venture capitalists for cash may have to surrender a significant share of ownership of the firm.

Aligning Employees' Interests

Another reason that employers might prefer stock is the desire to align the interests of employees with those of the company. According to the ERISA Industry Committee (ERIC), "Employer stock plans serve the important purpose of aligning the interests of the employees with the interests of the employer's business and encouraging employees to be attentive to the inter-

---

30. Schultz and Francis, "Hot Tax Break: 401(k)s—Why Firms Stuff Plans with Stock."

31. Liang and Weisbenner (2002).

32. The reason does not appear to be that firms are cash constrained. Liang and Weisbenner (2002) in a cross-section regression find a positive relationship between cash flow and employer match in company stock.

33. One strain of finance literature—the pecking-order theory of capital structure—argues that firms should rely on internal cash for their activities rather going to the market. See Myers (1984). One reason is that firms that make seasoned equity offerings typically see their stock price decline. Investors suspect that the firm is issuing more stock because it believes its stock is overvalued and react by depressing the stock price.

ests of business."[34] To reinforce the argument, the statement includes an anecdote from a company that suffered large losses because delivery people regularly discarded expensive containers after they delivered the company's product to retailers rather than bringing them back to the company to be used again. The company tried to persuade the deliverers to save the containers but to little effect. Finally, the company placed the company's stock plan logo on the containers, and the delivery people changed their behavior. ERIC contends that they saw the connection between returning the containers to the company for reuse and the value of their stock in the company plan.

Employers often cite improving employee motivation as an important reason for providing employer stock.[35] The notion is that tying employee income and wealth to company performance will increase productivity and performance by decreasing labor-management conflicts and encouraging employee effort. However, the evidence is not robust. A review of thirty-one studies found a positive but weak relationship between employee ownership and employee attitudes and motivation.[36] Of the nine studies analyzing the relationship between ESOPs and productivity, only two found a significant positive effect. Nevertheless, considering the nine studies as a whole, positive and significant coefficients appear more often than would be expected if there were no relationship between ESOPs and productivity.[37] It is important to remember that these weak results are derived from studies that focused primarily on ESOPs and small cooperatives. One would expect the results for broad-based ownership in 401(k) plans to be even less compelling since most employees have little influence on the stock price.[38] Indeed, one study that broke firms down by size found a significant positive relationship between employee ownership and profit measures for small firms, but the relationship disappeared or became negative for large firms.[39]

34. ERIC (2002).

35. In a study by the U.S. General Accounting Office (1986), 70 percent of employers cited improving productivity as a major motivation for forming an ESOP.

36. Kruse and Blasi (1997); Kruse (2002).

37. Kruse and Blasi (1997). The average estimated productivity difference between ESOP and non-ESOP firms was 6.2 percent, while the average pre- and post-adoption difference was 4.4 percent. These estimates should be interpreted cautiously, however, since large standard errors kept most of the individual estimates from being statistically significant.

38. Theory suggests that the number of employees in large firms dilutes individual incentives. Employees are tempted to become free riders, that is, they themselves do not work hard but they hope to enjoy the payoff from the efforts of others. In small firms, creating a cooperative workplace and employing peer pressure can overcome the free-rider problem, but such efforts are more difficult in larger establishments.

39. Blasi, Conte, and Kruse (1996).

Fending off Hostile Bids

Although employers rarely mention that putting shares in friendly hands is a major motivation for 401(k) investment in company stock, it has been an important consideration in some celebrated cases. Certainly fending off a hostile takeover by Shamrock Holdings in 1988 was the reason that Polaroid created its ESOP. Polaroid fought the takeover bid by creating 10 million new shares and depositing them in the ESOP, which gave Polaroid workers 14 percent of the common stock. The ESOP created a major hurdle for Shamrock to overcome, since under Delaware law Shamrock needed 85 percent of the shares to acquire the company immediately.[40] Mandatory contributions to the new ESOP meant that many employees did not have resources available to continue contributing to the company's diversified 401(k) plan. As a result, when Polaroid declared bankruptcy in 2001, employees were highly invested in company stock and many lost the bulk of their retirement savings. More generally, of the roughly 1,000 companies that introduced or maintained plans with company stock during the 1980s, 102 reported that the plans were introduced or used in response to takeover bids.[41]

Among Standard and Poor's top 100 companies with company stock in defined contribution plans, these employee holdings account for an average of 7 percent of outstanding shares. The figure is considerably more in companies such as Ford, Lucent, and Honeywell (table 5-5). The Securities and Exchange Commission classifies a 5 percent owner as a major shareholder, and experts say that most chief executive officers (CEOs) would be delighted to control a block that size.[42] In Hewlett-Packard's controversial 2002 bid to buy Compaq Computer, considerably smaller blocks proved pivotal. Other than shares held by the family foundations, most institutional investors held less than 3 percent.[43] Some serious players in the proposed deal, such as the California Public Employee Retirement System, controlled less than 0.5 percent.[44] It was reported that Walter Hewlett went out of his way to visit Boston firms that owned as little as 0.05 percent.[45]

---

40. Richard L. Wentworth, "ESOP Gains as an Anti-Takeover Defense," *Christian Science Monitor,* January 18, 1989, p. 9.

41. Blasi, Conte, and Kruse (1996).

42. Blasi, Conte, and Kruse (1996).

43. The David and Lucile Packard Foundation controlled 10.37 percent and the William R. Hewlett Revocable Trust held 3.75 percent. See D. C. Denison, "HP-Compaq Vote Starts Today, Results Seen Taking Weeks," *Boston Globe,* March 19, 2002, p. D2.

44. Denison, "HP-Compaq Vote Starts Today, Results Seen Taking Weeks."

45. Steven Syre, "HP, Compaq Make Their Pitches, One by One," *Boston Globe,* March 17, 2002, p. C1.

Table 5-5. *Employee Holdings of Company Stock, Highest and Lowest of Standard and Poor's Top 100 Companies, 2001*

Company	Total company stock (millions of dollars)	Company stock in defined contribution plans (millions of dollars)	Company stock in defined contribution plans as percent of total stock[a]
Highest			
Ford Motor	32,974	11,400	34.6
Lucent Technologies	24,982	4,928	19.7
Honeywell	26,949	3,668	13.6
McKesson HBOC	10,659	1,277	12.0
Procter & Gamble	100,359	10,424	10.4
Lowest			
Wachovia Corp.	42,119	331	0.8
Dell Computer	72,814	471	0.6
PepsiCo	85,083	516	0.6
J.P. Morgan	74,923	297	0.4
Wal-Mart Stores	245,808	82	>0.1

Source: Authors' calculations based on COMPUSTAT/CRSP, Center for Research in Security Prices (www.crsp.uchicago.edu); Institute of Management and Administration (2001).

a. Average is 7 percent.

The Harm to Employees from Investing in Company Stock

Employers clearly encourage employees to purchase company stock. The question is whether they understand the risks. Some of the quotations reported in the press suggest that employers, especially those that are prospering, do not understand the risks associated with a lack of portfolio diversification. Others suggest that they do. For example, Reuben Mark, CEO of Colgate-Palmolive, which has 80 percent of its 401(k) plan assets in company stock, states: "One school of thought says, Don't put all of your eggs in one basket. Another says, Put them in one basket but watch it pretty closely. Our people feel they know the company well, they are involved in it and working their tails off to be successful, so they feel comfortable investing in Colgate stock."[46] In other words, lack of diversification is risky but it can be justified on the basis of superior knowledge.

A more interesting view is that equity diversification is not the whole story. Under the auspices of the Employee Benefit Research Institute, a nonprofit organization financed largely by plan sponsors and other members of

46. Blake (2001), pp. 68–71.

the pension industry, Jack VanDerhei made the following argument in testimony before Congress. Yes, it is true, he said, that a diversified portfolio of stocks has less risk than investing in a single stock. But what this simple analysis leaves out, he argues, is that many extremely risk-averse employees would avoid stocks altogether were it not for their employer's contribution of company stock into the 401(k) plan. Improved asset allocation could thus accompany company stock investment and the argument of "more risk for no additional return" is too limited a framework. Left to their own devices, many employees might invest less in stock and have a lower expected return overall. The inclusion of company stock thus might work to the benefit of such employees.[47]

Whether one agrees with the argument or not, it is clear that finance experts involved with the industry recognize that diversification reduces investment risk. It is less clear whether employers in general recognize the dangers of overinvestment in company stock. Nor is it clear that employers generally recognize the risks they bear. Although ERISA explicitly allows investment in company stock in defined contribution plans, the practice can put the company in a tricky legal position. Investment in company stock, for example, may not always be consistent with ERISA's "prudent person" requirements.

Take the case of a firm in financial trouble. Is it prudent for the firm to continue directing the employer match into company stock? If the sponsor of the plan knows that the company's stock has become highly risky, its fiduciary duty may require that it stop loading employee accounts with this imprudent investment. But such a shift sends a scary message to outside investors. Directing employee investment into company stock can thus create a serious conflict of interest for the sponsor. Indeed, a federal judge in Texas has ruled that Enron's former president and Northern Trust could be sued over losses suffered on Enron stock in the company's 401(k) plan.[48]

The most obvious harm from overinvestment of 401(k) plans in company stock is big losses when things go wrong at the firm. When companies fall into bad times, workers can lose their jobs and see their retirement savings devastated at the same time. Table 5-6 shows the investment in company stock at several large companies that saw their stock values plummet between March 2000 and the end of 2001. In most of these cases, many employees also lost their jobs. In other words, it is not simply the losses but rather the

47. VanDerhei (2002).
48. Theo Francis, "Ruling Lets Enron Workers Sue Lay, Northern Trust over Lost Savings," *Wall Street Journal*, October 2, 2003.

Table 5-6. *Stock Losses, Twelve Companies, March 2000 to December 2001*
Percent

Company	Change in stock price	Company stock as share of pension assets
Polaroid	−99.6	19
Enron	−99.6	41
Global Crossing	−97.5	16
Weirton	−96.4	16
Providian Financial	−91.8	19
Kansas City Southern	−91.8	80
Lucent Technologies	−89.2	16
Owens Corning	−88.5	26
Montana Power	−88.0	25
Northern Telecom	−86.6	30
Corning	−86.0	32
ADC Telecom	−80.4	46

Source: Chris Farrell. 2002. "The Problem with Pension Plans." Business Week Online Sound Money 1/11/02. New York: McGraw-Hill. (www.businessweek.com/bwdaily/dnflash/jan2002/nf20020111_3044.htm).

fact that these losses occurred at the same time that participants' jobs were in jeopardy.

Enron is the poster child for the risks associated with investment in company stock. A major portion of its retirement income program was a 401(k) plan. Employees could invest their own 401(k) contributions in several options, including Enron stock. Regardless of what they chose, the company's matching contribution ($0.50 per $1.00, up to a maximum of 6 percent of pay) was invested entirely in Enron stock.[49] Since Enron employees also put a lot of their own contributions in company stock, at the end of 2000, 60 percent of 401(k) assets were in Enron stock. Although employees faced no restrictions on the sale of company stock purchased with their own contributions, they could not sell employer-match stock until they reached age fifty. As Enron stock plummeted from a high of $88 in September 2000 to $0.60 by the end of 2001, employees lost most of their retirement saving (figure 5-2).

Enron had a defined benefit plan as well as the 401(k) plan. In 1986 Enron closed down its overfunded defined benefit plan and used the extra funds to set up an ESOP. It then transferred the liabilities and remaining assets of the old plan to a new defined benefit plan. This new plan had a floor-offset arrangement with the ESOP, so the benefits earned in the ESOP

49. Enron's form 11-K.

Figure 5-2. *Stock Price of Enron, January 1987 to December 2001*

Dollars

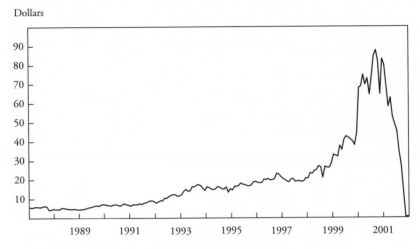

Source: CNBC, *MSN Money* (http://moneycentral.msn.com).

reduced those from the defined benefit plan.[50] This meant that, by the time Enron imploded, the defined benefit plan had little value. Most of the employees' retirement assets were in the defined contribution plan and in company stock.

As discussed above, some observers suggest that there is no need to worry about company stock if the employer also offers a defined benefit plan, and some legislative proposals would place fewer restrictions on employers with a defined benefit plan. One lesson from Enron is that the mere presence of a defined benefit plan does not ensure an adequate retirement income.

Although bankruptcies of firms with large pension stakes in company stock make the headlines, the more fundamental point is that overinvestment in company stock is never a good idea. It exposes participants to firm-specific risk. Usually, higher risk is associated with higher returns; that is why large company stocks yielded a real annual return of 7.2 percent over the period 1926–2001 compared to 0.8 percent for U.S. Treasury bills.[51] But investing

50. In determining the offset from the ESOP, Enron calculated the ESOP offsets based on the price of the stock over the period 1996–2000, when it was selling at about $40 a share. It then used these higher values to permanently reduce the value of pensions that employees had earned between January 1987 and January 1995, when the Enron stock price was considerably lower. See Schultz and Francis, "Fair Shares? Why Company Stock Is a Burden for Many—And Less So for a Few."

51. Ibbotson Associates (2003).

in one stock rather than in a diversified portfolio creates more risk without providing any increase in expected returns.

A 2002 study attempts to measure the value lost by employees who hold company stock.[52] Not surprisingly, the amount of loss depends on the risk associated with the particular stock. A well-diversified portfolio of stocks in the last 150 trading days of 1998 had a volatility of 23 percent, meaning that the value of the portfolio had a standard deviation equal to 23 percent of its trend-line value. The average volatility of a single stock from companies listed on the New York Stock Exchange (NYSE) was 45 percent, roughly twice as great. The comparable volatility for NASDAQ stocks was 86 percent and for Internet-based firms 117 percent, five times as great as the volatility of the diversified portfolio.

One way to measure the loss associated with company stock is to calculate the relative price of a diversified portfolio that would provide investors the same risk-adjusted return as the company stock investment. The loss depends not only on the particular stock, as discussed above, but also on the size of the investment relative to the participant's total wealth and how long the stock is held. If pension holdings constitute 50 percent of an individual's wealth, and if 25 percent of pension assets is invested in the stock of a company on the NYSE, an employee with a ten-year holding period sacrifices 16 percent of the value of the initial contribution by not being diversified.[53] The average loss for all companies is 27 percent and for Internet companies 48 percent. If the employee's holdings in company stock account for 50 percent of pension assets, then the loss of value of the initial contribution rises to 42 percent.[54]

The fundamental point is that the risk-adjusted value of company stock in a nondiversified portfolio is significantly less than its market value. This result has important implications not only for company stock in 401(k) plans but also for stock purchase plans in which employees can buy stock at a discount. These plans may not be such a good deal unless investors sell immediately. Moreover, this study underestimates the total loss in value since it does not consider the critical correlation between the value of the stock and the individual's earning potential.

In some situations employees have sued their employers over loss of retirement funds. The following case studies are illustrations.

IKON OFFICE SOLUTIONS. In 1998 employees filed a suit against Ikon, a Pennsylvania provider of copier and printing systems, alleging that the com-

52. Meulbroek (2002).
53. Meulbroek (2002).
54. Meulbroek (2002).

pany breached its fiduciary duty by matching employee contributions with company stock.[55] Ikon's shares fell from about $60 in the fall of 1998 to about $3 by the end of the year after the company took a $100 million earnings charge. In March 2000 the judge in the U.S. District Court for the Eastern District of Pennsylvania ruled that the case could proceed as a class action suit.

LUCENT TECHNOLOGIES. On July 19, 2001, two former Lucent employees filed a class-action suit in the U.S. District Court of New Jersey alleging that Lucent breached its fiduciary responsibility by allowing employees to buy company stock as one of its investment options.[56] The suit also alleges that Lucent "withheld material information regarding the fiscal state of the company" during the period between January 1, 2000, and the date the suit was filed. As a result, the plaintiffs allege, Lucent "encouraged participants and beneficiaries to continue to make and to maintain substantial investments in stock in the company's 401(k) plan." When the suit was filed, Lucent shares had plunged from a high of $82 to about $6. With about 30 percent of 401(k) plan assets in company stock at the peak, employees suffered big losses, many at the same time that they lost their jobs.

RITE AID. In June 2001 Rite Aid Corporation settled with employees participating in its defined contribution plan for $193 million dollars, with $44 million in cash and the rest in stock. The complaint alleged that the company knew or should have known that unregistered shares of stock were being illegally sold to plan participants. The employees asserted that Rite Aid breached its fiduciary responsibilities by selecting and maintaining Rite Aid as an investment option for its plan as well as by providing participants with inaccurate and misleading information about Rite Aid stock.

ENRON. In 2001 members of the Enron Corporation Savings Plan filed three separate class action lawsuits against Enron Corporation. The suits allege that plan fiduciaries breached their duties in a number of ways. First, the fiduciaries maintained Enron stock as an investment option after it had become inappropriate to do so. Second, they provided misleading information to participants about Enron's financial health. Third, they did not provide an investment prospectus as required by law. Fourth, Enron imposed a blackout period, which prevented plan participants from disposing of com-

55. Blake (2001).
56. Blake (2001).

pany stock during a period of a precipitous decline in its price Enron failed to give proper notice of this blackout period.

PROVIDIAN FINANCIAL. In December 2001 beneficiaries of the Providian Financial 401(k) plan filed a class action lawsuit against Providian Financial for breaching its fiduciary responsibilities. The suit alleges that fiduciaries at Providian Financial were aware that Providian had become an inappropriate stock for the plan. The fiduciaries withheld this information and continued to promote investments in Providian Financial to plan participants and beneficiaries. During this period Providian Financial stock fell from a high of $60 down to $2, losing more than 90 percent of its value.[57]

Reforming the System

The idea of changing federal laws to improve diversification in pension plans is hardly new. The Tax Reform Act of 1986 mandated that employees covered by an ESOP who are age fifty-five and who have completed ten years of service must be allowed to transfer some of their company stock to other investment options. It is a fairly modest mandate in that these participants have the right during the following five years to sell only 25 percent of their company stockholdings; during the sixth year, they may diversify up to 50 percent, less any previously diversified shares.

Another flurry of interest in allowing participants to diversify developed in 1997, in the wake of the bankruptcy of the Fort Worth, Texas, floor-covering chain Color Tile. Color Tile's 401(k) plan had 90 percent of plan assets invested in the company's own stores, which were leased back to the company. When Color Tile filed for bankruptcy, the value of this real estate declined sharply. As a result, employees saw much of their retirement money evaporate just as they lost their jobs. Color Tile differs from current cases such as Enron and Polaroid in that plan investments were in the employer's real property instead of common stock and the sponsor directed the investment of employee contributions as well as the employer match.[58]

---

57. Keller Rohrback LLP (www.erisafraud.com [March 25, 2003]).

58. Before 1992 the Color Tile Investment Plan allowed maximum contributions of 5 percent of pay, with Color Tile providing a 50 percent match. In 1992 the company introduced a new benefits package, which allowed participants to contribute an additional 5 percent with no match. According to written testimony from the lead plaintiff in the lawsuit against Color Tile, Raymonda Handler Almand, "Participants were never given reports as to what the monies were invested in but were generally told that it was invested in stocks, real estate, and bonds." See PWBA (1997).

Color Tile's bankruptcy prompted a review by a working group of the Department of Labor's Pension and Welfare Benefits Advisory Council of the practice of holding employer assets in defined contribution plans.[59] The working group heard from a long list of witnesses with a variety of perspectives and in the end came to the following conclusions. First, it unanimously recommended limiting plan asset investments in the employer's real property to 10 percent and revoking the exemption from the diversification requirement for real property. Second, for publicly traded securities, it unanimously recommended, at a minimum, extending the ESOP diversification rules to all participants in defined contribution plans. A majority supported stronger measures—namely, that all participants be allowed to sell their company stock as soon as they were vested. Third, it recommended that plan sponsors disclose to plan participants the risks associated with investment in company stock. The members did not support a cap on investment in company stock, however, since they concluded that the burden of diversification rested with the participant. They were also concerned that imposing restrictions on 401(k) plans would lead employers to convert their plans to KSOPs—that is, to a 401(k) plan in which a portion of plan assets is invested in company stock through an ESOP.

The other major response to the Color Tile bankruptcy and similar losses was the introduction of legislation by Senator Barbara Boxer (Democrat from California) that would impose a 10 percent cap on holdings of company stock in 401(k) plans. While the proposal was enacted as part of the Taxpayer Relief Act of 1997, a large number of exemptions severely undercut its impact. The legislation places no restrictions on employer contributions and applies only to employee contributions in two rare situations. In the first situation employees have no choice over the investment of their own contributions; instead, the employer makes all the decisions, as in the case of Color Tile.[60] In the second situation the employer requires that more than 1 percent of employee contributions be directed to company stock. Given these limitations, observers conclude that the legislation would only affect 1 percent of corporate defined contribution plans.[61]

In response to the collapse of Enron, the Bush administration proposed some changes, and legislators introduced several bills to limit employee losses from investment in company stock. The two common themes were allowing employees greater freedom to sell employer contributions of company stock and providing employees more information. The most controversial issue is

59. PWBA (1997).
60. PWBA (1997).
61. Anand (1996).

whether to directly limit the amount of company stock that employees can hold in their 401(k) plans. Another issue is so-called lockdowns, or blackout periods.

Allowing Employees to Sell Employer Stock

Although ESOPs have provisions that allow employees to diversity their holdings (albeit not until age fifty-five and after ten years of service), 401(k) plans traditionally had none. That is, no law mandates that employees can sell their elective purchases of employer stock or diversify out of employer stock contributed by the employer. Most employers allow the immediate sale of elective purchases but permit diversification of employer-directed company stock only after the employee has satisfied some age and service requirement.

To encourage diversification the Bush administration proposed to allow 401(k) participants to sell employer stock after three years (the maximum vesting period). Every major legislative proposal includes a similar provision.[62] This does not appear to be a controversial issue; allowing employees to diversify will protect employees who want to sell and will provide a valuable option in times of distress. In terms of immediate impact, the change should be minimal. Employees generally like holding company stock, and much of their holdings arise from their own contributions.

Improving the Information Flowing to Employees

Although there is universal agreement that employees need more and better information about their investment options, how best to provide that information is slightly more controversial than it might seem. Starting with the most harmonious provisions, almost every bill wants employers to provide employees with regular information about their investment holdings and to inform them about the risks of concentrating investments in company stock. Where the harmony breaks down is over the question of making investment advice available to participants.

Insurance companies and investment managers have lobbied Congress to make it easier for them to gain access to 401(k) participants. In response, two bills have been introduced that would essentially protect employers from

---

62. By the end of March 2002, congressional committees had reported three bills: H.R. 3669, the House Ways and Means Committee's "Employee Retirement Savings Bill of Rights"; H.R. 3762, the House Committee on Education and Workforce's "Pension Security Act"; and S. 1992, the Senate Committee on Health, Education, Labor, and Pensions' "Protecting America's Pension Act." The other legislation that has received considerable attention is S. 1838, the "Pension Protection and Diversification Act of 2001," sponsored by Senators Barbara Boxer (D-Calif.) and Jon Corzine (D-N.J.). All four bills have similar diversification provisions.

being designated fiduciaries if they give investment firms the right to advise their employees on an individual basis. The two bills differ in the way they treat conflicts of interest. Senate bill 1677, the "Independent Investor Advice Act of 2001" (introduced by Senators Jeff Bingaman and Susan Collins), would prevent a representative from, say, Merrill Lynch from recommending investment in any Merrill Lynch fund. The "Retirement Security Advice Act of 2001," which was passed by the House in November 2001, simply requires the Merrill Lynch representative to disclose that his company will make money if the employee purchases a Merrill Lynch fund. In short, both Congress and the administration support the provision of investment advice, but proponents differ on how to handle the issue of conflict of interest.

Directly Limiting Employee Holdings of Company Stock

The argument in favor of limits on company stock is that pension plans are tax-subsidized retirement vehicles, and individuals should not be permitted to use these tax-favored vehicles for imprudent investments. But most defined contribution plans are exempt from the 10 percent limit on company stock imposed on defined benefit plans. The only exception is the 10 percent partial limit introduced in the Taxpayer Relief Act of 1997, which applies to very few plans.

Immediately after the collapse of Enron, Senators Barbara Boxer (Democrat of California) and Jon Corzine (Democrat of New Jersey) submitted Senate bill 1828, which would place a 20 percent cap on employee holdings of company stock in 401(k) plans. (To further discourage the use of company stock in 401(k) plans, the Boxer-Corzine bill would allow employers to deduct only 50 percent of the otherwise allowable value of company stock.) A cap is a direct way to prevent excessive holdings of company stock, but it raises the specter of forcing employees to sell their company stock just when the firm does well and the stock appreciates.

Perhaps to avoid this problem, the Senate Health, Education, Labor, and Pensions Committee took a somewhat different tack to accomplish the same goal. The legislation (Senate bill 1992) would require plan sponsors to select one of two options. Employers could either make their matching contributions in company stock or include company stock as an investment option for employee contributions. Employers could not do both unless they also sponsored a defined benefit pension. Since employees are enthusiastic purchasers of company stock, this provision would deter extremely high levels of company stock in participant accounts, but it does not limit employer contributions in company stock and would not necessarily keep participant holdings to prudent levels.

The Bush administration and many in Congress oppose placing any limitations on employee holdings of company stock in 401(k) plans. Their view is that employees generally make the decision to purchase on their own and that the government should not interfere with that freedom. Many are also concerned that if employer contributions were restricted in any way, they would cut back on the match. It is not clear why employers want to make their contributions in company stock. But they have certainly signaled that they will contribute less if they cannot make their 401(k) match in that fashion. Since studies show that the presence of an employee match has a positive effect on participation and contributions, changes that reduce the employer match could significantly reduce overall retirement saving.[63]

Regulating Lockdowns

The final area that has received legislative attention is lockdowns, or blackouts. Companies routinely suspend account activity in their 401(k) plans if they change administrators, install new software, or undertake other administrative tasks. In the case of Enron, the lockdown had been long planned but occurred as the price of the stock was plummeting. Although the stock only dropped from $15.40 to $9.98 between October 26 and November 13, 2001, the fact that many could not sell led to a cry of foul play.[64]

Enron employees have sued over the lockdown.[65] ERISA states that when employees have control over their assets, the plan sponsor or administrator is not liable for losses that the participant might incur. Whether the plan sponsor is relieved of such responsibility depends on whether the participant does indeed have control. The lawsuit says that employees were deprived of control at a time when revelations from the company caused the stock to drop. Since the employer rather than the employees had control, the suit alleges that Enron should have diversified the plan assets as required under ERISA. In other words, the employer should be liable for the losses.

The administration and all the proposed legislation would require that the employer provide employees with written notice thirty days before a lockdown. Some (for example, Representative Kenneth Bentsen's House bill 3509, "Retirement Account Protection Act") would require sixty days' notice and an exemption from the Secretary of Labor. The administration also argued that the safe harbor that relieves the sponsor from fiduciary liability should not apply during the blackout period. Moreover, the proposal would

---

63. Munnell, Sundén, and Taylor (2000); Munnell and Sundén (2003).
64. Schultz and Francis, "Hot Tax Break: 401(k)s—Why Firms Stuff Plans with Stock."
65. Purcell (2002b).

have prohibited company executives from selling any of their stock during the lockdown.[66]

Summary

The main areas of agreement on legislation are that individuals should be able to easily diversify out of company stock and should receive more information about investment generally and about the risks of excessive ownership of company stock. The options either to place a limit on company stock holdings or to make employers choose between a match in company stock or offering stock as an employee investment are more controversial proposals. Opinion is also split on how to respond, if at all, to the lockdown issue.

One issue that will have to be addressed in the legislative response is how 401(k) regulation will fit with the rules for ESOPs. It certainly seems possible at the current time that plan sponsors could circumvent any limits put on 401(k) plans by transforming the plan into a KSOP, which combines a 401(k) and an ESOP into a single plan. Remember that, in addition to requiring that more than 50 percent of assets be invested in company stock, ESOPs are becoming increasingly popular because they allow tax deductions for dividends paid to the plan. Most of the legislation does not address ESOPs directly, and perhaps any discussion might best be limited to the ESOPs of large publicly held companies.[67] But given that the activities of ESOPs and 401(k)s are increasingly intertwined, the future of ESOPs will also be affected by the nation's response to Enron.

Conclusion

A defining characteristic of 401(k) plans is that the employee rather than the employer bears the investment risk. Generally, the greater the risk, the higher the potential return. That is, if the employee invests in stocks rather than bonds, the employee takes on more risk but also can expect a higher return. This relationship between risk and return breaks down in the case of company stock; investing in only one stock rather than several creates more risk without providing any increase in expected returns. In addition, plan participants invest in an asset whose value is closely correlated with their own earnings. Finance theory screams, Don't do it!

---

66. This proposal was enacted as part of the Sarbanes-Oxley act on July 30, 2002 (P.L. 107-204).

67. The Boxer-Corzine legislation reduces the age and service requirements for diversification under an ESOP to age thirty-five and five years of service (from age fifty-five and ten years of service).

Yet more than 8 million 401(k) participants hold more than 20 percent of their 401(k) assets in company stock. The question is, Why? The evidence suggests that most participants are not sophisticated investors; they underestimate the risk of investing in company stock, and they tend to buy what they know. The problem is exacerbated when the employer matches in company stock. These contributions not only boost company stock holdings directly, but they are also interpreted as investment advice by employees and therefore encourage them to contribute more on their own. Employers strongly value the opportunity to match in stock rather than cash, apparently because it allows them to hold on to their valuable cash reserves and because they believe that it helps align the interests of the employee with those of the firm.

The challenge is to reduce the shortcomings of employee holdings of company stock without damaging the usefulness of 401(k) plans. Employers have indicated that if they cannot match in company stock they will cut back on their contributions. If that were to happen, it would undermine retirement security, since the presence of an employer match (if not the size of the match) strongly encourages employee participation and contributions. On the other hand, employers cannot cut back too dramatically: The match is part of the compensation they must pay to attract able employees in a competitive labor market. Even in a slack labor market, for many employers the employer match is critical in inducing enough highly compensated employees to participate in the plan to pass the nondiscrimination tests. Nevertheless, employer response must be one factor to weigh in any policy recommendation.

The other confounding factor is that employees like to buy company stock. They see executives getting rich and they want to have their chance to swing for the fences. Moreover, the mechanics of any fixed limit on company stock holdings means that employees would be forced to sell just as their company's stock was taking off. Although such rebalancing may be recommended by financial theory, it is certain to create a backlash among participants.

A consensus has emerged that employees should, at a minimum, be able to diversify more easily. The common proposal is that they should be able to sell their company stock as soon as they are vested. The other area of general agreement is that employees should be informed that they are taking on excessive risk in concentrating their 401(k) assets in a single stock. Current levels of company stockholdings are clearly imprudent and undermine the effectiveness of 401(k) plans by exposing participants to excessive and unnecessary risk.

The main area of disagreement is whether to directly limit the purchases or holdings of company stock. The notion of offering employees the choice of receiving the match in company stock or having it as an investment option may be the most promising proposal. It would not eliminate the problem, but it would reduce company stock holdings to less dangerous levels.

6

Leakages from 401(k) Plans

The previous chapters discuss how contribution and investment decisions affect retirement income from 401(k) plans. But the amount of retirement wealth a worker accumulates also depends on the extent to which the money is preserved for retirement. Participants are often allowed to borrow from their accounts and to withdraw funds to cover medical or education expenses before retirement. Workers also have the option of taking a lump-sum distribution when they change jobs, as do workers covered by new hybrid defined benefit plans. If these loans, withdrawals, and distributions are consumed rather than saved, retirement savings can be significantly reduced. A worker's retirement wealth also depends on the extent a 401(k) account affects other savings. This chapter examines possible leakages from 401(k) plans.

Borrowing from 401(k) Plans

Many 401(k) plans allow borrowing, adding an element of liquidity that does not exist in regular defined contribution plans or traditional defined benefit plans. Allowing participants to use their retirement savings for other purposes is a subject of controversy. Advocates argue that workers are more likely to participate and will contribute a larger share of their earnings if a 401(k) plan offers loans. As discussed in chapter 3, workers are indeed more likely to participate in the plan if they can borrow from it. Opponents argue that allowing loans reduces retirement savings and undermines the effort and expense of creating tax-preferred saving.

Most plans allow participants to borrow against their accounts. Tax law, however, limits how much can be borrowed to 50 percent of the account balance, up to $50,000. These loans do not require approval but must be paid back within one to five years. If the loan is used to finance the purchase of a primary residence, the payback time can be up to ten years. The interest rate on the loan is usually 1 or 2 percentage points above the prime rate, and many plans charge a one-time loan fee of $10 to $100.

When a worker takes out a 401(k) loan, assets in the worker's account are liquidated in the amount of the loan. Some plans allow workers to decide which assets to liquidate, while other plans reduce the investments proportionally. As the worker starts paying back the loan, the assets are bought back at current prices. The interest payments on the loan are paid into the worker's account. If a worker is unable to make loan payments and defaults, the amount of the loan is treated as a lump-sum distribution and is thus subject to income taxes and, for those younger than fifty-nine-and-a-half, a 10 percent penalty. Furthermore, most plans require that participants pay back 401(k) loans in full if they leave the firm. If a loan is not paid back when a worker is laid off or quits, it is treated as a lump-sum distribution.

Borrowing from 401(k) plans increased steadily during the 1990s. Three factors contributed to this trend. First, more workers were covered by 401(k) plans. Second, more plans offered loans. The share of participants who could borrow increased from 63.9 percent in 1992 to 76.2 percent in 2001.[1] According to the Employee Benefit Research Institute, 52 percent of 401(k) plans offered loans by 2001. Large plans were more likely to have the feature: 87 percent of firms with 5,000 or more participants offered loans but only 60 percent of plans with between 50 and 100 participants and less than 43 percent of plans with 25 or fewer participants.[2] Finally, more households borrowed from their plans.

Table 6-1 presents trends in 401(k) plan borrowing. Among those families that could borrow from their 401(k) plans, 14.1 percent had an outstanding

---

1. Sundén and Surette (2000) and authors' calculation of the 2001 Survey of Consumer Finances.
2. The average for all plans reflects that a majority of plans are small plans. See Holden and VanDerhei (2003).

Table 6-1. *Trends in 401(k) Plan Borrowing, 1992–2001*

Borrowing characteristics	1992	1995	1998	2001
Share of families with loans (percent)	12.5	16.1	17.5	14.1
Median 401(k) loan balance (2001 dollars)	2,200	2,100	3,100	3,500
Average ratio of loan amount to gross account balance (percent)	24.8	20.9	18.5	18.6

Source: Authors' calculations based on Board of Governors, *Survey of Consumer Finances* (SCF), 2001.

loan in 2001, up from 12.5 percent in 1992, although down from the peak of 17.5 percent in 1998. The typical loan balance in 2001 was relatively small, at $3,500, or 18.6 percent of the account balance.[3]

Reasons for 401(k) Borrowing

Families with 401(k) plans typically own their home, have financial assets, and have access to loans from traditional lenders. So why do they borrow from their pension plans? Three reasons come to mind. First, assets are costly to liquidate. Nonfinancial assets, for example one's home, are expensive and difficult to sell. Even financial assets, such as equities and mutual funds, often have costs associated with selling. Many assets are bought as long-term investments, and selling them may involve sacrificing returns. Second, 401(k) loans are a convenient way to borrow because they do not require loan approval and have low transaction costs. Finally, borrowing from 401(k) plans allows families to keep their precautionary savings intact. That is, taking out a 401(k) loan offers a possibility to keep the money in the rainy-day pile and still buy a new car or pay for a wedding.

People also like to borrow from their 401(k) plans because they are borrowing their own money, the interest gets credited to their account, and the loan is paid back to them. Loans from 401(k) plans generally have a low interest rate and appear to be a bargain. "It's the cheapest loan in town," says one 401(k) participant who frequently borrowed from his plan.[4] The prob-

3. The decrease in loan activity is consistent with data from the EBRI/ICI Participant-Directed Retirement Plan Data Collection Project. These data show that 16 percent of 401(k) participants who were eligible to borrow had an outstanding loan by the end of 2001, down from 18 percent in 1997. The average loan balance was 14 percent of the account balance net of the unpaid loan in the EBRI data. See Holden and VanDerhei (2003).

4. Ellen Schultz, "Many Borrow from Nest Egg to Live Better: It Isn't Always a Terrible Idea," *Wall Street Journal*, October 17, 1997, p. A1.

lem is that borrowing from a 401(k) may have negative effects on retirement income. This depends on two factors: the extent to which the loan increases current consumption and the extent to which the loan is paid back.

The Impact of 401(k) Borrowing

A loan used to buy other assets or to consolidate debt simply reshuffles the family's balance sheet, and net worth is essentially unchanged. This means that in the case the loan is paid back the effect on retirement income should be low. While the loan is outstanding the participant does not earn any investment return on the assets in the account that were used for the loan. Instead, the borrower pays himself the interest on the loan. If the interest rate is lower than the return on the 401(k) assets that were liquidated, the borrower will forgo some investment earnings. This was likely to be significant during the run-up in the stock market in the late 1990s. By borrowing, the participant also loses some of the advantages of tax deferral. The account earns interest tax free, while the loan is paid back with after-tax income. This means that more income is needed to pay back the loan. This loss should be modest, however, since the maximum loan is $50,000. Of course, if paying back the loan means that participants reduce their regular contributions, the implications for retirement savings would be more serious. In the case the loan is not paid back because the borrower defaults or leaves his job, the loan is treated as a lump-sum distribution and is subject to a 10 percent penalty and income taxes.[5] But since the loan was used to purchase an asset or pay down debt, the family's overall wealth has declined only by the penalty and by paying taxes on the distribution currently rather than deferring them to the future.

On the other hand, if a loan is used for current consumption, the effect on retirement savings can be more serious. If the loan is paid back, the borrower forgoes the earnings on the account as discussed above, but the major risk to retirement savings is that participants pay back the loan by reducing their regular contributions to the plan. But if the loan is not paid back, the effects on retirement wealth are severe because the funds in the account are permanently reduced. Because the loan was used to increase consumption, no equivalent increase in household assets or reduction in debt has taken place. Furthermore, the household has to pay the tax and penalty. Retirement income will be further reduced if the participant also reduces or stops making regular contributions to the plan.

The effect on retirement wealth also depends on at what point in the life cycle the worker takes out a loan. Younger workers are farther from retire-

---

5. No penalty is imposed if the borrower is older than fifty-nine-and-a-half.

Figure 6-1. *Reasons for Borrowing from a 401(k) Plan*

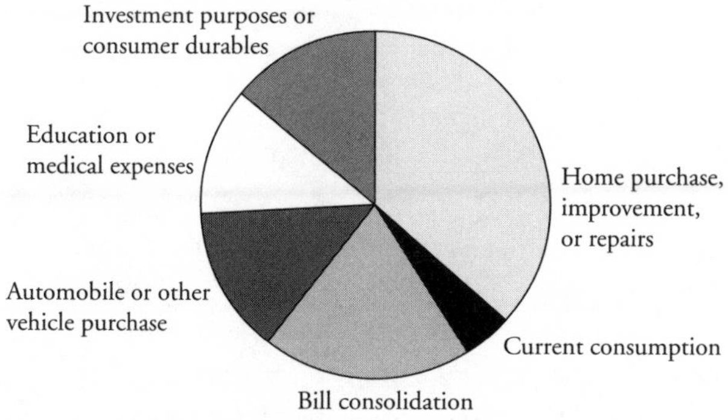

Source: Authors' calculations based on the 2001 SCF.

ment, and unless they use the loan for current consumption they have a longer time to recoup any forgone earnings.

When one evaluates how 401(k) loans affect retirement income, it is important to remember that a worker may have decided to participate in the pension plan because of the possibility to take out a loan. Evidence from the Survey of Consumer Finances and the Department of Labor's form 5500 shows that participation in 401(k) plans is positively related to being able to borrow from the plan.[6] So even if the worker participates in the plan and takes out a loan, retirement savings may be higher than if the worker had not participated in the plan at all. The level of contributions may also be affected by the ability to take out a loan. One study shows that participants who could borrow contributed significantly more to their 401(k) plans.[7]

Most 401(k) loans are used to reshuffle the balance sheet, typically to buy a home or to improve an existing residence (figure 6-1). The second most common use is to consolidate other debt, most likely credit card debt. These two uses represent almost 60 percent of all loans. Less than 5 percent was used for current consumption, such as vacations or weddings.

Who borrows from 401(k) accounts? Studies indicate that participants with relatively high account balances and relatively weak financial positions outside the plan are more likely to take out a 401(k) loan.[8] Data from the Employee Benefit Research Institute/Investment Company Institute (EBRI/ICI) 401(k) database show that, among participants with account bal-

6. Hungerford (1999); Munnell, Sundén, and Taylor (2002).
7. U.S. General Accounting Office (1997).
8. Sundén and Surette (2000).

Table 6-2. *The Effects of 401(k) Loans on Retirement Wealth*

Loan activity	Account balance at age sixty-two (dollars)	Percent of no-loan balance
No loan	353,408	100
Loan taken out		
Repay loan and maintain contributions	349,569	99
Repay loan and suspend contributions for five years	289,441	82
Default on loan and suspend contributions for two years	296,371	84

Source: Authors' calculations based on simulations discussed in chapter 2.

ances of less than $10,000, only 9 percent had loans outstanding.[9] Borrowers generally have a substantial amount in their retirement accounts but have fewer financial assets and more total debt than nonborrowers. In fact, families that have been turned down for traditional loans are much more likely to use 401(k) loans than families that are not credit constrained. "Most of the employees who take out loans against their 401(k)s are part of younger blue-collar families," says one vice president of human resources.[10] This suggests that the borrowers are a vulnerable group of 401(k) participants.

The simulation model presented in chapter 2 can be used to demonstrate how much retirement wealth is reduced if participants borrow money from their retirement accounts (table 6-2). If our hypothetical participant never borrowed from the account, he would reach retirement with an account balance of $353,408. Now assume that the participant, at age forty, borrows 50 percent of the accumulated account balance, that the loan is paid back over five years in equal installments, and that the interest rate on the loan is 1 percentage point over the prime rate. If the participant continues his regular contributions while paying back the loan, the effect on retirement wealth is small. The participant loses only the difference between the rate of return and the interest rate on the loan. But if the participant stops his regular contributions for five years while paying back the loan, the reduction in retirement wealth is much larger. Finally, if the participant defaults on the loan after two years but continues contributions the following year, the loss of retirement wealth is slightly less than stopping contributions while paying back the loan.

9. Holden and VanDerhei (2003).
10. Schultz, "Many Borrow from Nest Egg to Live Better; It Isn't Always a Terrible Idea." The EBRI/ICI 401(k) data show that borrowing is highest among participants in their thirties (17 percent of participants) and forties (19 percent of participants). See Holden and VanDerhei (2003).

Should we be concerned about pension loans? 401(k) plans constitute a relatively small fraction of households' overall wealth, and most participants are fifteen to twenty-five years away from retirement. But as contributions grow, the possibilities for larger loans increase. One of the most severe effects occurs when workers default on their loans, which most often occurs after a layoff. Many plans require outstanding loans to be paid back in full when employment ends; the participant cannot elect to continue making scheduled payments. If not paid back in full, the loan is treated as a lump-sum distribution, subject to tax and penalty charges. This means that economic downturns could generate 401(k) loan defaults, with large negative impact on retirement savings.

Lump-Sum Distributions

The second way participants can access the funds in their 401(k) plans before retirement is by taking a lump-sum distribution. This can be done in two ways. First, a participant can make a hardship withdrawal while still contributing to the plan. Many plans allow participants to withdraw funds to pay for medical expenses, education expenses, or to buy a house while still contributing to the plan. Second, participants can withdraw funds when leaving their jobs. This money can then be rolled over into another qualified plan, typically an individual retirement account (IRA) or another 401(k) plan, or used for some other purpose.[11]

To create an incentive for workers to preserve their 401(k) balances for retirement, Congress in 1986 enacted a 10 percent penalty on withdrawals before age fifty-nine-and-a-half that are not rolled over.[12] In addition to the penalty, a 20 percent income tax is withheld when the funds are withdrawn.

11. Increasingly, defined benefit plans also make lump-sum distributions. If the present value of benefits is less than $5,000, a firm can pay out a lump sum without the employee's consent. The conversion of traditional defined benefit plans to cash balance plans will increase the amount of distributions from defined benefit plans, since cash balance plans provide lump-sum payments at separation.

12. No penalty applies for workers between age fifty-five and fifty-nine-and-a-half if the lump sum distribution is due to retirement (job termination). The Unemployment Compensation Amendments of 1992 require employers to offer employees the option to have their lump-sum distributions transferred directly to an IRA or to another employer's plan. Employers are required to withhold 20 percent of preretirement distributions that are paid directly to employees. See Purcell (2000). The 20 percent withholding does not change the total tax burden but changes the timing of the tax payment. In addition, the Economic Growth and Tax Relief Reconciliation Act requires that distributions between $1,000 and $5,000 be rolled over into an IRA unless the participant elects to take the distribution directly or directs that it be rolled over into another qualified plan.

Table 6-3. *Summary Characteristics of Lump-Sum Distributions, 2001*

Characteristic	Figure
Workers who have received a lump-sum distribution (percent)	15.9
Average age of participant at receipt (years)	37
Median lump-sum distribution amounts (2001 dollars)	
Total	9,000
Rolled over	14,800
Cashed out	6,000

Source: Authors' calculations based on the 2001 SCF.

Data on lump-sum distributions come from three sources: tax returns, benefit administrators, and household surveys. Almost all sources combine lump-sum distributions for defined benefit plans with those for defined contribution plans. Because hybrid plans are relatively new and traditional defined benefit plans limit lump-sum distributions to instances in which the expected value of the benefit is less than $5,000, it is likely that only a modest percentage of the total lump-sum distributions come from defined benefit plans. Hence for the remainder of this discussion, we assume that 90 percent of distributions from pensions come from 401(k)-type pensions. Of course, an increasing portion will be attributable to hybrid defined benefit plans in the future.

Lump-sum distributions are sizable. Tax data show that, in 1995, lump-sum distributions from 401(k) accounts were $78.5 billion, or 9.1 percent of 401(k) assets. Most of these distributions (77 percent) were rolled over into a qualified account. The remaining distributions were used for some other purpose and therefore subject to the 10 percent penalty.[13] The share of participants who received a lump-sum distribution between 1988 and 1993 increased by more than 60 percent; the average amount rose by almost 40 percent.[14] The most recent data, from the 2001 Survey of Consumer Finances, show that 16 percent of workers had at some point received a lump-sum distribution and that the median amount of those distributions was $9,000 (table 6-3).[15]

The Rollover of Lump-Sum Distributions

In the infancy of 401(k) plans, the rollover rate was low. The low account balances and the absence of a penalty for withdrawing funds created incen-

13. Sabelhaus and Weiner (1999).
14. Burman, Coe, and Gale (1999). The data for 1988 to 1993 come from the Current Population Survey.
15. Data from the Survey of Income and Program Participation show that the median lump-sum distribution was $5,000 in 1998, while the mean was $15,402, indicating that most lump-sum distributions are relatively small. See Copeland (2002).

Table 6-4. *Rollover Behavior for Recipients Aged Sixty and Younger,*
by Earnings, Age, and Year, 2001
Percent

Earnings, age, and year	Share of participants who rolled over lump-sum distributions	Lump-sum dollars rolled over
Earnings		
Less than $20,000	35.2	56.7
$20,000–39,999	32.6	50.3
$40,000–59,999	42.2	84.6
$60,000–79,999	57.2	87.9
$80,000–99,999	84.6	97.2
$100,000 and more	80.3	89.2
All	44.8	79.3
Age		
20–29	19.6	41.1
30–39	42.9	56.7
40–49	47.5	76.6
50–59	48.2	86.3
Year received		
1980–86	31.8	37.1
1987–91	48.7	78.8
1992–96	55.0	83.8
1997–2001	42.0	83.5

Source: Authors' calculations based on the 2001 SCF.

tives for participants to use their 401(k) accounts for other purposes and to sacrifice future retirement income. Another factor that may have contributed to the low rollover rate during the first half of the 1980s was that 401(k) plans often complemented defined benefit plans, and workers were less reliant on them for their retirement savings.

Rollover rates increased after the introduction of the 10 percent penalty in 1986 and the 20 percent withholding on lump sums not rolled over in 1992. Estimates show that the introduction of the 10 percent penalty increased the probability to rolling over by 6 percentage points.[16] In 2001, 44.8 percent of recipients rolled over their lump sums, and these rollovers represented 79.3 percent of all lump-sum dollars (table 6-4).[17]

16. Chang (1996).
17. The dollar amount of rollovers reported in household surveys is lower than that shown by tax data. One explanation for the discrepancy is that recall error in survey data tends to bias the amount downward. See Sabelhaus and Weiner (1999). Data from the Health and Retirement Study indicate that a significant share of participants leave their pensions with the previ-

One common reason workers do not roll over a lump-sum distribution is that they want to use it for current consumption or to pay off debt. To make a decision, a participant has to compare the loss in retirement saving by taking the lump sum to the cost of liquidating other assets or taking out a loan. If participants are young, they are likely to cash the lump-sum distribution to pay for their expenses.[18] Young workers tend to have low incomes, fewer nonpension assets, and less access to credit. In fact it may be optimal for those who are liquidity constrained to spend small accounts. Because of their current low marginal tax rate and higher cost of borrowing, the costs are lower and the benefits greater. On the other hand, the 10 percent penalty represents a significant increase in their marginal tax rate. In contrast, participants with lower borrowing costs (for example, those who can borrow against their homes and deduct the interest) or with a large amount of other assets are not likely to cash their 401(k) plan to finance current consumption. For this group, high marginal tax rates combined with the 10 percent penalty make such a move costly.

Although most lump-sum distributions are not rolled over, most lump-sum dollars are.[19] The larger the distribution, the more likely a participant is to roll it over; large lump sums account for most of the money distributed. Data from the Survey of Income and Program Participation show that 70 percent of participants who received lump-sum distributions of $50,000 or more rolled over the entire distribution, while less than 30 percent of participants with distributions of $10,000 or less rolled over their funds.[20] Researchers estimate that the probability of a rollover is greater than 50 percent for distributions of $25,000 or more and 10 percent for distributions of $1,000 or less.[21] On reason that participants are more likely to roll over large distributions is that they might view large distributions as different from small distributions. People create "mental accounts" to classify their money into current income, assets, and future income.[22] They might classify a small distribution as current income rather than as an asset and, therefore, feel more comfortable about using it for current consumption. A large lump-sum distribution is more likely to be put in the mental account for assets,

---

ous employer. See Hurd, Lillard, and Panis (1998). This means that the share of funds from prior employers that remains in a qualified account is actually higher than reported in surveys and on tax returns. Thus the share of retirement funds that is preserved for retirement is actually higher than that shown in the rollover numbers.

18. Burman, Coe, and Gale (1999).

19. This is because most lump-sum distributions involve small amounts.

20. Copeland (2002).

21. Poterba, Venti, and Wise (1995b, 1999).

22. Thaler (1994a).

Figure 6-2. *Use of Lump-Sum Distributions, Recipients and Dollars, 2001*

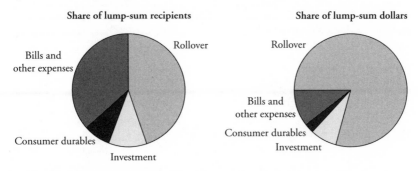

Source: Authors' calculations based on the 2001 SCF.

which means it should be preserved. The closer a worker is to retirement and the higher the earnings, the more likely the distribution will be rolled over (table 6-4).

When researchers examine the effects of age, income, size of distribution, and other characteristics, they find that the single most important determinant of whether a lump-sum distribution will be rolled over or not is the size of the distribution.[23] Workers with liquidity constraints or short planning horizons are also less likely to roll over a lump-sum distribution. A related factor is the reason for leaving the job: Those who are laid off are more likely to be liquidity constrained and therefore to cash in their lump-sum distribution. Participants who do not roll over their distributions use the money for everyday expenses (figure 6-2).

The Impact of Lump-Sum Distributions on Retirement Wealth

What workers decide to do with lump-sum distributions has important implications for how much money they will have in retirement. As in the case with taking out loans, the effect on retirement wealth depends on how it affects the household balance sheet. When the lump sum is rolled over into another qualified account, such as an IRA or another employer's 401(k) plan, the whole account balance is preserved and retirement wealth is unaffected. If the lump sum is used for other investments or to consolidate other debt, wealth is only reduced by the amount of the penalty and income taxes. (If the participant pays the tax and penalty by reducing current consumption, wealth remains unchanged). If the lump sum is used for current consumption, however, retirement wealth is permanently reduced by the full amount withdrawn.

23. Purcell (2000); Moore and Muller (2002).

Table 6-5. *Effects of Rolling Over or Spending a Lump-Sum Distribution*

Action	Lump sum spent (dollars)	Balance at age sixty-two (dollars)	Percent of balance at age sixty-two
Rolling over	0	353,408	100
Spending			
Age thirty-five	27,866	277,007	78
Age forty	60,461	208,232	59
Age forty-five	103,832	146,539	41

Source: Authors' calculations based on the 2001 SCF.

The simulation model presented in chapter 2 illustrates how much retirement wealth is reduced if a participant spends a lump-sum distribution rather than rolling it over. If our typical participant rolled over her 401(k) account every time she changed jobs, she would reach retirement with an account balance of $353,408 (table 6-5). But assume the worker changes jobs at age thirty-five and uses the distribution of her account balance to buy a new car and go on vacation. She then starts her new job and begins contributing to the new firm's 401(k) plan. By using the lump-sum distribution for consumption, her retirement wealth is only 78 percent of what it would have been had she left the money in the 401(k) plan. If the participant changes jobs at forty-five and spends the lump-sum distribution, her retirement wealth would be less than half of what she could have accumulated. Such an outcome is less likely, however, because, as shown earlier, lump sums larger than $25,000 are rolled over more than 50 percent of the time.

Several researchers used the Health and Retirement Study to estimate the actual effects on retirement wealth of spending lump-sum distributions. One study estimates that 8–11 percent of Social Security and pension wealth is lost by workers spending their lump-sum distributions.[24] Another study predicts that cohorts retiring in 2025 or 2035 will have, on average, 5 percent less retirement savings in their 401(k) plans because all lump-sum distributions were not rolled over.[25] These estimates might understate the true losses to retirement wealth because they rely on Health and Retirement Study data, which are for workers born between 1931 and 1941, whose main pension arrangement is a defined benefit plan. If they have 401(k) plans they are likely to be supplemental, and the amounts cashed out are likely to be small—and a small part of their retirement wealth.

24. Engelhart (1999).
25. Poterba, Venti, and Wise (1999).

401(k) Plans and Other Saving

To evaluate how successful 401(k) plans are in providing income security in retirement it is important to know how they affect other savings. That is, to what extent do workers reduce other savings as a result of participating in a 401(k) plan? For example, if workers offset most of their other savings, 401(k) plans would do little to improve overall retirement savings. If on the other hand workers reduce other savings less or not at all, 401(k) plans would increase retirement saving. What is important for the analysis in this book is the net effect of 401(k) plans on the accumulation of retirement wealth and how it is different from the defined benefit world.

In a world without pensions, people would save during their working years and use the savings for consumption during retirement. If people had no other reason to save than for retirement and had no intention of leaving bequests, a pension plan would simply lead to a reduction in other savings and have no effect on lifetime wealth. This simple outcome is not likely because people save for many reasons other than retirement, and retirement wealth is also not as liquid as other forms of wealth. An illiquid pension plan cannot serve as a buffer against unforeseen events. Also complicating the simple story is the fact that having a pension may also encourage people to retire earlier than otherwise, encouraging them to save more to support the longer time in retirement.

Relative Impact of Defined Benefit versus 401(k) Plans

A number of studies have examined how pensions affect other saving. Studies done in the 1970s and 1980s, when the defined benefit plan was the most common pension arrangement, conclude in general that defined benefit plans reduce other saving but at less than dollar for dollar.[26] The question is how the shift to 401(k) plans has affected how workers view pensions in relation to other saving. In other words, do people reduce other savings more or less when they have a 401(k) plan instead of a defined benefit plan?

Defined benefit plans are a rather abstract form of saving. Benefits are typically based on final earnings and years of service, and the workers know neither until they are close to retirement. By contrast, 401(k) plans are more like regular savings accounts. Workers get monthly or quarterly statements and direct the investments. If they view 401(k) plans more like regular savings accounts, the reduction in other savings could be larger than for defined benefit plans. People might also reduce their other savings more with a 401(k)

26. Munnell (1976); Gale (1999).

plan because of "wealth illusion." When people look at how much they have accumulated for retirement they see a dollar amount, while in a defined benefit plan they only know that they will receive a monthly payment when they retire. The psychology literature shows that people view lump sums differently from periodic payments: When a lump sum is compared to a monthly benefit, the lump sum looks like much more money than the monthly benefit, even if they are worth the same in terms of present discounted value.

On the other hand, it is possible that 401(k) plans have a smaller effect on other savings than defined benefit plans because people do not intend to spend the money in their 401(k) accounts. This reluctance is evident in the limited dissaving in retirement, the small size of the U.S. annuity market, the aversion of older homeowners to reverse annuity mortgages, and the holdings of life insurance by retirees.[27] One reason people want to hold onto their 401(k) money and other retirement wealth is that they want to leave bequests. In fact people's interest in bequests is likely to increase when they gain access to accumulated assets. Accumulating wealth out of current income to leave a bequest is too difficult. But if people receive a pile of wealth, as in a 401(k) plan, leaving a bequest becomes plausible. 401(k) plans could also increase other saving because they help workers realize the need for saving. Thus 401(k) plans could either have a larger or smaller effect on other saving than defined benefit plans.

When one considers the impact of 401(k) plans on other saving, it is useful to consider families' entire balance sheets. These balance sheets consist of financial assets (such as savings accounts, mutual funds, and bonds), nonfinancial assets (such as primary residences and cars), and debts (such as mortgages, credit card debts, and installment loans). The difference between total assets and total debts is a family's net worth. According to the Survey of Consumer Finances, the typical family in the United States had net worth of $86,100 in 2001. For most families the most important asset on their balance sheet is equity in their primary residence. Overall, families have few financial assets outside retirement accounts. Only 18 percent of all families owned shares in mutual funds outside of a plan. In general, those with 401(k) plans are better off—they own more assets, including more financial assets, they have less debt, and their net worth is higher—than those without a 401(k). The question is how pensions in general and 401(k) plans in particular affect families' balance sheets. Total saving increases if families maintain their other saving and make their 401(k) contribution by reducing consumption. But they may offset some or all of the contributions to the 401(k) plan by reducing other assets or by taking out more debt. Most studies have exam-

27. Munnell and others (2003).

ined the effect of defined benefit plans and 401(k) plans on financial assets, but financial assets are only a small part of a household's balance sheet. It is possible that other substitutions could be made. In particular, households may reduce the equity in their homes by taking out a larger mortgage, a home equity loan, or a home equity line of credit.

Empirical Studies of 401(k) Plans and Saving

Two groups of researchers have had a long-standing discussion over how 401(k) plans affect other saving and assets. One group claims that most of the money in 401(k) plans constitutes new savings and therefore increases assets.[28] The second group concludes that 401(k) plans reduce other savings to a much larger extent and in some cases have no effect on overall savings.[29] One reason it is difficult to reach a consensus is the statistical problems involved in estimating the offset between 401(k) saving and other saving (see below).

Although further research has narrowed the differences in the two groups' estimates somewhat, the issue remains unsettled.[30] However, the researchers agree that 401(k) plans have a positive effect on savings for middle- and low-income workers, while they are unlikely to add to savings for the highest income groups. The two groups also agree that the positive effects on saving of 401(k) plans are likely to increase over time and that automatic enrollment in 401(k) plans can significantly influence workers' saving behavior.

These studies examine only the effect of 401(k) plans on saving. To address the question of whether people's savings respond differently to 401(k) plans than to defined benefit plans, both types of plan need to be included in the analysis. The results from a recent study suggest that 401(k) plans reduce other saving less than defined benefit plans.[31] However, the results are inconclusive and could depend on the fact that 401(k) participants have more taste for saving than participants in defined benefit plans. The problem with this and other studies is to find variables that adequately measure people's taste for saving. People with pensions are likely to have a stronger taste for saving than those without and tend to save more in all forms.[32] But because participation in 401(k) plans is voluntary, while participation for workers who are eligible for defined benefit plans is mandatory, those who

---

28. Poterba, Venti, and Wise (1995a, 1998).

29. Engen and Gale (1997); Engen, Gale, and Scholz (1996).

30. Today, the first group of researchers concludes that two-thirds or more of contributions to 401(k) plans constitutes new saving, while the second group estimates that one-third or less of 401(k) savings represents new saving.

31. Munnell and others (2003).

32. As discussed in chapter 2, firms that offer 401(k) plans often do so to attract workers with a taste for saving because such workers tend to be more productive. Only workers with a

participate in 401(k) plans are likely to have an even stronger taste for saving. Unless a study includes a measure of taste for saving in the statistical analysis, the results may falsely show that 401(k) plans increase saving. (The study comparing defined benefit and 401(k) plans includes a common measure of taste for saving—having an IRA—but with limited success.)[33]

Estimation Problems

Most studies that investigate how much 401(k) plans affect other savings use the same data—the Survey of Income and Program Participation for 1984, 1987, and 1991—and look at the same time period. So the question is, Why do the two groups of researchers come to different conclusions?[34] One explanation is the statistical problems associated with estimating the offset between 401(k) and other saving. The results will depend on how the following problems are tackled:

—Workers who like to save are more likely to participate in 401(k) plans.

—Saving differs by income.

—Financial markets and other economic factors have changed over time.[35]

The decision to offer a 401(k) plan is made by the employer, who may take employees' preferences into account when offering a plan. Furthermore, as discussed above, participants in 401(k) plans are likely to save more in all forms, and unless this taste for saving is included in the analysis, the results may falsely show that 401(k) plans increase saving. An additional complication is that the average taste for saving among workers with 401(k) plans could have changed over time. The number of 401(k) participants increased dramatically during the 1980s and early 1990s, and if their taste for saving

---

taste for saving would be willing to give up cash wages for deferred compensation to work for such firms. See Ippolito (1993).

33. Other researchers control for saving by comparing 401(k)-eligible people with noneligible people instead of participants to nonparticipants. See Poterba, Venti, and Wise (1994, 1995a); Engen and Gale (2000); Engelhart (1999). Because eligible people include those who choose not to participate, the taste for saving might be similar between eligible and noneligible people. In the absence of a 401(k) plan, the two types of household would then have similar wealth accumulation patterns. So if 401(k) plans add to a household's savings, the wealth of those households eligible for a 401(k) plan should increase faster than the wealth of those without a 401(k) plan. Some researchers find that eligible households have more financial wealth than ineligible households and conclude that 401(k) plans add to savings. But as other researchers point out, being eligible for a 401(k) plan is not necessarily independent of taste for saving. Engen, Gale, and Scholz (1996).

34. The data mostly come from the Survey of Income and Program Participation (SIPP) from 1984, 1987, and 1991. The SIPP is the only nationally representative data source that includes information on 401(k) eligibility and wealth. The Survey of Consumer Finances added questions on eligibility for 401(k) plans in the 1995 survey.

35. Engen and Gale (2000).

differs depending on when they entered the program, it is difficult to make simple comparisons of 401(k) participants who joined at different times.

In addition, saving propensities and 401(k) coverage vary significantly by income level. Low-income workers have few other savings and therefore fewer assets to reduce. This makes it essential to control for household income differences, and it appears that the results are sensitive to alternative ways of controlling for income. The researchers agree that 401(k) savings do not add to savings for those in the highest income groups but reach different conclusions for workers slightly lower down on the income distribution. One group finds that 401(k) plans constitute substantial new savings for workers earning $75,000–$100,000.[36] The other group finds that 401(k) plans do not represent new saving for this group.[37]

Finally, financial markets and other economic factors have changed dramatically since the early 1980s. This is important for the analysis because those with 401(k) plans are more likely than others to own financial assets in addition to their homes. The general increase in the stock market until the late 1990s affected workers' financial assets positively. But because those with 401(k) plans are more likely than others to hold stocks and mutual funds, it is difficult to disentangle the effects on savings of 401(k) plans and the run-up in stock prices. It could be that the increase in savings depended solely on the increase in stock prices. A similar question arises when one considers the offset between 401(k) plans and home equity. Over time, borrowing against home equity has become easier. Those with 401(k) plans have higher home-ownership rates and may therefore be more likely to borrow against their homes irrespective of having a 401(k) plan.

Thus it appears that the effect of 401(k) plans on other savings varies both with income and over time. Most studies examine these two factors separately, which could be an explanation for the difference in results. A possible avenue to reconcile the research is, therefore, to allow the impact of 401(k) plans to vary simultaneously over both time and earnings groups.[38]

In summary, what matters for this book is the net effect of 401(k) plans on the accumulation of retirement wealth. The current state of the debate indicates that 401(k) plans increase savings for low-income earners but have little effect on savings for high-income earners. This makes sense, since lower income workers often have no savings other than their 401(k) plan. A similar pattern probably also occurred with defined benefit plans. As discussed above, it is possible to tell a plausible story in which 401(k) plans reduce

36. Poterba, Venti, and Wise (1998).
37. Engen and Gale (2000).
38. Engen and Gale (2000).

other saving less than defined benefit plans do. But even with the best intentions, the statistical problems involved make it difficult to prove the point.

Conclusion

Compared to defined benefit plans, 401(k) plans look much more like ordinary savings accounts—participants receive a statement monthly or quarterly, they can take out a loan from the account, and they can withdraw money when they change jobs or for emergency purposes. Because 401(k) accounts look much more like regular nonpension savings, participants may also treat them more like regular savings. This chapter shows that withdrawing funds from a 401(k) account before retirement can reduce retirement wealth substantially. The most serious effect comes from taking a lump-sum distribution and failing to roll it over to another qualified retirement plan and, instead, spending it on current consumption. On the other hand, taking out a loan and using it for a down payment for a house has a small effect on retirement wealth. Young workers and workers with low incomes are the groups that are most likely to use their lump-sum distributions for consumption rather than saving. So while the average rollover pattern indicates that lump-sum distributions have a relatively modest effect on retirement saving in the aggregate, those who are hurt the most are the lower paid, for whom 401(k) participation could have the most positive effect on their total saving.

In terms of pension loans, the most significant reduction in retirement wealth occurs when a worker defaults on the loan, and the loan becomes a withdrawal. Defaults are most likely when workers change jobs or are laid off. As laid-off workers tend to be cash constrained, paying off the loan is often a serious hardship, more serious than paying the penalty and taxes.

The question is, How can workers better manage the risks associated with loans and withdrawals? When it comes to 401(k) loans, one option would be to allow them to continue paying back the loans after they have left the firm, which requires that the company allow the participant to keep the account with the firm. This would avoid involuntary lump-sum distributions being made when the employee is laid off. Another option is to take advantage of workers' inertia to reduce the cashing out of lump-sum distributions. The Unemployment Compensation Amendments of 1992 require employers to offer workers the option of having their lump-sum distributions transferred directly to an IRA or to another employer's plan. If instead lump-sum distributions were automatically rolled over into an IRA when a worker changes jobs, the rollover rate, especially for smaller distributions, is likely to increase dramatically.

7

Withdrawing 401(k) Funds at Retirement

A s earlier chapters show, 401(k) plans shift most of the responsibility for retirement planning from employers to employees. Employees decide whether or not to join the plan, how much to contribute, how to invest the funds, and whether to roll over lump-sum distributions into another retirement plan when changing jobs.

All these decisions are relatively easy, however, compared to figuring out what to do with 401(k) balances at retirement. Unlike defined benefit plans that provide participants with steady benefits for as long as they live, 401(k) plans generally pay out benefits as lump sums. Lump-sum payments mean that retirees have to decide how much to withdraw each year. They face the risk of either spending too quickly and outliving their resources or spending too conservatively and consuming too little. These risks could be eliminated through the purchase of annuities, but the individual annuity market in the United States is tiny.[1] This chapter

---

1. The following discussion focuses on the single premium immediate annuity, since it is designed specifically to insure against longevity risk. Other types of annuities exist. For example, the rapid growth in variable annuities, sales of which increased from $5.3 billion in 1985 to $137.2 billion in 2000, has received considerable publicity. Sales actually declined to $111.0 billion in 2001. See LIMRA International (2002). But variable annuities, where payouts are linked to returns

explores the challenge retirees face in living off their funds in retirement and explanations for the limited interest in annuities.[2]

The Challenge

Traditionally, defined benefit plans have paid retirees benefits in the form of a life annuity, which guarantees benefits for as long as retirees live and thereby insures them against outliving their resources.[3] Defined contribution plans generally do not pay annuities; they offer participants a lump sum or a phased withdrawal.[4] Also, as discussed in earlier chapters, the new hybrid defined benefit plans, such as cash balance and pension equity plans, provide lump sums rather than annuities. Lump sums offer participants liquidity and flexibility but no easy way to protect themselves against outliving their pension accumulations. Since the 2001 Survey of Consumer Finances (SCF) shows that of those households with pensions roughly 60 percent rely exclusively on a defined contribution plan, the shift in pension type involves a major change in the mode of payment at retirement. This trend has been reinforced with the emergence of hybrid defined benefit plans.

Why do defined benefit plans provide annuities and 401(k) plans do not? The short answer is that defined benefit plans are required by law to provide annuities and that 401(k) plans are not. Technically, employer-sponsored plans fall into three categories: pensions, profit-sharing plans, and stock bonus plans. Pensions include defined benefit plans and money purchase defined contribution plans. Money purchase plans differ from other defined contribution plans in that the sponsor commits to contribute on a fixed basis. Profit-sharing plans, which include thrift plans and 401(k) plans, are not considered pension plans because the employer has discretion over contributions.

---

on stocks or other underlying assets, are more like mutual funds and are generally purchased as a form of tax-deferred investment while people are working. The payouts from these annuities are not required to be converted to a stream of payments but rather can be taken as a lump sum and may ultimately not play an important role in protecting against the risk of outliving savings. See Mitchell and others (1999).

2. Much of the organization and discussion on the importance of annuities comes from Brown (2001).

3. Lump-sum payments are becoming more frequent options among defined benefit plans in large part due to the conversion of conventional defined benefit plans to cash balance plans.

4. The data on distributions show that, in 1997, 91 percent of full-time participants had the option of receiving their 401(k) accumulations as a lump sum and 41 percent could elect a phased withdrawal. Only 27 percent of participants had an annuity option at retirement. That number would be considerably lower in 2003, given that the Internal Revenue Service (IRS) issued regulations in 2000 permitting sponsors of defined contribution plans to discontinue all options other than lump-sum payments. See U.S. Internal Revenue Service (2000).

A sponsor of a pension plan is required to "provide systematically for the payment of definitely determinable benefits to his employees over a period of years, usually for life, after retirement."[5] Defined benefit plans and money purchase plans have traditionally met this requirement by providing a life annuity as the normal form of payment.

401(k) plans and other profit-sharing or stock bonus plans are not required to purchase an annuity, but they could if they wanted to. They have generally resisted this option and, in fact, sponsors have lobbied Congress for legislation limiting disbursements to lump sums.[6] Providing annuities adds extra administrative burdens. Making sure that employees conform to the rules for selecting a joint-and-survivor option is particularly costly. Sponsors that provide an annuity directly from a profit-sharing plan face a host of regulatory, administrative, and financial problems. If they provide the annuity through an insurance company, they still must evaluate the company's ability to pay and select the safest annuity possible.[7]

Without an annuity, 401(k) beneficiaries risk outliving their resources. At first, that risk may not sound that serious. Government life expectancy tables indicate that, with the expected improvements in longevity, a man turning sixty-five in 2000 could expect to live to eighty-one and a woman to eighty-five.[8] Therefore, an easy answer might be simply to spread out the original assets (and the expected interest on those assets) in equal monthly payments over the expected remaining life—sixteen years for the man and twenty years for the woman.

The problem is that not every man and woman will live the average life expectancy. The variation around these life expectancies at age sixty-five is enormous. As shown in table 7-1, 17 percent of men and 31 percent of women will live to age ninety or older and will need to support themselves for twenty-five years or more. People may know something about whether they are likely to die early or late based on their personal and family medical history, but date of death for most remains uncertain. This uncertainty about longevity creates two types of risk. The most obvious is that retirees will use

---

5. McGill and others (1996).

6. U.S. Internal Revenue Service (2000).

7. Brown and Warshawsky (2001).

8. The Social Security Administration prepares two types of mortality table. One is a period life table, which shows how many people in each age group are expected to die in a given year, which is useful for comparing death rates across age groups. To value annuities, however, the question is how long a sixty-five-year-old is expected to live. Answering this question requires a cohort life table, which incorporates mortality improvements. All the numbers presented in this chapter, except where otherwise indicated, are from the cohort life table for those born in 1935 (becoming sixty-five in 2000).

Table 7-1. *Survival Rates, Sixty-Five-Year-Olds Born in 1935,*
Men and Women
Percent

Age	Men	Women
70	88	92
75	74	82
80	56	69
85	36	51
90	17	31
95	6	13

Source: Unpublished data from the Social Security Administration.

up their money too quickly and not have enough to support themselves when they are very old. The second is that they will worry too much about outliving their resources and deprive themselves of things they want or need, often to the point of hardship, and will die with a substantial amount of money on hand. The importance of these issues will intensify over time as life expectancy rises and people's uncertainty about how long they will live increases. Today, a sixty-five-year-old man is expected to live for sixteen years, but that should rise to nineteen years by 2040 and to twenty-one years by 2080 (table 7-2). The projections for females are even more dramatic. By 2080 a sixty-five-year-old woman can be expected to live for another twenty-four years. So the possibility of living for a long time complicates financial planning after retirement.

Exhausting resources raises the possibility of a large number of the very old living in poverty. Poverty rates among the elderly already increase with age, and poverty is particularly acute among elderly nonmarried women (table 7-3). In 2000 the majority of women aged eighty-five and older were not married, and over a third of these women were classified as either poor or near-poor (125 percent of the poverty line). Given that the poverty line for an older single individual was only $8,259, many women were facing serious hardship. If people exhaust their pension resources early in retirement, more retirees—particularly women—will end up in poverty. On the other hand, given how few resources many people have, too cautious spending of accumulated assets can also cause serious hardship.

Annuities as a Solution

Fortunately, a product exists that removes both the risk of outliving one's resources and the hardship created by inadequate consumption. This product

Table 7-2. *Cohort Life Expectancy, Sixty-Five-Year-Old Men and Women, Selected Years 2000–80*[a]

Year	Men	Women
2000	16.5	19.5
2020	17.8	20.8
2040	19.0	22.0
2060	20.1	23.0
2080	21.1	24.0

Source: Social Security Administration (www.ssa.gov/OACT/TR/TRO3/V_demographic.html).
a. Cohort life expectancy reflects mortality improvement expected in the future.

is a life annuity, which is offered by insurance companies and pays monthly amounts for as long as the individual lives, in exchange for an initial premium. The annuity not only protects people from outliving their resources but also allows them to enjoy a high level of consumption. The insurance company can provide this high guaranteed income because it pools the experience of a large number of individuals and pays benefits to those who live longer than expected out of the premiums received from those who die early. In this way, the insurer can provide a higher payment than people could receive by investing safely on their own. The precise amount of the annuity payment depends on the purchaser's life expectancy and on the return that the insurer can earn on the initial premium. Thus annuity payments are high when interest rates are high and low when they are low.

The simplest annuity is the single-life, single-premium immediate annuity, which involves a one-time payment from the individual, and payments to the individual begin immediately. Other options are available. Annuities can

Table 7-3. *Prevalence and Poverty Status, Nonmarried Women, 2000*
Percent

Age	Nonmarried women as a share of total population sixty-five and older	Poor and near-poor nonmarried women as share of all nonmarried women sixty-five and older[a]
65–69	31	27
70–74	39	29
75–79	47	30
80–84	52	27
85 and older	62	33

Source: Social Security Administration (2002).
a. Near-poor is defined as 125 percent of the poverty line. Poverty income for a single person aged sixty-five and older was $8,259.

Figure 7-1. *Income Produced from $100,000 by Annuitization versus Alternative Asset Management Strategies*[a]

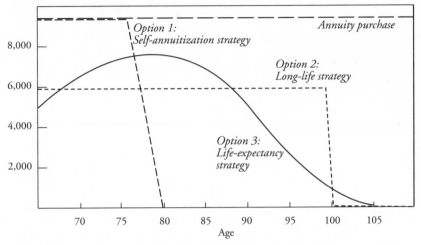

Annual income, nominal dollars

Source: American Council of Life Insurance (2002); Gebhardtsbauer (1998).

a. Assumed rate of return on investments is 5 percent. Mortality is based on the Internal Revenue Service Single Life Expectancy Table (unisex).

cover both the husband and wife (joint and survivor), they can begin at a later date (deferred), they can provide payments based on some underlying portfolio (inflation indexed or linked to stocks), or they can guarantee payments for a certain period, such as ten or twenty years.

Economic theory suggests that people would be interested in buying annuities. Rational life-cycle consumers with no interest in leaving a bequest would always choose to annuitize 100 percent of their wealth.[9] After all, they face a choice between a traditional investment with a market return or an annuity with a market return plus a "mortality premium." As noted, this mortality premium arises because the insurance company pools experience and uses the assets from deceased annuitants to pay those who survive. The only cost to consumers is that the annuity payments stop at death. But if they place no value on wealth after death—that is, they have no bequest motive—the cost of the annuity is zero.

The gains from buying an annuity are substantial. As shown in figure 7-1, sixty-five-year-olds could expect to receive $9,240 each year for the rest of

9. Yaari (1965). Davidoff, Brown, and Diamond (2002) show that the 100 percent annuitization also depends on "complete markets," that is, people must be able to insure themselves against all major contingencies, including the need for long-term care.

their lives from annuitizing $100,000, assuming a 5 percent return. People often think, however, that they can do better managing their own investments and withdrawing money from those investments over time. But this is not true. Consider three alternative options. Option 1 is self-annuitization. That is, the retiree invests $100,000 in a risk-free asset with the same 5 percent return and withdraws $9,240 each year. This option works well for a period of time. But the assets are depleted after fourteen years, and the retiree still has a 60 percent chance of being alive. Option 2 would be a long-life strategy. That is, the retiree selects some distant age such as a hundred and spends down assets evenly over this period. The problem here is that the retiree would be able to spend only $5,756 each year over the thirty-five-year period and would have no resources to support himself should he live beyond one hundred. Option 3 is based on life expectancy. Under this option, the retiree spends a fraction of assets each year based on expected remaining years of life. For example, life expectancy at sixty-five is twenty years, so the person would spend one-twentieth of the $100,000, or $5,000. Income under this option is always lower than that provided by an annuity, and the withdrawals rise and then fall with age, creating a significant chance of impoverishment in very old age.

Researchers have attempted to calculate the value to individuals of access to an annuity market. The concept they use is annuity equivalent wealth.[10] Calculating this number involves comparing levels of well-being with and without an annuity. Since this concept is used throughout the chapter, it is worth taking a moment to explain how it is derived. The experiment starts with the assumption that an individual has $100,000 of annuitized wealth and then looks at the consequences of eliminating the annuity market. Specifically, it asks, How much additional wealth would an individual need to be as well off without annuities as with them? Economists would say, How much additional wealth would the individual need to remain on the same indifference curve? The answer depends on many factors, such as the individuals' attitudes toward risk, the extent to which they have access to other sources of annuitized income, and whether they are married or single. Because the ability to annuitize has value, as discussed above, annuity equivalence wealth typically will be greater than $100,000. For example, in the case of an average sixty-five-year-old male with no other annuitized income, the ratio of annuity equivalent wealth to $100,000 is 1.45. This means that the individual would be indifferent between $100,000 of annuitized wealth and $145,000 of nonannuitized wealth.

10. Brown, Mitchell, and Poterba (2001); Brown and Poterba (2000); Brown (1999).

Resistance to Annuities

Despite the enormous potential gains from annuitization, the market for immediate annuities in the United States is minuscule. In 2001 sales of so-called single-premium immediate annuities amounted to only $10.3 billion.[11] In comparison, total long-term care expenditures for the elderly amounted to $120.5 billion.[12] Researchers have done a lot of work to find out why people do not buy annuities, and the reasons fall into three categories: market problems, other practical reasons, and gut feelings.

Market Problems

One reason people do not buy annuities is that annuities are expensive for the average person—that is, they are not actuarially fair. The high costs come from two sources. The first is adverse selection. Annuities are most attractive to people who are likely to live for a long time; those with a serious illness keep their cash. (Annuitants live, on average, about 3.5 years longer than the rest of the population.)[13] To address the adverse selection problem, private insurers raise premiums, which makes the purchase of annuities expensive for the person with average life expectancy. The second source of the high price is the insurance company's need to cover administrative and marketing costs and profit.

Researchers have measured the impact of adverse selection and administrative and marketing costs on the price of annuities by calculating money's worth ratios for these products.[14] They calculate a present discounted value of the annuity payments, discounting the projected monthly payments by the probability that the purchaser will be alive to receive them and by the return on assets underwriting the annuity. They then divide this value by the purchase price of the annuity to determine its money's worth ratio. If the ratio equals one, the annuity is actuarially fair; if it is less than one, it is not. The next step is to estimate how much of the reduction in money's worth is due to administrative and marketing costs and how much to adverse selection. This involves reestimating money's worth using mortality tables for annuitants. The cost of adverse selection is the difference between the money's worth for the annuitant population and that for the whole popula-

---

11. LIMRA International (2002). In fact even this number overstates the sale of life annuities because it includes products that are period certain only and have no life-contingent payments (Brown and Poterba 2000).
12. American Council on Life Insurance (2001b).
13. Unpublished data from the Social Security Administration; Brown and others (2001).
14. Mitchell and others (1999); Brown, Mitchell, and Poterba (2001).

Table 7-4. *Present Discounted Value of Annuity Payments Relative to Price for Male Annuitant Age Sixty-Five, Selected Years 1985–98*

Basis of calculation	1985	1990	1995	1998
Population mortality table	0.75	0.81	0.82	0.86
Annuitant mortality table	0.83	0.91	0.92	0.98

Source: Mitchell and others (1999); Brown, Mitchell, and Poterba (2001).

tion. Administrative and marketing costs are the price of the annuity less the money's worth for the annuitant population.

Calculations for 1990 and 1995 show that the money's worth for the average man was 81–82 percent of the price of an annuity; for the typical annuitant, the money's worth ratio was 91–92 percent (table 7-4). These numbers imply that about 10 percent of the 20 percent reduction in benefits per dollar of cost was attributable to adverse selection and 10 percent to administrative and marketing costs. In 1998 the money's worth ratios improved significantly. It is unclear whether the 1998 numbers were due to more competition, to greater operational efficiencies, or to less perceived interest rate risk on the part of insurance companies. Or perhaps these more attractive money's worth ratios reflect a failure to incorporate mortality improvements into the annuity prices, in which case the insurers priced their plans too favorably and the money's worth ratios will fall back in the future.

Other Practical Considerations

In any event, the fact that annuity prices are not actuarially fair is one explanation offered for retirees' lack of interest. The money's worth shortfall on its own, however, cannot explain the reluctance to buy annuities. Other considerations are also relevant

The presence of preexisting annuitized wealth reduces the value of further annuitization. People already have a lot of their retirement wealth annuitized because Social Security, which is most people's largest asset as they enter retirement, provides an inflation-indexed annuity (table 7-5). With the annuity equivalent wealth approach discussed above, the value of annuities declines when some wealth is already annuitized. As shown in table 7-6, $100,000 of fully annuitized wealth would be equivalent to $145,000 of nonannuitized wealth to a single sixty-five-year-old with no existing annuitized wealth. If 50 percent of that person's wealth were already annuitized, $100,000 of annuitized wealth would be equivalent to only $130,000 of nonannuitized wealth.

The outcome is highly dependent on people's attitude toward risk. The annuity equivalent wealth values reported above are for individuals with

Table 7-5. *Wealth Holdings of a Typical Household Prior to Retirement*[a]

Source of wealth	Amount in dollars	Percent of total
Primary house	81,900	16.9
Business assets	9,653	2.0
Financial assets	36,806	7.6
Defined contribution	28,516	5.9
Defined benefit	86,792	17.9
Social Security	220,791	45.4
Other nonfinancial assets	21,335	4.4
Total	485,793	100.0[b]

Source: Authors' calculations based on Board of Governors, *Survey of Consumer Finances* (SCF), 2001.

a. The "typical household approaching retirement" refers to the mean of the middle 20 percent of the sample of households headed by an individual aged fifty-five through sixty-four.

b. May be more or less due to rounding.

Table 7-6. *Annuity Equivalent Wealth, by Family Type and Risk Aversion*

Family type and annuity characteristics	Low risk aversion[a]	High risk aversion[b]
Single individual	1.45	1.62
Single individual, 50 percent annuitized	1.30	1.52
Married couple	1.18	1.34
Married couple, 50 percent annuitized, and a 12 percent load factor (money's worth = 0.88)	0.97	1.07

Source: Brown and Warshawsky (2001).

a. Coefficient of relative risk: 1.

b. Coefficient of relative risk: 5.

some tolerance for risk (low risk aversion) and those more averse to risk (high risk aversion). To assess the relative merits of annuitization, it would be helpful to have some sense about people's attitude toward risk. Unfortunately, different approaches to measuring risk tolerance yield different answers. The results from household surveys and from experiments that present people with lotteries suggest a level of risk aversion slightly above that described as low risk aversion in table 7-6.[15] On the other hand, only a much higher level of risk aversion can explain the difference between the return on equities and the return on risk-free U.S. Treasury bonds, far above what is characterized as higher in table 7-6.[16] On balance, it is probably reasonable to assume that most people are rather risk averse, but this chapter—like the academic literature—uses lower risk aversion as the base case.

15. Laibson, Repetto, and Tobacman (1998).
16. Mehra and Prescott (1985).

Another factor that may explain people's reluctance to buy annuities is that families provide a certain amount of self-insurance.[17] Husbands and wives generally pool their resources while both are alive and name each other as the major beneficiary in the case of death. If one spouse lives to be very old, the probability is high that the other spouse has already died and left a bequest to help finance consumption. In effect, the potential death of each spouse hedges the risk of the other spouse living too long and exhausting his or her resources. As a result, the two can set a level of consumption that takes account of the expected bequest. Simulations suggest that marriage provides 46 percent of the protection offered by a fair annuity for a fifty-five-year-old individual.[18] Adding risk sharing between parents and children, the risk-sharing potential within families is substantial.

The importance of risk pooling among couples, the presence of existing annuity income, and the lack of an actuarially fair annuity market can be quantified within the annuity equivalent wealth framework. As reported above, $100,000 of fully annuitized wealth would be equivalent to $145,000 of nonannuitized wealth to a single sixty-five-year-old with no existing annuitized wealth; that is, an annuity equivalent wealth ratio of 1:45. The ratio declines to 1:18 for a couple who can share mortality risk. And if that couple already has 50 percent of its wealth annuitized and faces an annuity market characterized by adverse selection and administrative costs, the ratio drops to 0:97. The ratio is somewhat higher for more risk averse couples (1:07) but still pretty close to even money.

An obvious reason that people might be reluctant to annuitize is their desire to leave a bequest. Individuals without a bequest motive place no value on any wealth that they hold at death, so it would be irrational for them not to select the higher guaranteed income that annuities provide.[19] But individuals with a bequest motive do value the wealth left to their heirs and, therefore, will not want to annuitize all their assets.

An extensive amount of research has focused on bequests. Do people have a bequest motive, or do they leave bequests accidentally because they are uncertain about when they will die (see box 7-1)?[20] If people do have a bequest motive, is it because they have altruistic feelings about their children, or are they trying to control their children's behavior? To what extent does a desire to leave a bequest affect saving and asset allocation decisions? Unfortu-

---

17. Kotlikoff and Spivak (1981); Brown and Poterba (2000).
18. Kotlikoff and Spivak (1981).
19. Yaari (1964).
20. For a discussion of the role of bequests, see Munnell and Sundén (2003).

Box 7-1. *Bequests and Lum-Sum Payments*

Bequests are likely to increase as retirees receive more of their pension benefits as lump sums rather than as annuity payments.[1] The increase in lump-sum payouts reflects not only the shift in coverage from traditional defined benefit plans to 401(k)s but also the transformation of defined benefit plans into cash balance plans or other hybrids. With less annuitization, bequests will inevitably rise because of uncertain lifetimes and little interest in life annuities. Elderly individuals will conserve wealth to self-insure against the risk of outliving their resources and will die with precautionary balances on hand. Moreover, evidence suggests that people are reluctant to spend accumulated wealth once they get it. Thus the shift to lump-sum payouts will produce more people who will die with substantial assets, and this will produce greater bequests.

In addition, the trend toward lump-sum payments might increase bequests by increasing people's interest in bequests. Accumulating wealth out of current income to leave a bequest is extremely difficult but becomes a plausible option when people receive a pile of wealth. Surveys indeed find that interest in leaving a bequest is positively related to the proportion of pension wealth received as a lump sum. Finally, the shift to 401(k) and hybrid plans could increase bequests by increasing savings rates. Workers do not reduce their other saving in anticipation of payments from defined contribution plans as they do in response to promised Social Security and defined benefit pension payments.

The quantitative effect on total bequests is potentially large and significant. Bequeathable wealth in the hands of decedents was $15 billion higher (3.2 percent) in 1998 than in 1992 as a result of the increase in defined contribution plans as a share of total pension wealth. Thus the shift in pension form has already significantly increased potential bequests. And the transition in coverage to defined contribution plans was far from complete in 1998, and hybrid plans were in their infancy. By the time the transition to plans with lump-sum payouts is complete, the impact should be twice as large.

1. Munnell and others (2003).

nately, economists have not reached any consensus about the importance of a bequest motive, its nature, or effects.

Two types of evidence suggest that people may well have a bequest motive. The first is survey data.[21] The Health and Retirement Study and the Survey

21. Early surveys asked whether people were saving in order to leave a bequest. Only 4 percent of respondents to the 1962 Survey of Financial Characteristics cited "providing an estate" as a saving objective. See Projector and Weiss (1966), table A30. The Brookings survey of affluent families ($10,000 and above in 1965 and $56,000 in 2001) found that only 23 percent were saving to make a bequest. See Barlow, Brazer, and Morgan (1966), p. 198.

Table 7-7. *Views of Households on Leaving a Bequest*
Percent

Questions and answers	Health and Retirement Study	Survey of Consumer Finances
Do you think it is important to leave an inheritance to surviving heirs?		
Very important or important	23	42
Somewhat important	44	31
Do you expect to leave a sizable inheritance to your heirs?		
Yes or probably	27	28
Possibly	15	20

Source: Authors' calculations based on the 2001 SCF; and on the Health and Retirement Study (http://hrsonline.isr.umich.edu).

of Consumer Finances ask respondents virtually the same questions: "Do you (and your spouse) think it is important to leave an inheritance to surviving heirs?" and "Do you (and your spouse) expect to leave a sizable inheritance to your heirs?" The responses show that 67–73 percent of families think leaving an inheritance is very important, important, or somewhat important; 42–48 percent responded either yes, probably, or possibly to expectations about leaving a sizable bequest (table 7-7).[22]

The second method for determining the strength of a bequest motive is through empirical tests. A study of 425 male TIAA-CREF annuitants found significant interest in leaving estates.[23] The average age of these annuitants was seventy, and they generally fell within the top 10–20 percent of the income distribution but were not the superrich. About half of the group was interested in leaving an estate. The net worth of these individuals was several hundred thousand dollars higher than those with no interest in bequests.[24]

22. We interpret positive responses to these questions as an indication of a bequest motive. This seems reasonable because 80 percent of those who "expect" to leave a bequest view leaving a bequest as "important." Others suggest that positive responses to the questions simply reflect the recognition that any household with nonannuitized wealth will end up leaving a bequest unless its members live for an exceedingly long time or have large nonreimbursed medical expenses.

23. Laitner and Juster (1996).

24. Laitner and Juster (1996) were particularly interested in determining the extent to which intergenerational altruism explained saving for bequests. They found that among households for whom leaving a bequest is important the projected bequest tends to be largest for those with the lowest assessment of their children's likely earnings, suggesting substantial intergenerational altruism. In the sample as a whole, however, altruistic bequests did not appear to be the major motive for saving.

Many researchers argue that a strong bequest motive helps explain why the rate of dissaving among the elderly is so low. The main critic of this position is Michael Hurd, who has examined dissaving among the elderly using several data sets.[25] Like other researchers, he finds a small amount of dissaving among the elderly and sometimes even a growth in wealth. In each study, however, Hurd compares the savings patterns of households with children to those without children and finds no significant difference. He therefore concludes that no evidence for a bequest motive exists and that bequests are simply the result of people holding on to their assets in the face of uncertain lifetimes.[26]

A final reason that people may be reluctant to annuitize is that they are worried about large unanticipated expenses, especially those related to their health. If people annuitize all their wealth, they leave themselves without a buffer to cover such large unexpected expenditures. They cannot go back to the insurance company and cash in their annuity; it is an irrevocable decision. If it were not irrevocable, people would ask for their money back as soon as they got a serious illness, and the whole system would collapse.

The cost of regular illness is not a particularly serious problem. Most people age sixty-five and older have Medicare coverage for both doctor's visits and hospital stays. Although Medicare requires deductibles and copayments, the vast majority is protected by supplemental insurance. In 1997 more than one-third of beneficiaries in Medicare's fee-for-service program had supplemental insurance provided by their employer, and 28 percent had individually purchased Medigap policies.[27] Another 20 percent of low-income people were protected from the bulk of out-of-pocket medical expenses by Medicaid. Thus most elderly are protected from the costs of a regular illness.

The real problem is long-term care. Medicare does not cover nursing home care, and most people do not have long-term care insurance. Medicaid will cover nursing home costs for the low-income once they have fully exhausted their assets, but the rest of the population is unprotected. Roughly 40 percent of the population aged sixty-five and older will require a nursing

25. Hurd has analyzed the Longitudinal Retirement History Survey, the Survey of Income and Program Participation, the Health and Retirement Study, the Asset and Health Dynamics among the Oldest Old, and the New Beneficiary Data System.

26. In collaborative work with Haider and others (2000) using the Asset and Health Dynamics of the Oldest Old (AHEAD) and the New Beneficiary Data System (NBDS), Hurd and his coauthors once again tested whether parents dissave more slowly than nonparents. Again they found no difference and concluded that a desire to leave a bequest is not the motive for the slow rate of dissaving. See Hurd, Lillard, and Panis (1998); Hurd and Rohwedder (2003).

27. AARP, "The Medicare Program" (research.aarp.org/health/fs45r_medicare.html).

home stay sometime in their lives.[28] The average nursing home stay in 1997 was 2.5 years. The average annual cost of a nursing home in 1998 was $56,000, which is roughly $62,200 in 2002 dollars.[29] Thus older people face the prospect of a large expenditure and may want to retain at least some wealth to cover uninsured long-term care and other health-related costs of aging.

Gut Feelings

Nonrational factors may also explain the small size of the immediate annuity market—specifically a preference to retain and control wealth and a lack of understanding of the advantages that annuities offer.

People appear to be completely satisfied with receiving retirement benefits in the form of annuities. No one complains about their benefits from Social Security or traditional defined benefit plans, demanding that they be paid as a lump sum. On the other hand, people who start with a pile of assets rarely exchange it for a stream of income. The real world and the psychological literature are full of examples showing that people prefer lump sums to income flows. Employers exploit this preference by offering athletes and other prospective employees immediate signing bonuses, rather than streams of future payments, to induce them to accept positions. The great majority of taxpayers (75 percent) overpay their income taxes to ensure themselves a lump-sum refund, when they could easily adjust their withholding to avoid making an interest-free loan to the Internal Revenue Service.

A recent study illustrates this preference for lump-sum payments.[30] Participants were offered either an annuity that pays $12,500 a year or an annuity that pays $10,000 annually plus a lump-sum bonus of $25,000 disbursed immediately upon retirement. The two plans are virtually equivalent at a real interest rate of 2.8 percent. But respondents preferred the one-time bonus to the increased annuity by a margin of three to one.[31]

Why do people prefer lump sums? An immediate lump sum allows for big-ticket purchases, such as paying off a mortgage or taking a vacation, which are not possible with small annuity payments. This preference for lump sums, however, more likely reflects a high discount rate—that is, peo-

28. Murtaugh and others (1997).

29. AARP, "The Medicare Program" (research.aarp.org/health/fs45r_medicare.html).

30. Fetherstonhaugh and Ross (1999).

31. For the typical male born in 1960, the expected present value of the $2,500 additional annuity payment at a 3 percent discount rate is roughly $30,000, which is larger than the $25,000 lump-sum payment offered in the experiment. For the typical woman, the expected present value of the increased annuity is even larger, at roughly $35,000.

ple simply do not put much value on money they will get in the future. For example, one researcher found that the median respondent would give up $3,000 today in exchange for a payment ten years in the future only if the delayed payment was at least $10,000.[32] This implies a discount rate (continuously compounded) of 12 percent. (As inflation was then running about 3 percent, this suggests a real discount rate of about 9 percent.) High discount rates can reflect the desire for immediate gratification at the expense of long-term well-being, a concern about how long one will live, or the belief that the satisfaction money can buy will decline with age. High discount rates also have an irrational component in that people's discount rates appear to vary depending on how the proposition is phrased, the size of the prize, and the time horizon.[33] Regardless of whether the standard preference for lump sums is rational or not, people given the choice typically prefer a pile of money to a stream of payments. This makes an annuity very unattractive.

The American Council on Life Insurance (ACLI) assembled a task force in 1999 to examine why people were so reluctant to buy immediate annuities. The task force found that, in addition to their lack of understanding about annuities, people had a strong desire to keep, control, and invest their money for its own sake. They had little interest in handing it over to a life insurance company in exchange for a flow of income; some even viewed money management as a form of entertainment.[34] The task force also asked 321 financial planners why so few people buy annuities.[35] The responses are shown below:

—Loss of control, 31 percent

—Bequest motive, 18 percent

—Low payout, 15 percent

—Lack of inflation adjustment, 12 percent

—Not well informed, 9 percent

—Do not need annuity, 5 percent

In addition to having rational and nonrational preferences for lump sums, most people also fail to understand or appreciate the benefits of annuitization. A common misunderstanding focuses on the risk of dying early and receiving less than they pay in.[36] This ignores the primary rationale of annuitization: the possibility of living longer than expected and receiving much more than the initial premium. Many people unfortunately view annuities as a gamble,

---

32. Thaler (1994b).
33. Thaler (1994b).
34. Brown and Warshawsky (2001).
35. Brown (2001).
36. Brown and Warshawsky (2001).

with the odds in the favor of the insurance company. They ignore the fact that annuities provide insurance against the risk of outliving one's resources.

One piece of evidence demonstrating people's aversion to leaving the insurance company with their money is the strong preference for annuities that guarantee payments for a fixed period of time if the purchaser should die early. This guarantee costs money in terms of lower monthly benefits. For example, the monthly benefit for a $100,000 annuity is reduced from $669 to $593 if the benefits are guaranteed for twenty years.[37] If leaving a bequest is the concern, it makes far more sense not to annuitize a portion of one's wealth.

Despite the reduction in monthly benefits, the guarantee option is popular even among those who should know better. TIAA-CREF is the retirement system for those employed in education and research. The system has been active in educating its participants about the advantages of annuities, and before 1988 TIAA-CREF provided basic pensions only in the form of annuities or death benefits. Although more distribution options have become available, most TIAA-CREF participants still choose a life annuity.[38] TIAA-CREF annuitants are well educated and relatively affluent and probably like TIAA-CREF better than most people like their insurance company. Nevertheless, among a sample of TIAA-CREF annuitants in 2000, 80 percent of men and 75 percent of women purchased an annuity with some form of guarantee (table 7-8). Even those who purchased joint-and-survivor annuities—that is, those who could be sure that their spouse was provided for—generally opted for period-certain payment. These choices must reflect some compromise between the recognition of the need for a guaranteed lifetime income and the sense of not wanting the insurance company to "win the bet."

Annuities and Inflation

Even if participants in 401(k) plans purchase annuities, virtually all annuities in the United States are fixed in nominal terms and therefore do not protect the individual against inflation. This problem plagues annuities provided through traditional defined benefit plans as well, since they are also fixed in nominal terms. In the 1990s only 10 percent of full-time defined benefit plan participants in medium and large firms were in plans that provided any cost-of-living adjustment.[39] The most recent survey reports only on auto-

---

37. www.immediateannuity.com/rates.asp.

38. Over the period 1994–96, almost 60 percent of people aged sixty-five opted for a life annuity within one year of retiring. Ameriks (1999).

39. U.S. Department of Labor (1998).

Table 7-8. *Distribution of New Immediate Annuities, TIAA-CREF, Men and Women, 2000*

	Men		Women	
Type of annuity	*With guarantee*	*Without guarantee*	*With guarantee*	*Without guarantee*
Single life	19.0	9.9	47.9	21.2
Full to survivor	44.2	6.7	17.9	2.3
Half to second annuitant	3.8	1.0	4.4	0.6
Two-thirds to survivor	12.9	2.5	4.6	1.1
All types of annuities	79.9	20.1	74.8	25.2

Source: Abel (2003).

matic cost-of-living adjustments, which applied to only 3 percent of participants in defined benefit plans in 2000.[40]

Inflation has been low in recent years, but it is important to remember that even moderate inflation can erode the real value of an income stream over time. For example, 3.0 percent inflation cuts the purchasing power of a nominal annuity in half in twenty-five years (figure 7-2). If inflation were totally predictable, a graded annuity could solve the problem nicely. It would pay a lower initial benefit than a nominal annuity so that the amount could rise over time in line with expected inflation. A graded benefit however cannot protect retirees against unexpected inflation. The only option here is explicit indexing.

In the past, insurers have not been able to offer inflation-indexed annuities primarily because they did not have inflation-indexed investments with which to underwrite such policies. With the introduction of Treasury inflation-protected securities (TIPS) in 1997, TIAA-CREF began offering a variable annuity backed by an inflation-linked bond account. Although this product offers substantial inflation protection, few annuitants have elected this option.[41] The product has some technical peculiarities.[42] But the more

40. U.S. Department of Labor (2003).

41. As of the end of 2002, the number of current contributors using the inflation-linked bond account in their retirement portfolios increased by more than 50 percent by year end 2001. However, the number of users is still the lowest of any of the ten TIAA-CREF pension accounts, with only 8 percent of the contributing population using the account (John Ameriks, TIAA-CREF, personal correspondence with author).

42. First, all CREF annuities use an assumed interest rate of 4 percent to establish the initial payment. If the nominal return on TIPS does not exceed 4 percent plus inflation, the payment will decline in real terms. Second, the value of the underlying portfolio is marked to market

Figure 7-2. *Purchasing Power of $100 with a 3 Percent Inflation, over Forty Years*

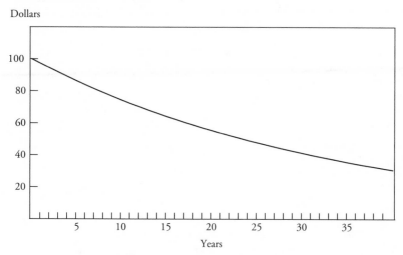

Source: Authors' calculations.

likely reason people do not select this option is that they are simply not willing to accept a low initial benefit relative to a fixed annuity in return for inflation protection. Even in the United Kingdom, where inflation-indexed bonds have been around for two decades, approximately 90 percent of individuals who purchase annuities do not opt for inflation protection.[43]

Some researchers have raised the notion that a variable annuity, in which the payments are linked to equity returns, might be an attractive vehicle to address inflation risk.[44] They do not argue that equities are a good inflation hedge; they are not. Real equity returns decline as inflation increases both on a year-to-year basis and over longer horizons. Rather, they suggest that the higher average return available though a variable annuity—even with its higher risk—would offset some of the erosive effect of inflation. As shown in table 7-9, the variable annuity does indeed appear better than either the nominal or the inflation-adjusted annuity for individuals with lower risk aversion. That is, people who are denied access to a variable annuity would

---

daily, so its value will vary over time. Finally, TIAA-CREF annuities are "participating" and thus change value based on the mortality experience of the contract owners.

43. Diamond (1997).

44. Brown, Mitchell, and Poterba (2001).

Table 7-9. *Annuity Equivalent Wealth, by Annuity Type and Risk Aversion*

Annuity	Low risk aversion[a]	High risk aversion[b]
No preannuitized wealth		
Nominal	1.45	1.62
Inflation indexed	1.50	1.86
Variable[c]	1.62	0.92
Fifty percent of wealth already in a real annuity		
Nominal	1.30	1.52
Inflation indexed	1.33	1.62
Variable[c]	1.57	1.43

Source: Brown, Mitchell, and Poterba (2001).
a. Coefficient of relative risk: 1.
b. Coefficient of relative risk: 5.
c. Real return is 6 percent.

need an even larger increment to their nonannuitized wealth to be equally as well off.[45] The results are reversed, however, for more risk-averse individuals. Here, the greater risk associated with stock investment offsets the advantages of the higher return.

To summarize: To be fully protected in retirement, people need a source of income that they cannot outlive and that is protected against the erosive impact of inflation. Traditionally, people lucky enough to be covered by a pension plan got a nominal annuity from their defined benefit plan and an inflation-adjusted annuity from Social Security. Two things are changing.

First, Social Security benefits relative to earnings are scheduled to drop under current law and could well drop further to bring the program back into balance. The replacement rate for average earners at age sixty-five will decline under current law from 41.0 percent today to 36.7 percent by 2022. Adjusting for rising Medicare premiums, increased taxation of benefits, and cuts in benefits to cover a portion of the current shortfall, the net benefit will fall even more.[46] As a result, retirees' access to inflation-indexed retirement income will decline.

Second, the shift in coverage under private retirement plans from traditional defined benefit plans to 401(k) and hybrid plans means that retirees will not automatically be provided an annuity by their employer-sponsored plan. They could purchase an annuity from an insurance company, but they

45. One of the reasons that people find variable annuities as attractive as they do is that the exercise is constructed so that the only way they can purchase equities is through the variable annuity. If they had access to equities outside the annuity, variable annuities would probably be less appealing.
46. Munnell (2003).

probably will not. And even if they did approach the insurance company for an annuity, they cannot—and probably would not—purchase an inflation-indexed annuity.

Possible Approaches

Although retired individuals rarely annuitize their 401(k) balances, this chapter presents evidence that annuitization could offer significant advantages. This is the case even when these advantages are mitigated by factors such as bequest motives, the ability to pool risks within families, and the desire to hold precautionary balances. As we have seen, the value of annuitization will rise as Social Security and employer pensions (the primary forms of annuitized wealth for retired individuals) decline in importance. Most people would be better off today, and much better off tomorrow, if they annuitized at least a portion of their pension wealth.

Three possible approaches come to mind to encourage greater annuitization of retirement wealth. The first is to establish annuities as the default payout mode for 401(k) plans. The second is to educate employees about longevity risk and the advantages of annuities and to design innovative annuities. The third is to have the government enter the annuity business.

Annuities as the Default in 401(k) Plans

Participants in 401(k) plans exhibit an enormous amount of inertia. Adopting automatic enrollment significantly increases participation in 401(k) plans, especially among the lower paid.[47] One option for increasing annuitization is to take advantage of that inertia and make annuities the default payout mechanism under all defined contribution plans. This would force participants to affirmatively select an alternative distribution option. Given the importance of inertia, and the fact that participants are likely to interpret default options as advice, making annuities the default would almost certainly increase annuitization rates. This approach still allows participants the freedom to choose other distribution methods. And some may. Many elderly face risks—prescription drugs, long-term care, and so on—for which insurance markets are not fully developed, and they will want to retain some assets to cover these contingencies.[48]

---

47. Choi and others (2001a, 2001b).

48. Davidoff, Brown, and Diamond (2002) suggest that the lack of demand for annuities may rest more with underdeveloped insurance markets for various contingencies than with the annuity market itself.

The default annuity for married couples should be a joint-and-survivor plan. The lesson learned from defined benefit plans is that employees otherwise fail to provide for their spouses. Husbands typically selected the single-life annuity, which pays higher monthly benefits. Wives, who typically outlive their husbands, then lose all pension income when their husband dies. The Employee Retirement Income Security Act of 1974 required that all pension plans that provide annuities automatically pay married couples in the form of a joint-and-survivor annuity. (The 1984 Retirement Equity Act amends this protection by requiring the spouse's notarized signature when the joint-and-survivor option is rejected.) Instituting the default significantly increased protection for wives.[49] A joint-and-survivor annuity should also be the default option for married couples in defined contribution plans. Those who want to opt out for a single-life annuity should be free to do so, with a signature from their spouse, as they are under current law for pension plans.

The default annuity should probably be indexed for inflation, since most people need to protect their purchasing power over a long period of time. Again, participants can affirmatively change to a nominal annuity or a variable annuity. For those who already have a significant share of their wealth in an inflation-adjusted annuity through Social Security, taking on the higher risk and greater expected returns of a variable annuity might be an appropriate way to diversify their portfolio. Legislating the default as inflation indexed, however, sends the message that this is the most sensible payment option for most people.[50]

This proposal raises two issues. The first is the additional cost to 401(k) plans. As discussed above, sponsors of these plans have always had the option to disburse benefits in the form of annuities, but they see providing annuities as more burdensome and costly than making lump-sum payments. Thus care must be taken to minimize the burden on plan sponsors so as not to endanger pension coverage.

The second issue is that the private market for inflation-indexed annuities is nearly nonexistent. As noted earlier, Treasury inflation-protected securities have been available in the United States since 1997. The explanation for the lack of indexed annuities must be lack of demand. If left on their own, individuals tend to select annuity options with the highest initial payment. The

49. Holden and Nicholson (1998) find that 62 percent of married men whose pensions began after 1974 indicate that they elected a pension that would continue to their widow; the share is 48 percent for married men whose pension began before 1974.

50. It might make sense to extend this provision to defined benefit plans as well, so that the default payment for all employer-provided pensions would be an inflation-indexed, joint-and-survivor annuity. This proposal raises a variety of issues, however, that are beyond the scope of this book.

evidence from the United Kingdom, which has had reasonably similar inflation experience, indicates that the initial payment for an inflation-adjusted
annuity could be 25–30 percent below that for a nominal instrument, which
may explain the lack of demand. But inertia is also a powerful force, and setting inflation-indexed annuities as the default would almost certainly increase
demand. If insurance companies perceive a growing demand and a chance for
profit, they will inevitably respond. If not, the third option discussed below
explores the possibility of the government entering the annuity market.

Education and Design Innovation

Various nonrational factors diminish the public's interest in annuities. Most
prominent are a visceral reluctance to part with cash and a lack of understanding of the benefits of annuities. People think only of losing the annuity gamble by dying early and leaving their money to the insurance company, and
they generally do not much like insurance companies. Equally troubling, even
financial planners rarely appreciate the advantages of annuities. Almost no
financial planning websites and software packages recommend annuities as
part of a financial plan.[51] Instead they typically deal with uncertainty about
date of death by recommending that people plan to finance retirement over a
conservative estimate of life expectancy, such as life expectancy plus ten years.

An underlying explanation for this lack of appreciation of annuities on the
part of both individuals and financial planners is that people are not worried
about outliving their resources. In a recent survey by the American Council
on Life Insurance, only 32 percent of respondents said they were "very concerned" about outliving their retirement resources (figure 7-3). It is hard to
appreciate a plan that solves what people see as an unimportant a problem—
or better, a problem that people are reluctant to recognize. Given the general
lack of understanding about the real potential for exhausting one's resources,
as well as for underconsuming, an education program seems warranted. It
should begin now, as the first employees dependent exclusively on defined
contribution plans are about to enter retirement.

In addition to education, the insurance industry might design products
that respond to the concerns that people do have. The major concern is medical expenses, especially the cost of long-term care. One proposed product
combines a fairly priced annuity with extra benefits payable at the onset of a
disability. This product would overcome some of the concerns about liquidity, since more money would be available if the purchaser's health declines.
By covering the costs of long-term care, the combined product would also

51. Warshawsky and Ameriks (2000).

Figure 7-3. *Retirement Concerns among the General Public, by Level of Concern*

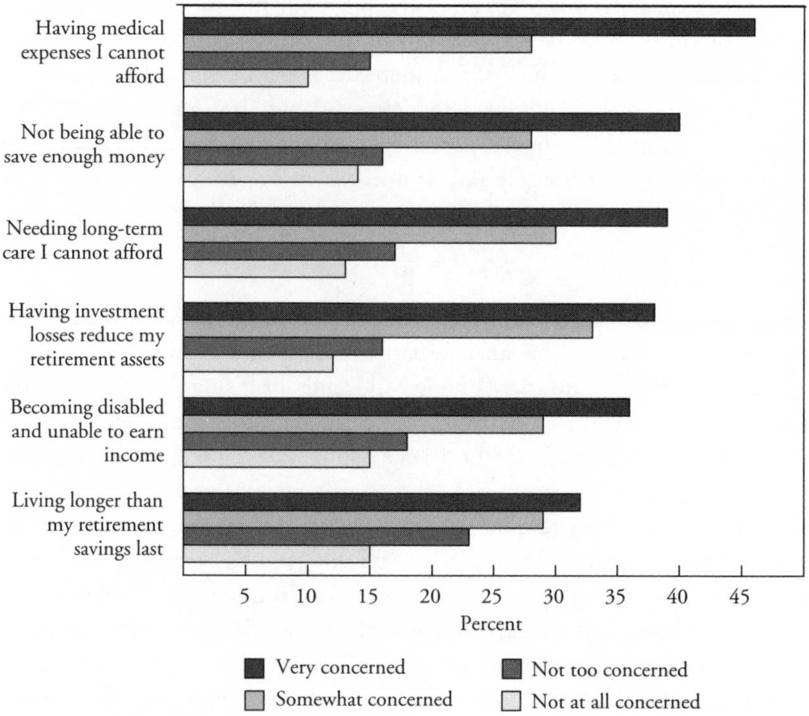

Source: American Council of Life Insurers (2001b).

protect other assets so that money would be available for bequests. Other options are surely available. The trick is to find out what people worry about and package the product to meet those needs.

Similarly, if people do not want to lose the bet and leave their money to the insurance company, perhaps the annuity could be designed so that they explicitly leave their money to people they like. That is, the annuity pool could consist of musicians, teachers, or maybe just extended family if large enough. If the purchaser dies early, he could be assured that people he cares about directly or indirectly will have a continued stream of income because of his participation. Of course, even in a regular annuity the money from those who die never "goes back to the insurance company" but is used to pay benefits for those who live for a long time. The notion is that making those long-lived people real and appealing might shift the potential annuitants' attention from the gamble with the insurance company to the true benefici-aries of their early death.

These are only suggestions. But it is clear that people are confused about the necessity and desirability of annuities. They need to be persuaded of both. A private sector solution is always the first choice. If the private sector cannot solve the problem, then a role may exist for government.

A Government Role in the Annuity Market

Individuals cannot purchase on their own the same annuity that they would have received under a traditional defined benefit plan. First, the voluntary nature of annuitization under a 401(k) plan creates a major adverse selection problem, which significantly increases the cost per dollar of annuity income. Second, administrative and marketing costs are significantly higher when annuities are purchased one by one rather than in bulk. Third, the explosion of 401(k) plans greatly changed the relative price of annuities for women and men (see box 7-2).

Voluntary individual annuities are riskier as well as costlier than defined benefit annuities. Participants must now worry about when they purchase an annuity. The amount the insurance company can offer in annual payments depends on how much it can earn on the principal invested. Payments will be high when interest rates are high and low when they are low. The variation is substantial. A $1,000 premium would have purchased a monthly income of $9.50 in 1989, when the yield on a ten-year Treasury note was about 8.5 percent; the monthly payment in March 2003 was about $6.69 per $1,000, as ten-year Treasury note yields fell below 4 percent. Under a traditional defined benefit regime, individual participants were insulated from these fluctuations. This is because the plan sponsor promised a given benefit and absorbed the interest rate risk associated with purchasing an annuity. In a 401(k) environment, the interest rate risk shifts to the individual participant. Experience with interest rate fluctuations suggests that different cohorts of retirees who annuitize will likely end up with different monthly benefits for the same total accumulations.

One further issue that no one had to think about in the past is the safety of the insurance company. To date, few annuitants have taken a loss on fixed annuities, but it has happened. Two relatively large insurance companies ended up paying only seventy cents on the dollar after they got into trouble as a result of bad investments.[52] The main purchasers of annuities to date, moreover, have been large sophisticated sponsors of defined benefit pension plans, not millions of relatively unsophisticated consumers. If individuals have to shop for annuities on their own, they will have to consider the health

---

52. U.S. General Accounting Office (1999).

Box 7-2. *Sex and 401(k) Plans*

The reason for the disparity in prices faced by women and men is that annuities provided under defined benefit and defined contribution plans are regulated by different legal regimes. Federal labor law covers annuities provided through defined benefit pension plans and requires equal pay for equal work. The Supreme Court has interpreted this to mean that a man and a woman with equal earnings histories should receive equal monthly benefits, even though women live longer on average than men and would be expected to receive higher lifetime benefits.

In contrast, 401(k) plans provide lump-sum payments at retirement, and retirees who want to annuitize must take their money to an insurance company. (Only a few 401(k) plans offer an annuity withdrawal, which would also be required to provide equal benefits to men and women.) Insurance companies, which are regulated by state insurance law, provide a smaller monthly benefit to women than to men, all else equal, to compensate for their longer life expectancy. According to online quotes in March 2003 from Immediateannuity.com, a sixty-five-year-old woman purchasing a $100,000 lifetime annuity contract could expect to receive $630 a month, whereas a man of the same age would get $669 a month.

What's fair? Insurance companies use average life expectancy to calculate the income provided under an annuity contract. On average, life expectancy at age sixty-five is twenty years for women and sixteen years for men. Insurance companies thus pay a larger monthly benefit to men, since on average they expect to make fewer such payments to men than to women. In the end, insurers expect that the present value of the amounts paid out to men and women will be equal.

In determining fairness in employer pension plans, the Supreme Court considered the full distribution of mortality rates and the uncertainty implicit in the distributions, instead of average life expectancy. The figure shows that the death ages of men and women overlap significantly. Because of this overlap, the Court disallowed the use of sex as a predictor of an individual's life expectancy and, instead, required equal monthly benefits for equal contributions.

It is important to note that requiring unisex pricing in traditional defined benefit plans does not raise problems of adverse selection, since individuals must generally take their benefits as annuities. In contrast, individuals who receive lump

---

of the insurance company as well as all the other factors that play into the decision about allocating their 401(k) funds at retirement.

If the goal is to encourage annuitization, the annuity must be made as cheap, easy, and safe as possible. The government could potentially help eliminate many of the problems that make the private provision of individual annuities expensive, complex, and risky. It could lower administrative costs by pooling large numbers of participants. To the extent that lower adminis-

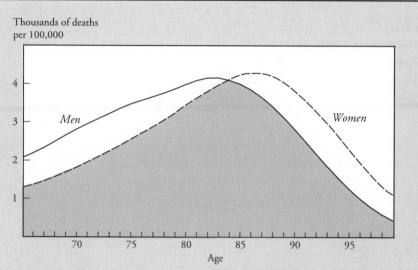

Source: "United States Life Tables, 1999" (www.cdc.gov/nchs/data/nvsr/nvsr50/nvsr50_06.pdf).

sums from their 401(k) plan can choose whether to purchase an annuity. One concern with unisex pricing in a voluntary environment is that it could amplify the adverse selection problem already associated with such annuities and make them even more expensive than they are today.[1]

1. The people who purchase voluntary annuities tend to be those who expect to live for a long time. If insurers are required to implement unisex pricing, they might choose to use a simple average of life expectancies for men and women to determine the price. As a result, men would face an even higher price than they do now, while women would find annuities more affordable. If sales to men fall while sales to women rise, the insurer would suffer from increased adverse selection. Therefore, insurers might price annuities on the assumption that only long-lived women will buy a unisex annuity. To the extent that companies choose this approach, women with average life expectancy would remain at the same disadvantage as they do today, while men would face a price even higher than under some blended unisex pricing. Such an outcome would result in an even greater adverse selection problem than exists in the current sex-differentiated market.

trative costs increases participation, it would also reduce adverse selection and thereby further improve the payout per dollar of premium. The government at this time is also the most likely entity to provide inflation-indexed annuities at a reasonable cost in a short period of time. Finally, the government is in a much better position to absorb interest rate risk than the individual. It could smooth out payments over time so that different cohorts did not end up with dramatically different benefits for the same accumulations.

The government could address the provision of annuities in one of two ways. The most aggressive would be to set up a government agency that received premiums from individuals, invested the money, and paid the monthly benefits. That is, the government would take on the full administrative, underwriting, and investment responsibilities. An alternative approach would be for the government to specify a standard type of annuity, perhaps including inflation indexing and a maximum load factor (that is, a minimum money's worth ratio), and issue requests for proposals to private sector insurers. If the private insurance companies could satisfy these requirements, the government could serve as a clearinghouse and direct consumers to companies that offered these standard annuities. The government could also act as a purchaser or reinsurer of the approved annuity sold by private companies. The goal would be to establish a public-private partnership that provides 401(k) participants, and now retirees from hybrid plans, with the annuities they need at retirement.

Conclusion

401(k)s have transferred almost all the responsibility and risks of retirement planning from the employer to the employee. The hardest decision is what to do with a 401(k) account at retirement. The way to have the highest standard of living and to not outlive one's resources is to buy an annuity and duplicate the payment stream provided by defined benefit plans.

But most people do not buy annuities. They are expensive for the average person because of administrative and marketing costs and adverse selection. Moreover, Social Security and defined benefit plans have annuitized a considerable portion of the wealth of today's retirees. Married couples achieve some degree of risk sharing within the family. People may also want to hold onto their wealth for a bequest or in anticipation of large health-related expenses.

The amount of retirement income that will be automatically annuitized will decline sharply. Social Security replacement rates are scheduled to fall, and annuities from defined benefit plans are on the wane. Nothing suggests that individuals can easily duplicate previous levels of annuitization on their own. Once people are given a pile of wealth, they typically want to hold on to it and manage and control it themselves. Too few individuals understand the risk of outliving their resources or appreciate the higher level of income that annuities offer. They instead view an annuity as a gamble with the insurance company, in which the company wins if they die early.

In short, the 401(k) environment must change so that people are not significantly worse off than they were in the defined benefit world. These changes could involve instituting inflation-indexed, joint-and-survivor annuities as the default in 401(k) plans, educating the public about the risks of outliving resources and the advantages of annuities, and exploring what role the federal government might play. Without such an effort, the baby-boom generation, which is the first to rely predominantly on 401(k) plans, will have a difficult time in retirement. And if this large generation runs into trouble, it will put enormous pressure on existing government programs, from Social Security and Medicare to the Supplemental Security Income program and Medicaid.

8

Making Pension Plans Do Their Job

The U.S. employer-sponsored pension system faces many challenges. First, the majority of people with pensions now rely on 401(k) and similar plans, and as previous chapters show, these plans are coming up short. The problems go beyond investment losses from the collapse of the stock market and abusive trading practices by mutual funds. Rather, these plans shift most of the responsibility for participation, contributions, investment, and withdrawal to the workers, and many lack the experience to make wise decisions. Further, many employers have transformed their traditional plans into cash balance or other hybrid plans. These plans improve the benefits for mobile workers, but they also provide lump-sum benefits rather than a stream of payments. Thus many workers in these plans are cashing out accumulations when they change employers and face the daunting task of allocating fixed sums over their expected remaining lifetimes at retirement. At the same time, it is important to remember that at any point about half of the work force aged twenty-five through sixty-four has no pension coverage at all, so people with 401(k) plans and hybrids are the lucky ones.

This chapter explores three possible changes. The first involves improving the effectiveness of existing 401(k)s by establishing defaults in these plans that reflect reasonable outcomes for most people. The second relates to possibilities for designing a better mousetrap through modifying cash balance plans, introducing a defined benefit plan with 401(k) features, or allowing people to move from one type of plan to another as they near retirement. The third centers on the possibility of introducing a new universal pension plan to alleviate reliance on 401(k) plans and provide coverage for those who have no employer-provided plan.

The Ideal Pension Plan

In our view, an ideal pension system would provide secure retirement benefits to all workers to supplement Social Security. To achieve this goal, all workers would be covered by a plan. Within each plan, participation and contributions would be automatic. Participants would not be able to cash benefits when they change jobs. The pattern of benefit accrual would not impede mobility or cause uneconomic incentives to retire early. Investment risk would be minimized, and benefits would be paid as an annuity and adjusted for inflation after retirement.

Our current system is far from this ideal. Less than half of all workers have any pension coverage at a given moment in time, and even those with coverage face a number of risks. In the old days, most workers with pensions had a traditional defined benefit plan. Participation in the plan was automatic, and the employer made contributions on behalf of workers. The worker who stayed with one employer was guaranteed an annuity to replace a substantial percentage of final pay. Alas, the benefit was not indexed for inflation, so purchasing power eroded as prices increased. But the real problem with defined benefit plans was that mobile employees forfeited benefits when they changed employers.

Today pension coverage has shifted from defined benefit to defined contribution plans, in particular 401(k) plans. The reasons for the shift are many and include a movement away from manufacturing, high administrative costs for defined benefit plans, and workers' preferences for individual accounts. At this point, about 58 percent of households with pension coverage have only a 401(k) plan or other form of defined contribution plan to supplement Social Security.

As shown in this study, 401(k) plans come up short in a number of ways. Although workers in theory could accumulate substantial pension wealth under 401(k) plans, in practice they do not. Balances—even for long-service employees—are substantially less than those produced by even the most sophisticated simulations. The reason for these low balances appears to be that the entire burden is on employees, and they make mistakes at every step along the way. A quarter of those eligible to participate in a plan fail to do so. Less than 10 percent of those who do participate contribute the maximum. Over half fail to diversify their investments, many overinvest in company stock, and almost none rebalance their portfolios in response to age or market returns. Most important, many take cash when they change employers. And few annuitize at retirement. Changes are clearly needed.

Resetting the Defaults in 401(k) Plans

One finding that emerges from this study is that participants in 401(k) plans exhibit a high degree of inertia when it comes to participation, contribution, and investment. An explanation for this outcome is that the decisions are complicated. In general, workers do not have sufficient financial experience, training, or time to figure out what to do, and the cost of understanding the options appears greater than the benefits. As a result, they simply stay put.

Public policy could leverage this inertia by setting the defaults in 401(k) plans to the desirable outcome. This would eliminate the cost for participants of trying to figure out what to do, and it would help workers avoid mistakes by pointing them in the right direction. Of course, individuals could opt out at any stage, allowing them the flexibility to make different decisions if their circumstances warrant it.

The experience with setting defaults to date indicates that the effects on participant behavior could be substantial. Internal Revenue Service regulations allow firms to enroll participants automatically and then to let those who do not want to participate opt out. The firms that have adopted automatic enrollment show a dramatic increase in participation, because workers who are automatically enrolled generally do not withdraw.

One problem that has emerged is that contribution rates for automatic enrollees are set much lower than those typically selected by 401(k) participants. Because workers are creatures of inertia and are unlikely to increase contributions, they risk ending up at retirement with inadequate resources. Workers also tend to stay with the default investment option and, in fact, interpret this option as investment advice from the firm. Even workers who subsequently change their allocations used the default option as a standard against which they evaluate other investment choices.

The conclusion is that the design of the default options is crucial. The question is how to set the defaults and who chooses them. The results from this study indicate that, to ensure a sufficient and reliable retirement income, the defaults should be designed so that all eligible participants are automatically enrolled; their contributions are set at the level that maximizes the employer match; the portfolios of thirty-year-olds are allocated to 70 percent stocks and 30 percent bonds and automatically rebalanced as they age; investments in company stock are restricted; lump-sum distributions automatically roll over; and retirement benefits are paid in the form of a joint-and-survivor inflation-indexed annuity.

The next question is, Who decides on the defaults? Having Congress set the defaults is fully consistent with other measures for private plans. Traditional defined benefit plans typically paid workers a single-life annuity. As a result, the wife was left destitute when the husband died and pension payments ceased. To remedy this situation, Congress passed legislation that requires plan sponsors to provide benefits in the form of a joint-and-survivor annuity, so that benefits continue after the death of the husband. Couples can opt out of this default by presenting a request signed by both spouses. Despite the ability to opt out, the number of joint-and-survivor annuities has increased markedly.

Of course, policymakers do not want to impose a regulation that discourages employers from sponsoring plans or contributing to existing plans. For example, requiring employers to set the default employee contribution so that it maximizes the employer match may cost employers more than they want to spend on retirement benefits. This might lead some employers to reduce the matching contribution. Currently, the typical employer contributes 3 percent of earnings. As our simulations show, this level of employer contribution ensures sufficient retirement income if workers contribute continuously throughout their working life. One way of creating an incentive for employers to maintain this contribution level could be to tie it to nondiscrimination testing. That is, employers who automatically enroll all eligible workers, set contributions to maximize the employer match, and provide a match of at least 3 percent that is vested immediately would automatically pass nondiscrimination testing.

Because of fiduciary concerns, another area in which firms may be reluctant to adopt defaults is investment allocation. To date, companies with automatic enrollment programs generally invest contributions in money market funds. To provide a default investment allocation with higher risk and return, companies would need Labor Department approval to protect them against litigation if results were unfavorable. One way to set the default investment option is to use life-cycle, or life-stage, funds.

To summarize, defaults lead people in the right direction while providing the freedom to choose a different outcome. And all the evidence indicates that a default approach will put participants in a better place and that retirement income will be more reliable. This may be particularly important for low-income workers, who have the lowest participation rate in 401(k) plans but the most to gain in terms of future retirement income from participating.

Building a Better Mousetrap

Establishing defaults for 401(k) plans may solve many of the problems associated with this pension arrangement. But some will remain. Even though the default option described above will reduce the share of 401(k) plan assets allocated to equities over time, plan participants will continue to face substantial investment risk. The risks associated with stocks seem particularly serious. Sustained periods of low equity returns means that even workers fifteen years from retirement will not have enough time to accumulate adequate retirement assets. A recent book about 401(k) plans argues that the next twenty years may be one of those periods.[1] And the Yale economics professor Robert Shiller, author of *Irrational Exuberance,* contends that stocks are still expensive by historic standards and could end the decade where they began.[2] Thus it is important to consider ways of reducing the investment risk faced by employees.

What about cash balance and other hybrid plans that combine features of both defined benefit and defined contribution plans? These plans, typically found in large companies that have converted their traditional defined benefit plans, have some obvious strengths. The most notable is that they protect employees against most investment risk during the accumulation phase by providing a guaranteed return. Although the employer may invest in assets with higher risk and return than those associated with the guaranteed credit on the employee's notional account, employees are not at risk for investment losses. The employer guarantees the return, and if the employer should fail, benefits are insured by the Pension Benefit Guaranty Corporation.

Cash balance plans also relieve employees of the participation, contribution, and investment decisions they must make with 401(k) plans. Participation is automatic, and the employer makes the contribution on behalf of the employee and guarantees the return. For the mobile employee, cash balance plans offer the same advantage as 401(k) plans in that benefits accrue at a steady rate over the employee's working life, rather than being related to final pay. Therefore, unlike in the case of traditional defined benefit plans,

1. Wolman and Colamosca (2002).
2. Craig Karmin and Michael R. Sesit, "Prescient Professor Favors Tactic Often Scorned: Timing the Market," *Wall Street Journal,* July 29, 2002, p. C1.

employees' benefits are not affected by a job change if they move to an identical plan.

The weaknesses of cash balance plans are twofold. First, they pay lump-sum benefits both at termination and at retirement. Because workers often cash lump sums when changing employers—especially when they are young and the sum is small—the provision of lump sums reduces the accumulation of retirement wealth. But even more worrisome, cash balance plans provide the employee a lump sum at retirement: a predictable lump sum, but a lump sum all the same. At a minimum, employees have to translate lump sum amounts into rates of income replacement to determine whether or not to save additional amounts on their own. More important, at retirement employees face the daunting task of how to allocate the lump sum over an uncertain lifetime. An annuity would produce a life-long guaranteed monthly income, but individuals are reluctant to invest in them. Moreover, the retiree faces interest rate risk. If interest rates are low, insurance companies will have low returns on the initial premium, and the resulting retirement income stream will be low. Unfortunately, this is when annuities are most needed—when investment income alone provides little support. In short, lump sums are a major drawback of cash balance plans.

The second weakness of cash balance plans is that both contributions and investment earnings on these plans, as currently constituted, are low. Employers typically contribute about 5 percent of earnings, and the average guaranteed return is usually linked to a U.S. Treasury security. As demonstrated by the simulation model in chapter 2, a plan with such low contribution levels cannot on its own provide an adequate level of retirement benefits. It is highly likely that most of the cash balance conversions have occurred in companies that also offer 401(k) plans, so the low level of benefits is not a serious problem for those fortunate enough to have two plans. But if cash balance plans are the sole source of support, contributions would need to be closer to 8–9 percent. Moreover, tying the return to Treasury securities is like locking people into an all-bond portfolio from the beginning of their working lives. As discussed in chapter 4, young people, with a lifetime of earnings ahead of them, are in a position to take on higher risk in order to earn higher returns and, therefore, should have some stock investment.

To build on the cash balance framework would require a number of modifications. The most important would be to restrict lump-sum payouts and to require that retirement benefits be paid as an annuity—or at least that the annuity be the default. Another challenge would be to devise some way to encourage employers to increase their contributions, recognizing that employees will pay for these contributions in the form of slower wage growth. At the same time, it would also be desirable to raise the guaranteed return. The certainty offered by cash balance plans is worth some reduction in expected returns. The question is, How much?

Another approach would be to start with the structure of traditional defined benefit plans. These plans have many of the characteristics of an ideal pension: automatic coverage and contributions, no investment risk for the employee, limited lump-sum payments upon termination, and retirement benefits paid as annuities. The main problem with these plans is that mobile employees lose benefits under plans that base benefits on final earnings, and both workers and employers see mobility as increasingly important. Young workers also prefer the simplicity and control of having their own 401(k) accounts, the chance to make pretax contributions, and the opportunity to earn market rates of return. Employers believe that individual accounts are easier to explain to workers, and they avoid much of the administrative costs associated with sponsoring a defined benefit plan. 401(k) plans also shift the interest rate risk of acquiring an annuity from the employer to the employee. Since participants generally do not buy annuities, they do not appear to view this as a serious problem.

The American Academy of Actuaries has been concerned for some time about the decline in coverage under traditional defined benefit plans.[3] It attributes the decline to many of the developments discussed in chapter 2 but also places considerable emphasis on the lack of a level playing field. One provision in particular, the academy claims, gives 401(k) plans an enormous advantage, namely, the ability for the employee to make pretax contributions. To support this argument, they point to the prevalence of defined benefit plans in Canada and in the state and local sector in the United States, where employees can contribute on a pretax basis.

One way to level the playing field is to modify defined benefit regulations. The academy proposes to allow voluntary employee contributions and employer matches in defined benefit plans.[4] For those who worry about allowing such contingent accruals in defined benefit plans, the academy notes that nonprofits already do it successfully and that for-profits can do it through profit-sharing plans. Not allowing contingent accruals in defined benefit plans only encourages more profit-sharing plans and employee stock ownership plans, which increase the investment risks for the employee. The academy also offers suggestions for simplifying the regulation of defined ben-

3. Gebhardtsbauer (1999).
4. Gebhardtsbauer (1999, 2002).

efit plans to make them more competitive. A defined benefit 401(k) plan may or may not be the answer, but it certainly merits consideration.

Instead of adopting a hybrid plan such as a defined benefit 401(k), another approach is to have workers move from a 401(k) plan to a defined benefit plan either at their choice or at a certain age.[5] The ability to switch between plans would allow workers to take advantage of the higher risk, higher return when they are young and the predictable replacement rate offered by defined benefit plans when they are older. But most employers do not provide both a defined benefit and 401(k) plan and therefore would not be able to offer such an option. One possibility is for the federal government—perhaps through the Pension Benefit Guaranty Corporation—to offer a defined benefit plan for those who want to switch their pension arrangement. However, the cost of switching could be significant, and the pricing of this kind of option is key for determining its feasibility. One peripheral advantage is that, if the government provided this option, it could reverse the trend away from annuities.

An alternative is for defined contribution plans to guarantee a real or nominal rate of return. Such an approach has been introduced in Germany, where the new individual account system guarantees the nominal value of principal.[6] Guarantees can be expensive, however, if they are to be significant.[7] Furthermore, they raise the issue of moral hazard. That is, if individuals understand that they will be bailed out, they have every incentive to undertake risky investments. Moreover, guaranteeing a rate of return is not the same as guaranteeing a replacement rate, so the individual still lacks retirement security.

The purpose here is not to decide upon an alternative to the 401(k) plan, but merely to note that defined benefit plans have enormous advantages and that incorporating some of their advantages into the 401(k) world might substantially strengthen the private pension system.

Introducing Another Pension Layer

Even with appropriate defaults and reduced risk, 401(k) plans by themselves may not be able to produce an adequate retirement income for the nation's workers. As noted, half of the work force aged twenty-five to sixty-four at any point in time has no pension coverage at all. Even considering pension cover-

---

5. The state of Florida has enacted such an option for its public employees (www.leg. state.flus). Lachance and Mitchell (2003) analyze the costs associated with the Florida proposal.

6. Turner and Rajnes (2002).

7. Lachance and Mitchell (2003).

Table 8-1. *Social Security Replacement Rates, Age Sixty-Five,
under Current Law, 2003 and 2030*
Percent

	Share of earnings		
Year	Low earner	Medium earner	Maximum earner
2000	55.5	41.2	27.3
2030	49.1	36.7	24.0

Source: U.S. Social Security Administration (2003b), table VI-E11.

age over people's entire lifetimes and on a household basis, many retirees will have nothing other than Social Security when they retire. And a large portion of those with partial pension coverage over their lifetimes still run the risk of accumulating an inadequate retirement income.

What makes the situation especially serious is that Social Security will become a less important source of retirement income going forward, even under current law. Social Security today provides benefits equal to 41.3 percent of preretirement earnings for the average worker retiring at age sixty-five. But the replacement rate will decline to 36.3 percent for the average worker who retires at age sixty-five in 2030 (table 8-1). The reason for this decline is the increase in the normal retirement age from age sixty-five to age sixty-seven, which will be fully phased in for workers attaining age sixty-two by 2022. An increase in the normal retirement age is equivalent to an across-the-board benefit cut at any given age, and that cut reduces the replacement rate.

The second development that will affect future Social Security replacement rates is the rising cost of Medicare. Premiums for Medicare part B, which are automatically deducted from Social Security benefits, are scheduled to increase from 6.8 percent of benefits for someone retiring today to 10.2 percent for someone retiring in 2030. The third factor that will reduce Social Security benefits is that they will be taxed more extensively under the personal income tax.[8] In addition to these already scheduled cuts, further reductions are likely as part of any compromise to eliminate the program's structural deficit. The net replacement rate for a sixty-five-year-old in 2030 is likely to be about 27 percent. As workers who retire before age sixty-five have their benefits actuarially reduced, the net replacement rate for a sixty-two-year-old will be about 21 percent.[9] These are very low numbers.

8. Munnell (2003).
9. Munnell (2003).

With a diminished Social Security program, uncertain outcomes from 401(k) plans, and 35 percent of retirees with no pensions at all, it might be worth considering the introduction of an additional tier of retirement income. This is not a new idea. The President's Commission on Pension Policy recommended in 1981 a mandatory universal pension system (MUPS). Under this proposal, every employer would contribute a minimum of 3 percent of payroll to a tax-deferred defined contribution pension plan. All employees over age twenty-five with one year of service would participate; vesting would be immediate; and benefits would not be integrated with Social Security. Company MUPS plans would be managed as company plans are today—through pension trusts, insurance companies, and other financial institutions. If employers did not want to administer their own plans, they could send their contributions to a clearinghouse under the authority of the Social Security Administration to be invested in private capital markets. An independent board appointed by the president would administer the investments.

Any proposal of this kind hinges on its cost. Employers are unlikely to swallow the additional expense and would probably recoup their contributions by slowing the wage growth of their employees. The workers would thus bear the burden. Another cost is the forgone revenues to the federal government, because an expansion of the pension system would increase the tax expenditure numbers reported in the introduction. To compensate for this loss, the government would have to raise additional revenues through increased taxes to maintain its current level of expenditures.

Nevertheless, introducing a MUPS-type arrangement and reducing wage growth in exchange for future retirement benefits is probably a reasonable trade-off for middle-income workers. The story for lower paid workers is different. The poverty level for a four-person household with two children was $18,244 in 2002, and for families with income close to this amount it probably makes more sense to try to increase take-home pay rather than reduce it. Thus people with a lifetime of low wages are often not in a position to sacrifice current consumption for additional retirement income. Although low-wage individuals also require additional retirement income to supplement what they receive from Social Security, relying on employer or employee contributions might not be the right mechanism to meet their needs.

An alternative approach is a program like the USA account proposal, introduced by the Clinton administration. Under this proposal, the government would make an automatic contribution in the form of a refundable tax credit deposited directly to each individual's account. As proposed, the tax credit for workers and their spouses in low- or moderate-income households would be $300 a year, and the automatic credit would be phased out for higher income families.[10] Individuals could make additional contributions to their USA accounts, and the government would match their contributions up to a certain amount. The proposed match was dollar-for-dollar for low- and moderate-income individuals, phased down to 50 percent for contributors with higher incomes. Workers would not need to shift out of private sector plans, as the government would pay these matching contributions either to USA accounts or 401(k) plans. Individuals would also be able to invest their accounts in a retirement plan similar to the federal thrift savings plan or with private sector fund managers.

Again, the purpose of this discussion is not to generate a particular recommendation. The point is that a government-supported second tier offers the flexibility of providing automatic credits for low-income workers without affecting their wages.

Conclusion

The argument presented in this book is that the advent of 401(k) plans has shifted most of the responsibility for retirement income from the employer to the employee. Employees must decide whether or not to join the plan, how much to contribute, how to invest the contributions, when to rebalance their portfolios, whether to invest in company stock, whether to roll over accumulations when changing employers, and how to use the lump-sum payments for retirement. The evidence indicates that, at every step along the way, a significant fraction of participants make serious mistakes. If 401(k) plans are to be a successful vehicle for providing retirement income, the system has to be changed.

This chapter sketches out three possible avenues of reform that would improve the current pension system. Our goal is not to recommend a specific proposal, but to stimulate a debate that we hope will generate other ideas and options. The time has come—once again—to begin a serious conversation about making our private pension system work better. It's a Studebaker moment!

10. This automatic credit would be phased out between $40,000 and $80,000 of adjusted gross income for a couple; $20,000–$40,000 for singles; and $30,000–$50,000 for heads of households.

Appendix: The Regulatory Framework for Eligibility, Participation, Contributions, and Withdrawals

The goal of pension policy has been to provide tax incentives to encourage—through favorable tax provisions—the use of tax-qualified pension and profit-sharing plans to ensure greater retirement security for all employees, not just highly paid executives. To ensure that employers do not establish pension plans just for the owners and other high-income workers, Congress requires all plans to pass a nondiscrimination test and limits how much can be contributed to and provided by a tax-qualified plan.

In spite of the favorable tax treatment and nondiscrimination testing, only about 50 percent of the work force ages twenty-five through sixty-four is covered by a pension plan at any point in time.[1] Some of the workers without pension coverage are not eligible even though they work for firms that sponsor plans, since these firms can exclude any worker under age twenty-one or who has less than one year of employment with the firm. A year of service is defined as working at least a thousand hours during a twelve-month period, which means that many part-time and seasonal workers are excluded from participating. In addition, firms can

1. For a discussion of trends in pension coverage, see Alicia H. Munnell and Annika Sundén, "Private Pensions: Coverage and Benefit Trends" (www.pensioncoverage.net/Papers.htm).

exclude up to 30 percent of the remaining nonhighly compensated workers from the plan.[2]

Once a worker is eligible to participate, enrollment is generally automatic in a defined benefit plan. In 401(k) plans, on the other hand, participation is voluntary. This means that employers often provide matching contributions to encourage participation by the rank and file in order to allow the plan to pass the nondiscrimination tests. Voluntary participation also means that many workers who could have a source of retirement income do not because they elect not to participate in the plan.

Among individual account plans, the 401(k) plan is the most common. However, similar plans exist for nonprofit organizations and state and local government. The different types of individual plan include:

—401(k) plan: Any size employer, including government and tax-exempt employers, may establish this type of plan.

—403(b) plan: Tax-exempt 501(c) employers, such as educational institutions and hospitals, typically offer this type of plan. Generally, employees contribute and employers match the contribution. However, some 403(b) plans do not require employee contributions.

—457 plan: State and municipal governments typically offer this plan, but any tax-exempt organization can have a 457 in addition to other plans. Only employees contribute to these plans.

—SIMPLE:[3] Firms with a hundred or fewer employees can offer a SIMPLE (savings incentive match plan for employees of small employers). A SIMPLE can be set up as an IRA for each employee or as a 401(k) plan. Employees contribute to the plan, and employers are obligated to contribute to the plan either through a match or through a nonelective contribution for all employees.

This book treats 401(k), 403(b), 457, and SIMPLE plans as one group of

2. Under the nondiscrimination rules, a firm's coverage of nonhighly compensated employees must be 70 percent of its coverage of highly compensated employees. So the firm can exclude 30 percent of the nonhighly compensated employees, with a highly compensated employee defined as someone earning $90,000 or more in 2002. A plan may exclude an even larger amount of nonhighly compensated employees in certain circumstances. If the firm excludes some of its highly compensated employees, it may exclude more than 30 percent of the other employees. Alternatively, the firm can use the average benefits antidiscrimination test, which permits the exclusion of more than 30 percent of employees. In some circumstances, a firm can use special "separate line of business rules" to exclude additional employees. A firm may also exclude employees covered by a collective bargaining agreement if retirement benefits were the subject of good faith bargaining.

3. SIMPLE plans have generally replaced SARSEPs (salary reduction simplified employee pensions), which was the earlier pension provision for small employers.

plans, since they are fundamentally similar retirement savings vehicles and because that is how defined contribution data are reported in household surveys.

Contribution Limits

Three limits apply to 401(k) plans: a limit on the employee's elective contributions to the plan, a limit on the total contributions by the employee and the employer to the account, and a limit on the total amount of compensation that can be taken into account for contributions. When the Employee Retirement Income Security Act (ERISA) was passed in 1974, the maximum annual contribution to a defined contribution plan was limited to the lesser of $25,000 or 25 percent of compensation. The dollar amount was adjusted annually for inflation and by 1982 had reached $45,472. In 1983 the contribution limit was reduced to $30,000, and in 1984 the inflation adjustment was frozen. The Tax Reform Act of 1986 left the limit on the total contribution amount unchanged but reduced the maximum employee contributions to $7,000. This amount has been adjusted for inflation annually, and by 2001 the maximum elective employee contribution was $10,500.

Congress limited the maximum earnings that can be used for contributions to defined contribution plans to make sure that low earners do not end up with excessively low contribution rates. In 2001 the maximum compensation that could be considered for calculating contributions was $170,000. For example, if the owner of the firm earns $500,000 and the maximum contribution is limited to $35,000, this contribution level would represent 7 percent of pay. But since earnings were limited to $170,000, the $35,000 contribution represents about 20 percent of pay. Nondiscrimination rules require that the difference in contribution rates between highly compensated and other workers cannot be too large. If discrimination is tested on the basis of income contributed, low-income workers must have similar contribution levels for the plan to be nondiscriminatory. The tax code does not limit total benefits or how much can be accumulated in the account.

In the last few years pressure has grown to increase the contribution limits in 401(k) plans. Those favoring an increase argue that allowing higher limits would increase retirement savings. More employers would be encouraged to establish plans if they themselves could benefit, and more plans mean more retirement savings for the rank and file. Opponents point out that few workers actually contribute the maximum amount allowed and that increasing

Table A-1. *Contribution Limits under Prior Law and under the Economic Growth and Tax Relief Reconciliation Act (EGTRRA)*[a]

Limit	Prior law	EGTRRA
Elective contribution	$10,500 and indexed for inflation in $500 increments	$11,000, 2002 $12,000, 2003 $13,000, 2004 $14,000, 2005 $15,000, 2006 After 2006, the limit will be indexed for inflation in $500 increments.
Total contribution	$35,000 or 25 percent of compensation for 2001, whichever is lower. The limit is indexed for inflation in $5,000 increments.	$40,000, 2002 The limit will be indexed for inflation in $1,000 increments.
Maximum compensation	$170,000, 2001 The limit is indexed in $10,000 increments.	$200,000, 2002 The limit is indexed in $5,000 increments.

Source: Watson Wyatt Worldwide, "The Unfolding of a Predictable Surprise" (www.watsonwyatt. com/research/resrender.asp?id=w-326).

a. After 2006 the limit for 401(k)s and 403(b)s will continue to be indexed for inflation in $500 increments. The defined contribution limit and the catch-up contributions are both indexed in $1,000 increments; compensation is indexed in $5,000 increments. Figures for 2003–06 are estimated assuming a 3 percent inflation rate. To encourage low-income taxpayers to make contributions, EGTRRA also provides tax credit incentives targeted at low-income workers. These tax credits have almost no practical value, however, because they are not refundable, and low-income workers have little or no income tax liability.

limits would only benefit high-income workers. After much debate, the contribution limits were increased as part of the 2001 Economic Growth and Tax Relief Reconciliation Act (EGTRRA).[4] The contribution limits in prior law and under EGTRRA are presented in table A-1.

To make it possible for older workers to increase their savings just before retirement, in 2002 catch-up provisions allowed workers aged fifty and older to contribute an additional $1,000. This means that workers approaching retirement could contribute $12,000 in 2002 on a pretax basis, with a maximum contribution to the account of $41,000. The catch-up contribution limit is to be increased by $1,000 annually until it reaches $5,000 in 2006. Participants can take advantage of these provisions regardless of how much

4. Pension provisions will expire at the end of 2010. However, the Portman-Cardin bill, "The Preservation and Savings Enhancement Act of 2003," introduced in the House of Representatives during spring 2003, proposes that the increases in contribution limits be accelerated to 2003 and made permanent.

they have contributed to their plans in the past.[5] In addition to increasing contribution limits, EGTRRA also increased the employer deduction limit for 401(k) plans.

Vesting

In many cases, workers have to be employed for a full year before they are eligible to participate in the plan. Once workers start to participate, most firms require a minimum number of years of employment before they can claim earned pension benefits. Once workers have rights to pension benefits, they are considered vested in the plan. ERISA regulates the maximum number of years that firms are allowed to require before workers are vested in the plan.

In 401(k) plans, the employees' contributions are immediately vested. Employers' matching contributions, however, must be vested following one of two rules:

—Three-year cliff vesting: Employees must own 100 percent of the employer contribution after no more than three years of service. Before 2002 this was five years. Any contribution that is not a matching contribution follows the five-year schedule.

—Six-year graded vesting: After no more than two years, 20 percent of employers' contributions must be vested, with the share increasing by 20 percent a year until (after six years) employees are fully vested. Before 2002 this was seven years. Any contribution that is not a matching contribution follows the seven-year schedule.

In defined benefit plans, employees' benefits must be vested following one of two rules:

—Five-year cliff vesting: Employees' benefits must be fully vested after no more than five years of service.

—Seven-year graded vesting: After no more than three years, 20 percent of employees' benefits must be vested, with the share increasing by 20 percent a year until (after seven years) employees are fully vested.

Nondiscrimination Testing

The Tax Reform Act of 1986 revised the nondiscrimination requirements for qualified pension plans to provide comprehensive guidelines for employers. The nondiscrimination rules limit how much highly compensated workers (those earning more than $90,000 in 2002) can contribute relative to the

---

5. Employers have discretion in implementing the catch-up provisions. One survey indicates that 80 percent of employers will implement the catch-up provisions. See Miller (2002).

rank and file so that the benefits from a 401(k) plan do not unduly favor highly compensated employees. This means that highly compensated employees can take advantage of the tax benefits in 401(k) plans only if a large share of rank-and-file employees also participates in the plan. Employers have two ways to ensure that a 401(k) plan is not discriminatory: to test the contributions and benefits allocated to participants under the plan or to meet safe harbor requirements.[6] If a plan fails the nondiscrimination test, a share of the highly compensated employees' contributions must be returned until the plan meets the requirements.[7]

For a plan to be nondiscriminatory, two criteria must be satisfied: actual deferral percentage or actual contribution percentage.

—Actual deferral percentage: The average deferred percentage (ADP) of salary deferred in the plan for the highly compensated (HC) cannot exceed that for the nonhighly compensated (NHC) by more than the allowable percentage, which depends on the ADP of the nonhighly compensated: If ADP_{NHC} is less than 2 percent, then ADP_{HC} cannot exceed two times ADP_{NHC}. If ADP_{NHC} is between 2 percent and 8 percent, then ADP_{HC} can exceed ADP_{NHC} plus 2 percent. If ADP_{NHC} is 8 percent or more, then ADP_{HC} cannot exceed 1.25 times ADP_{NHC}.

For example, if the average contribution is 1 percent for the nonhighly compensated, the average contribution for the highly compensated cannot exceed 2 percent. If the nonhighly compensated on average contributes 4 percent, the average contribution for the highly compensated cannot exceed 6 percent. And if the nonhighly compensated contributes as much as 10 percent, the highly compensated cannot contribute more than 12.5 percent. Note that the rule determines the maximum for the average among the highly compensated. As long as the average ADP for the group is less than or equal to the limit, an individual in the group can contribute in excess of the allowable percentage.

—Actual contribution percentage: The sum of employee and employer contributions as a percentage of compensation for the highly compensated (HC) cannot exceed that for the nonhighly compensated (NHC) by more than the allowable percentage.

To simplify nondiscrimination testing, the Small Business Job Protection Act of 1996 introduced "safe harbor" regulations. If a plan fulfills the safe harbor requirement it is automatically considered nondiscriminatory. The

6. The safe harbor concept was introduced in the Small Business Job Protection Act of 1996.

7. In addition to limits imposed by the Internal Revenue Code, many plans limit how much highly compensated employees can contribute to ensure that the plan will pass the nondiscrimination test without having to return contributions to highly compensated employees.

employer must meet one of the following two conditions for a safe harbor 401(k) plan:

—Employers match 100 percent of the first 3 percent of pay plus 50 percent of the next 2 percent of pay.

—Employers contribute 3 percent of pay to all employees' accounts whether the employee contributes or not.

In both cases, employers' contributions must vest immediately. Before EGTRRA the top-heavy rules required a minimum of 3 percent of pay for all 401(k) participants if 60 percent of the account balances were earned by key employees.

Restrictions on Withdrawals

Participants' withdrawals are restricted to ensure that savings in 401(k) plans are used for retirement.[8] Funds generally cannot be withdrawn before age fifty-nine-and-a-half, and at this time participants pay income taxes on the amount withdrawn. If money is taken out before this age a penalty of 10 percent is paid on the taxable amount withdrawn (in addition to income tax). However, workers between ages fifty-five and fifty-nine-and-a-half are exempted from the 10 percent penalty if the withdrawal is associated with retirement. Withdrawals that are based on life expectancy or made in the form of an annuity are exempt from penalty at any age. Before age fifty-nine-and-a-half and during employment, the worker can claim a distribution only in the case of hardship, which includes paying for medical expenses, paying for educational expenses, and buying a house. When workers leave their employers, the money in the account is usually withdrawn as a lump-sum distribution, even though alternative payment options may be available.

Because of the tax-exempt status of 401(k) plans, workers may want to leave their money in the plans to take advantage of the tax-preferred status or as a means to pass on the money in the form of a bequest. To ensure that 401(k) plans provide taxable retirement benefits, participants must start making minimum required withdrawals at retirement or at age seventy-and-a-half, whichever is later, or pay a penalty equal to 50 percent of the difference between the required payments and the actual payments.[9]

8. Withdrawals from 401(k) accounts before retirement are discussed in more detail in chapter 6 and withdrawals at retirement in chapter 7.

9. If the participant chooses to withdraw the account balance over a period of time but not in the form of an annuity, the minimum required payment is determined by dividing the participant's account balance by remaining life expectancy. The Portman-Cardin bill, "The Preservation and Savings Enhancement Act of 2003," introduced in the House of Representative in spring 2003, would increase the age at which withdrawals must start to age seventy-five.

References

Abel, Andrew. 2003. Comment on "How Do People Leave Bequests: Accidents or Purpose?" by Michael D. Hurd. In *Death and Dollars: The Role of Gifts and Bequests in America,* edited by Alicia H. Munnell and Annika Sundén, 93–117. Brookings.

Agnew Julie. 2001. "Inefficient Choices in 401(k) Plans: Evidence from Individual Level Data." Ph.D. dissertation, Boston College.

Agnew, Julie, Pierluigi Balduzzi, and Annika Sundén. 2003. "Portfolio Choice, Trading, and Returns in a Large 401(k) Plan." *American Economic Review* 93: 193–215.

Aizcorbe, Ana, Arthur B. Kennickell, and Kevin B. Moore. 2003. "Recent Changes in U.S. Family Finances: Evidence from the 1998 and 2001 Survey of Consumer Finances." *Federal Reserve Bulletin* (January): 1–32.

Allen, Steven, Robert Clark, and Ann McDermed. 1993. "Pensions, Bonding, and Lifetime Jobs." *Journal of Human Resources* 28 (3): 463–81.

American Council of Life Insurers. 2001a. *Life Insurance Fact Book.* Washington.

———. 2001b. *Public Perceptions of Retirement.* Washington.

———. 2002. *Promoting Annuitization.* Washington.

Ameriks, John. 1999. *The Retirement Patterns and Annuitization Decisions of a Cohort of TIAA-CREF Participants.* Research Dialogues 60. New York: TIAA-CREF Research Institute.

Ameriks, John, and Stephen P. Zeldes. 2001. "How Do Household Portfolio Shares Vary with Age?" Working Paper 6-120101. New York: TIAA-CREF Research Institute.

Anand, Vineeta. 1996. "Boxer's 401(k) Bill to Affect Few Plans." *Pensions & Investments*, June 10, p. 4.

Andrews, Emily S. 1992. "The Growth and Distribution of 401(k) Plans." In *Trends in Pensions 1992,* edited by John Turner and Daniel Beller, 14–76. U.S. Department of Labor.

Bajtelsmit, Vickie L., and Jack L. VenDerhei. 1997. "Risk Aversion and Pension Investment Choices." In *Positioning Pensions for the Twenty-First Century,* edited by Robert S. Gordon, Olivia S. Mitchell, and Marc M. Twinney, 45–66. University of Pennsylvania Press.

Banks, James, Richard Blundell, and Sarah Tanner. 1998. "Is There a Retirement-Savings Puzzle?" *American Economic Review* 88: 769–88.

Barber, Brad M., and Terrance Odean. 2000. "Trading Is Hazardous to Your Wealth: The Common Stock Investment Performance of Individual Investors." *Journal of Finance* 55 (2): 773–806.

———. 2001. "Boys Will Be Boys: Gender, Overconfidence, and Common Stock Investment." *Quarterly Journal of Economics* 116 (1): 261–92.

Barlow, Robin, Harvey E. Brazer, and James N. Morgan. 1966. *Economic Behavior of the Affluent.* Brookings.

Barsky, R. B., and others. 1997. "Preference Parameters and Behavioral Heterogeneity: An Experimental Approach in the Health and Retirement Study." *Quarterly Journal of Economics* 112 (2): 537–79.

Bayer, Patrick J., B. Douglas Bernheim, and John Karl Scholz. 1996. "The Effects of Financial Education in the Workplace: Evidence from a Survey of Employers." Working Paper 5655. Cambridge, Mass.: National Bureau of Economic Research.

Benartzi, Shlomo. 2001. "Excessive Extrapolation and the Allocation of 401(k) Accounts to Company Stock." *Journal of Finance* 56 (5): 1747–64.

Benartzi, Shlomo, and Richard H. Thaler. 2001. "Save More Tomorrow: Using Behavioral Economics to Increase Employee Saving." Working Paper. Center for International Business and Economic Research, University of California, Berkeley.

———. 2002. "How Much Is Investor Autonomy Worth?" *Journal of Finance* 57 (4): 1593–616.

Bernheim, B. Douglas, and Daniel M. Garrett. 1996. "The Determinants and Consequences of Financial Education in the Workplace: Evidence from a Survey of Households." Working Paper 5667. Cambridge, Mass.: National Bureau of Economic Research.

Bernheim, B. Douglas, Jonathan Skinner, and Steven Weinberg. 2001. "What Accounts for the Variation in Retirement Wealth among U.S. Households?" *American Economic Review* 91: 832–57.

Blake, Rich. 2001. "Bracing for a Backlash." *Institutional Investor* (November): 68–71.

Blasi, Joseph, Michael Conte, and Douglas Kruse. 1996. "Employee Stock Ownership and Corporate Performance among Public Companies." *Industrial and Labor Relations Review* 50 (1): 60–79.

Board of Governors of the Federal Reserve System. 2003. *2001 Survey of Consumer Finances.* Washington.

———. Various years. *Flow of Funds Accounts of the United States.* Washington.

Bodie, Zvi, and D. B. Crane. 1997. "Personal Investing: Advice Theory, and Evidence." *Financial Analysts Journal* 53 (6): 13–23.

Bodie, Zvi, and Robert C. Merton. 2000. *Finance.* Upper Saddle River, N.J.: Prentice-Hall.

Brown, Charles. 1980. "Equalizing Differences in the Labor Market." *Quarterly Journal of Economics* 94(1): 113–34.

Brown, Jeffrey R. 1999. "Are the Elderly Really Over-Annuitized? New Evidence on Life Insurance and Bequests." Working Paper 7193. Cambridge, Mass.: National Bureau of Economic Research.

———. 2000. "Taxing Retirement Income: The Case of Nonqualified Retirement Annuities." Paper prepared for Stanford Life Insurance taxation workshop, Washington, December.

———. 2001. *How Should We Insure Longevity Risk in Pensions and Social Security?* Issue in Brief 4. Chestnut Hill, Mass.: Center for Retirement Research, Boston College.

Brown, Jeffrey R., Olivia S. Mitchell, and James M. Poterba. 2001. "The Role of Real Annuities and Indexed Bonds in an Individual Accounts Retirement Program." In *Risk Aspects of Investment-Based Social Security Reform,* edited by John V. Campbell and Martin S. Feldstein, 321–70. University of Chicago Press.

Brown, Jeffrey R., and James M. Poterba. 2000. "Joint Life Annuities and Annuity Demand by Married Couples." *Journal of Risk and Insurance* 67 (4): 527–56.

Brown, Jeffrey R., and Mark J. Warshawsky. 2001. "Longevity-Insured Retirement Distributions from Pension Plans: Market and Regulatory Issues." Working Paper 7812. Cambridge, Mass.: National Bureau of Economic Research.

Brown, Jeffrey R., and others. 2001. *The Role of Annuity Markets in Financing Retirement.* MIT Press.

Bulow, Jeremy I. 1982. "What Are Corporate Pension Liabilities?" *Quarterly Journal of Economics* 97 (3): 435–52.

Bureau of Economic Analysis. 2002 National Income and Product Accounts Tables (www.bea.gov/bea/dn/nipaweb/Index.asp).

Bureau of Labor Statistics. 2003. Labor Force Statistics from the Current Population Survey (www.bls.gov/cps).

Burman, Leonard E., Norma B. Coe, and William G. Gale. 1999. "Lump Sum Distributions from Pension Plans: Recent Evidence and Issues for Policy and Research." *National Tax Journal* 52 (3): 553–62.

Burtless, Gary. 2000. *How Would Financial Risk Affect Retirement Income under Individual Accounts?* Issue in Brief 5. Chestnut Hill, Mass.: Center for Retirement Research, Boston College.

Burtless, Gary, and Joseph F. Quinn. 2001. "Retirement Trends and Policies to Encourage Work among Older Americans." In *Ensuring Health and Income Secu-*

rity for an Aging Workforce, edited by Peter P. Budetti and others, 375–415. Kalamazoo, Mich.: W. E. Upjohn Institute for Employment Research.

Campbell, John, Andrew Lo, and A. Craig MacKinlay. 1997. *The Econometrics of Financial Markets*. Princeton University Press.

Campbell, John Y., and Luis M. Viceira. 2002. *Strategic Asset Allocation: Portfolio Choice for Long-Term Investors*. Oxford University Press.

Carroll, Chris, and Lawrence H. Summers. 1991. "Consumption Growth Parallels Income Growth: Some New Evidence." In *National Saving and Economic Performance*, edited by B. Douglas Bernheim and John Shoven, 305–43. University of Chicago Press.

Chang, Angela E. 1996. "Tax Policy, Lump-Sum Pension Distributions, and Household Saving." *National Tax Journal* 49 (2): 235–52.

Choi, James J., and others. 2001a. "For Better or for Worse: Default Effects and 401(k) Savings Behavior." Working Paper 8651. Cambridge, Mass.: National Bureau of Economic Research.

———. 2001b. "Defined Contribution Pensions, and the Path of Least Resistance." Working Paper 8655. Cambridge, Mass.: National Bureau of Economic Research.

Clark, Robert L., and Sylvester J. Schieber. 1998. "Factors Affecting Participation Rates and Contribution Levels in 401(k) Plans." In *Living with Defined Contribution Plans: Remaking Responsibility*, edited by Olivia S. Mitchell and Sylvester J. Schieber, 69–97. University of Pennsylvania Press for the Pension Research Council.

———. 2002. "Taking the Subsidy out of Early Retirement: Converting to Hybrid Pensions." In *Innovations in Managing Financial Risk in Retirement*, edited by Olivia Mitchell and others, 149–74. University of Pennsylvania Press.

Clark, Robert L., and others. 2000. "Making the Most of 401(k) Plans: Who's Choosing What and Why?" In *Forecasting Retirement Needs and Retirement Wealth*, edited by Olivia S. Mitchell, P. Brett Hammond, and Anna M. Rappaport, 95–138. University of Pennsylvania Press for the Pension Research Council.

Coile, Courtney, and Jonathan Gruber. 2000. "Social Security and Retirement." Working Paper 7830. Cambridge, Mass.: National Bureau of Economic Research.

Copeland, Craig. 2001. *IRA Assets Continue to Grow*. EBRI Notes 1. Washington: Employee Benefit Research Institute.

———. 2002. *Lump-Sum Distributions: An Update*. EBRI Notes 7. Washington: Employee Benefit Research Institute.

Davidoff, Thomas, Jeffrey R. Brown, and Peter Diamond. 2002. "Annuities and Individual Welfare." Working Paper 9714. Cambridge, Mass.: National Bureau of Economic Research.

Diamond, Peter A. 1997. "Macroeconomic Aspects of Social Security Reform." *BPEA*, 2: 1–66.

———. 1999. *What Stock Market Returns to Expect for the Future*. Issue in Brief 2. Chestnut Hill, Mass.: Center for Retirement Research, Boston College.

Duflo, Esther, and Emmanuel Saez. 2002. "The Role of Information and Social Interactions in Retirement Plan Decisions." Working Paper 8885. Cambridge, Mass.: National Bureau of Economic Research.

Employee Benefit Research Institute. 2000. *History of 401(k) Plans*. Facts from EBRI (December). Washington.

———. 2001. "401(k) Plan Asset Allocation, Account Balances, and Loan Activity in 2000." Issue brief. November. Washington.

———. 2003. "401(k) Plan Asset Allocation, Account Balances, and Loan Activity in 2001." Issue brief. March. Washington.

———. Various years. *Pension Investment Report*. Washington.

Engelhart, Gary V. 1999. "Have 401(k)s Raised Household Saving? Evidence from the Health and Retirement Study." Paper 24. Aging Studies Program, Syracuse University.

Engen, Eric M., and William G. Gale. 1997. "Debt, Taxes, and the Effects of 401(k) Plans on Household Wealth Accumulation." Mimeo. Brookings.

———. 2000. "The Effects of 401(k) Plans on Household Wealth: Differences across Earnings Groups." Working Paper 8032. Cambridge, Mass.: National Bureau of Economic Research.

Engen, Eric M., William G. Gale, and John Karl Scholz. 1996. "The Illusory Effects of Savings Incentives on Saving." *Journal of Economic Perspectives* 10 (4): 113–38.

Engen, Eric M., William G. Gale, and Cori E. Uccello. 1999. "The Adequacy of Household Saving." *BPEA,* 2: 65–187.

ERIC (ERISA Industry Committee). 2002. "Statement on Investments in Employer Stock." Submitted to the Committee on Health, Education, Labor, and Pension, U.S. Senate (February 7).

Eschtruth, Andrew D.. and Jonathan Gemus. 2002. *Are Older Workers Responding to the Bear Market?* Just the Facts on Retirement Issues 5. Chestnut Hill, Mass.: Center for Retirement Research, Boston College.

Even, William, and David MacPherson. 2001. "How Will the Growth of DC and 401(k) Plans Affect Pension Income?" Working Paper. Department of Economics, Miami University.

Fama, E. F., and K. R. French. 1998. "Value versus Growth: The International Evidence." *Journal of Finance* 53 (6): 1975–99.

Farber, Henry S. 1996. "Are Lifetime Jobs Disappearing? Job Duration in the United States: 1973–1993." In *Labor Statistics Measurement Issues,* edited by John Haltiwanger, Marilyn Manser, and Robert Topel, 157–203. University of Chicago Press.

———. 1997. "Trends in Long-Term Employment Arrangements as a Response to Job Loss." Working Paper 384. Department of Economics, Princeton University.

Fetherstonhaugh, David, and Lee Ross. 1999. "Framing Effects and Income Flow Preferences." In *Behavioral Dimensions of Retirement Economics*, edited by Henry J. Aaron, 187–214. Brookings.

Fidelity Investments. 2002. *Building Futures.* Volume 3 supp., *Company Stock and 401(k) Plans: A Supplemental Report*. New York.

Fields, Gary S., and Olivia S. Mitchell. 1984. *Retirement, Pensions, and Social Security.* MIT Press.

Friedberg, Leora, and Anthony Webb. 2000. "The Impact of 401(k) Plans on Retirement." Discussion Paper 2000-30. Department of Economics, University of California, San Diego.

Gale, William G. 1999. "The Impact of Pensions and 401(k) Plans on Saving: A Critical Assessment of the State of the Literature." Paper prepared for Brookings, Stanford Institute for Economic Policy Research, and TIAA-CREF Institute conference, "ERISA after Twenty-Five Years," Washington, September 17.

Gale, William G., Leslie E. Papke, and Jack VanDerhei. 2004. "The Shifting Structure of Private Pensions: Evidence, Causes, and Consequences." In *The Evolving Pension System: Trends, Effects, and Proposals for Reform,* edited by William G. Gale, John B. Shoven, and Mark J. Warshawsky. Brookings.

Gebhardtsbauer, Ron. 1998. Testimony before the Advisory Council on Employee Welfare and Pension Benefits Plan, U.S. Department of Labor Task Force on Leakage, June 9.

———. 1999. "Hybrid Pension Plan Coverage: Retirement into the Twenty-First Century." Testimony before the Committee on Health, Education, Labor, and Pensions, U.S. Senate, September 21.

———. 2002. "Retirement Security and Defined Benefit Plans." Testimony before the Subcommittee on Oversight, Committee on Ways and Means, U.S. House of Representatives, June 20.

Ghilarducci, Teresa. 1992. *Labor's Capital: The Economics and Politics of Private Pensions.* MIT Press.

Gokhale, Jagadeesh, Laurence J. Kotlikoff, and Mark Warshawsky. 2002. "Life-Cycle Saving, Limits on Contributions to DC Plans, and Lifetime Tax Benefits." Working Paper W8170. Cambridge, Mass.: National Bureau of Economic Research.

Gottschalk, P., and R. Moffitt. 1999. "Changes in Job Instability and Insecurity Using Monthly Survey Data." *Journal of Labor Economics* 17 (4): S91–S126.

Gustman, Alan, and Thomas Steinmeier. 1992. "The Stampede toward Defined Contribution Pension Plans: Fact or Fiction?" *Industrial Relations* 31 (2): 361–69.

———. 1993. "Pension Portability and Labor Mobility: Evidence from the SIPP." *Journal of Public Economics* 50: 299–323.

Haider, Steven, and others. 2000. "Patterns of Dissaving in Retirement." Paper prepared for the AARP Public Policy Institute, Washington.

Halperin, Daniel. 1983. "Cash or Deferred Profit-Sharing Plans and Cafeteria Plans." *Proceedings of the New York University Forty-First Annual Institute of Federal Taxation,* 39.01–39.02.

Halperin, Daniel I., and Alicia H. Munnell. 2004. "Ensuring Retirement Income for All Workers." In *The Evolving Pension System: Trends, Effects, and Proposals for Reform,* edited by William G. Gale, John B. Shoven, and Mark J. Warshawsky. Brookings.

Halperin, Daniel I., and Marla Schnall. 2000. "Regulating Tax-Qualified Plans in a Hybrid World." *Proceedings of the Fifty-Eighth Institute on Federal Taxation: Employee Benefits and Executive Compensation,* chap. 5.

Hewitt Associates. 2001. *Trends and Experience in 401(k) Plans.* Lincolnshire, Ill.

Hinz, Richard P., David D. McCarthy, and John A. Turner. 1997. "Are Women Conservative Investors? Gender Differences in Participant-Directed Pension Investments." In *Positioning Pensions for the Twenty-First Century,* edited by Robert S. Gordon, Olivia S. Mitchell, and Marc M. Twinney, 91–103. University of Pennsylvania Press.

Hinz, Richard P., and John A. Turner. 1998. "Why Don't Workers Participate?" In *Living with Defined Contribution Plans: Remaking Responsibility,* edited by Olivia S. Mitchell and Sylvester J. Schieber, 17–37. University of Pennsylvania Press for the Pension Research Council.

Holden, Karen C., and Sean Nicholson. 1998. "A Selection of Joint and Survivor Pensions." Working paper. Madison, Wis.: Institute for Research on Poverty.

Holden, Sarah, and Jack VanDerhei. 2001a. *401(k) Plan Asset Allocation, Account Balances, and Loan Activity in 2000.* EBRI Issue Brief 239. Washington: Employee Benefit Research Institute.

———. 2001b. "The Impact of Employer-Selected Investment Options on 401(k) Plan Participants' Asset Allocations: Preliminary Findings." Washington: Employment Benefit Research Institute.

———. 2001c. *Contribution Behavior of 401(k) Plan Participants.* EBRI Issue Brief 238. Washington: Employee Benefit Research Institute.

———. 2002. *Can 401(k) Accumulations Generate Significant Income for Future Retirees?* EBRI Issue Brief 251. Washington: Employee Benefit Research Institute.

———. 2003. *401(k) Plan Asset Allocation, Account Balances, and Loan Activity in 2001.* EBRI Issue Brief 255. Washington: Employee Benefit Research Institute.

Hungerford, Thomas. 1999. "Saving for a Rainy Day: Does Pre-Retirement Access to Retirement Saving Increase Retirement Saving?" Department of Economics, American University.

Hurd, Michael D. 1987. "Savings of the Elderly and Desired Bequests." *American Economic Review* 77: 298–312.

———. 1989. "Mortality Risk and Bequests." *Econometrica* 57 (4): 779–813.

———. 1991. *The Income and Savings of the Elderly.* Final Report to the Andrus Foundation. Washington: American Association of Retired Persons.

———. 1992. "Wealth Depletion and Life-Cycle Consumption by the Elderly." In *Topics in the Economics of Aging,* edited by David A. Wise, 135–62. University of Chicago Press.

Hurd, Michael, Lee Lillard, and Constantijn Panis. 1998. "An Analysis of the Choice to Cash out, Maintain, or Annuitize Pension Rights at Job Change or Retirement." Santa Monica, Calif.: Rand.

Hurd, Michael, and Susanne Rohwedder. 2003 "The Retirement-Consumption Puzzle: Anticipated and Actual Declines in Spending at Retirement." Working Paper 9586. Cambridge, Mass.: National Bureau of Economic Research.

Hustead, Edwin C. 1998. "Trends in Retirement Income Plan Administrative Expenses." In *Living with Defined Contribution Plans: Remaking Responsibility,* edited by Olivia S. Mitchell and Sylvester J. Schieber, 166–77. University of Pennsylvania Press for the Pension Research Council.

Ibbotson Associates. 2003. *Stocks, Bonds, Bills, and Inflation 2002 Yearbook.* Chicago.

Illinois Municipal Retirement Fund. 1999. "The Defined Benefit versus Defined Contribution Debate: The $250 Million Question." Oak Brook, Ill.

Institute of Management and Administration. 2001. *DC Plan Investing.* December. New York.

Investment Company Institute. 2000. *401(k) Plan Participants: Characteristics, Contributions, and Account Activity.* Washington.

———. 2001. "401(k) Plan Asset Allocation, Account Balances, and Loan Activity in 2000." *ICI Perspective* 7 (5).

———. 2002. "Mutual Funds and the U.S. Retirement Market in 2001." *Fundamentals* 11 (2): 1–2.

———. 2003. "401(k) Plan Asset Allocation, Account Balances, and Loan Activity in 2001." *ICI Perspective* 9 (2).

Ippolito, Richard A. 1993. *Selecting and Retaining High-Quality Workers: A Theory of 401(k) Pensions.* Philadelphia: Pension Benefit Guaranty Corporation.

———. 1995. "Toward Explaining the Growth of Defined Contribution Plans." *Industrial Relations* 34 (1): 1–19.

———. 1997. *Pension Plans and Employee Performance.* University of Chicago Press.

———. 1999. "The New Pension Economics: Defined Contribution Plans and Sorting." Paper prepared for EBRI policy forum on the next twenty-five years of ERISA.

Iyengar, Sheena S., and Mark R. Lepper. 2000. "When Choice Is Demotivating: Can One Desire Too Much of a Good Thing?" *Journal of Personality and Social Psychology* 79 (6): 995–1006.

Jacobius, Arleen. 2001. "P&G Debuts New, Improved DC Plan." *Pensions & Investments* (July 9): 1.

Jaeger, D. A., and A. H. Stevens. 1999. "Is Job Stability in the United States Falling? Reconciling Trends in the Current Population Survey and Panel Study of Income Dynamics." *Journal of Labor Economics* 17 (4): S1–S28.

Jagannathan, R., and N. R Kocherlakota. 1996. "Why Should Older People Invest Less in Stocks than Younger People?" *Federal Reserve Bank of Minneapolis Quarterly Review* 20 (3): 11–23.

John Hancock Financial Services. 2002. "Insight into Participant Investment Knowledge and Behavior." *Eighth Annual Defined Contribution Plan Survey.* Boston.

Kotlikoff, Laurence J., and Avia Spivak. 1981. "The Family as an Incomplete Annuities Market." *Journal of Political Economy* 89 (2): 372–91.

Kotlikoff, Laurence J., and Lawrence H. Summers. 1981. "The Role of Intergenerational Transfers in Aggregate Capital Formation." *Journal of Political Economy* 89 (4): 706–32.

Kotlikoff, Laurence, and David A. Wise. 1987. "The Incentive Effects of Private Pension Plans." In *Issues in Pension Economics,* edited by Zvi Bodie, John Shoven, and David A. Wise, 283–339. University of Chicago Press.

———. 1989. "Employee Retirement and a Firm's Pension Plan." In *The Economics of Aging*, edited by David A. Wise, 279–330. University of Chicago Press.

Kruse, Douglas L. 1995. "Pension Substitution in the 1980's: Why the Shift toward Defined Contribution Plans?" *Industrial Relations* 34 (2): 218–41.

———. 2002. "Research Evidence on Prevalence and Effects of Employee Ownership." Testimony before the Subcommittee on Employer-Employee Relations, Committee on Education and the Work Force, U.S. House of Representatives, February 13.

Kruse, Douglas, and Joseph Blasi. 1997. "Employee Ownership, Employee Attitudes, and Firm Performance: A Review of the Evidence." In *Human Resources Management Handbook*, pt. 1, edited by David Lewin, Daniel J. B. Mitchell, and Mahmood A. Zaidi, 113–51. JAI Press.

Kusko, Andrea L., James M. Poterba, and David W. Wilcox. 1998. "Employee Decisions with Respect to 401(k) Plans." In *Living with Defined Contribution Plans: Remaking Resonsibility*, edited by Olivia S. Mitchell and Sylvester J. Schieber, 98–112. University of Pennsylvania Press for the Pension Research Council.

Lachance, Marie-Eve, and Olivia S. Mitchell. 2003. "Understanding Individual Account Guarantees." Working Paper 2003-2. Pension Research Council, University of Pennsylvania.

Laibson, David, Andrea Repetto, and Jeremy Tobacman. 1998. "Self Control and Saving for Retirement." *BPEA*, 1: 91–196.

Laitner, John, and F. Thomas Juster. 1996. "New Evidence on Altruism: A Study of TIAA-CREF Retirees." *American Economic Review* 86: 893–908.

Lazear, Edward. 1979. "Why Is There Mandatory Retirement?" *Journal of Political Economy* 87 (6): 1261–84.

———. 1983. "Pensions as Severance Pay." In *Financial Aspects of the United States Pension System*, edited by Zvi Bodie and John Shoven, 57–90. University of Chicago Press.

———. 1985. "Incentive Effects of Pensions." In *Pensions, Labor, and Individual Choice*, edited by David A. Wise, 253–82. University of Chicago Press.

Liang, Nellie, and Scott Weisbenner. 2002. "Investor Behavior and the Purchase of Company Stock in 401(k) Plans: The Importance of Plan Design." Working Paper 9131. Cambridge, Mass.: National Bureau of Economic Research.

LIMRA International. 2002. *The 2001 Individual Annuity Market: Sales and Assets.* Windsor, Conn.

Loewenstein, George. 1999. *Is More Choice Always Better?* Social Security brief. Washington: National Academy of Social Insurance.

Lumsdaine, Robin, James Stock, and David A. Wise. 1992. "Three Models of Retirement: Computational Complexity versus Predictive Validity." In *Topics in the Economics of Aging*, edited by David A. Wise, 19–60. University of Chicago Press.

Madrian, Brigitte C., and Dennis F. Shea. 2002. "The Power of Suggestion: Inertia in 401(k) Participation and Savings Behavior." *Quarterly Journal of Economics* 116 (4): 1149–87.

Malkiel, Burton G. 1991. *A Random Walk Down Wall Street: Including a Life-Cycle Guide to Personal Investing.* Norton.

Markowitz, Harry M. 1991. "Foundations of Portfolio Theory." *Journal of Finance* 46 (2): 469–77.

McGill, Dan M., and others. 1996. *Fundamentals of Private Pensions.* 7th ed. University of Pennsylvania Press.

Mehra, Rajnish, and Edward Prescott. 1985. "The Equity Premium Puzzle." *Journal of Monetary Economics* 15: 145–61.

Meulbroek, Lisa. 2002. "Company Stocks in Pension Plans: How Costly Is It?" Working Paper. Harvard Business School.

Miller, Lynn. 2002. *The Ongoing Growth of Defined Contribution and Individual Account Plans: Issues and Implications.* EBRI Issue Brief 243. Washington: Employee Benefit Research Institute.

Mitchell, Olivia, and others. 1999. "New Evidence on the Money's Worth of Individual Annuities." *American Economic Review* 89: 1299–318.

Moore, James H., Jr., and Leslie A. Muller. 2002. "An Analysis of Lump-Sum Pension Distribution Recipients." *Monthly Labor Review* (May): 29–46.

Morris, Kenneth M., Alan M. Spiegel, and Virginia B. Morris. 1998. *The Wall Street Journal Guide to Planning Your Financial Future.* New York: Lightbulb Press.

Munnell, Alicia H. 1976. "Private Pensions and Saving: New Evidence." *Journal of Political Economy* 84 (5): 1013–32.

———. 1982. *The Economics of Private Pensions.* Brookings.

———. 2003. *The Declining Role of Social Security.* Just the Facts on Retirement Issues 6. Chestnut Hill, Mass.: Center for Retirement Research, Boston College.

Munnell, Alicia H., Kevin E. Cahill, and Natalia A. Jivan. 2003. *How Has the Shift to 401(k)s Affected the Retirement Age?* Issue in Brief 13. Chestnut Hill, Mass.: Center for Retirement Research, Boston College.

Munnell, Alicia H., Annika Sundén, and Catherine Taylor. 2002 *What Determines 401(k) Participation and Contributions?* Social Security Bulletin 64.

Munnell, Alicia H., and others. 2003. "The Impact of Defined Contribution Plans on Bequests." In *Death and Dollars: The Role of Gifts and Bequests in America,* edited by Alicia H. Munnell and Annika Sundén, 265–318. Brookings.

Murtaugh, Christopher, and others. 1997. "The Amount, Distribution, and Timing of Lifetime Nursing Home Use." *Medical Care* 35 (3): 204–18.

Myers, Stuart C. 1984. "The Capital Structure Puzzle." *Journal of Finance* 39: 575–92.

Neumark, D., D. Polsky, and D. Hansen. 1999. "Has Job Stability Declined Yet? New Evidence from the 1990s." *Journal of Labor Economics* 17 (4): S29–S64.

O'Donoghue, Ted, and Matthew Rabin. 1999. "Doing It Now or Later," *American Economic Review* 89: 103–24.

Papke, Leslie E. 1995. "Participation and Contributions to 401(k) Pension Plans." *Journal of Human Resources* 30 (2): 311–25.

Papke, Leslie, Mitchell Petersen, and James Poterba. 1996. "Do 401(k) Plans Replace Other Employer Provided Pensions?" In *Advances in the Economics of Aging*, edited by David A. Wise, 219–40. University of Chicago Press.

Papke, Leslie E., and James M. Poterba. 1995. "Survey Evidence on Employer Match Rates and Employee Saving Behavior in 401(k) Plans." *Economic Letters* 49 (3): 313–17.

Poterba, James, and L. Summers. 1988. "Mean Reversion in Stock Returns: Evidence and Implications." *Journal of Financial Economics* 22 (1): 27–59.

Poterba, James M., Steven F. Venti, and David A. Wise. 1994. "401(k) Plans and Tax-Deferred Saving." In *Studies in the Economics of Aging*, edited by David A. Wise, 105–42. University of Chicago Press.

———. 1995a. "Do 401(k) Contributions Crowd out Other Personal Saving?" *Journal of Public Economics* 58: 1–32.

———. 1995b. "Lump-Sum Distributions from Retirement Savings Plans: Receipt and Utilization." Working Paper 5298. Cambridge, Mass.: National Bureau of Economic Research.

———. 1998. "Personal Retirement Saving Programs and Asset Accumulation: Reconciling the Evidence." In *Frontiers in the Economics of Aging*, edited by David A. Wise, 23–24. University of Chicago Press.

——— 1999. "Pre-Retirement Cashouts and Forgone Retirement Saving: Implications for 401(k) Asset Accumulation." Working Paper 7314. Cambridge, Mass.: National Bureau of Economic Research.

———. 2001. "The Transition to Personal Accounts and Increasing Retirement Wealth: Macro and Micro Evidence." Working Paper 8610. Cambridge, Mass.: National Bureau of Economic Research.

President's Commission to Strengthen Social Security. 2001. *Strengthening Social Security and Creating Personal Wealth for All Americans.*

Profit Sharing/401(k) Council of America. 2001. *Automatic Enrollment 2001: A Study of Automatic Enrollment Practices in 401(k) Plans.* Chicago.

———. 2002. *Forty-Fifth Annual Survey of Profit Sharing and 401(k) Plans.* Chicago.

Projector, Dorothy S., and Gertrude S. Weiss. 1966. *Survey of Financial Characteristics of Consumers.* Board of Governors of the Federal Reserve System.

Purcell, Patrick J. 2000. *Pension Issues: Lump-Sum Distributions and Retirement Income Security.* Report, March 27. Congressional Research Service.

———. 2002a. *Employer Stock in Retirement Plans: Bills in the 107th Congress.* Report, March 28. Congressional Research Service.

———. 2002b. *The Enron Bankruptcy and Employer Stock in Retirement Plans.* Report, January 22. Congressional Research Service.

———. 2003a. *Employer Stock in Retirement Plans: Investment Risk and Retirement Security.* Report, January 28. Congressional Research Service.

———. 2003b. "Retirement Savings and Household Wealth in 2000: Analysis of Census Bureau Data." *Journal of Pension Planning and Compliance* 29 (2): 48–76.

PWBA (Pension and Welfare Benefits Administration). 1997. *Report of the Working Group on Employer Assets in ERISA Employer-Sponsored Plans.* Final report, November 13. U.S. Department of Labor.

———. 1998. *Study of 401(k) Plan Fees and Expenses.* Final report, April 13. U.S. Department of Labor.

Quinn, Jane Bryant. 1997. *Making the Most of Your Mo*ney. Simon and Schuster.

Richardson, David, and David Joulfaian, 2001. "Who Takes Advantage of Tax-Deferred Savings Programs? Evidence from Federal Income Tax Data." Office of Tax Analysis, U.S. Treasury Department.

Sabelhouse, John, and David Weiner. 1999. "Disposition of Lump-Sum Pension Distributions: Evidence from Tax Returns." *National Tax Journal* 52 (3): 593–614.

Salop, Joanne, and Steven Salop. 1976. "Self-Selection and Turnover in the Labor Market." *Quarterly Journal of Economics* 90 (4): 620–27.

Samwick, Andrew. 1998. "New Evidence on Pensions, Social Security, and the Timing of Retirement." *Journal of Public Economics* 70: 207–36.

Samwick, Andrew, and Jonathan Skinner. 2001. "How Will Defined Contribution Pension Plans Affect Retirement Income?" Working Paper 6645. Cambridge, Mass.: National Bureau of Economic Research.

Sass, Steven A. 1997. *The Promise of Private Pensions.* Harvard University Press.

Sengmuller, Paul. 2001. "Performance Predicts Asset Allocation: Company Stock in 401(k) Plans." Working Paper. Department of Economics, Columbia University.

Skolnik, Alfred M. 1976 *Private Pension Plans.* Social Security Bulletin 39.

Smiley, Robert W., and Gregory K. Brown. 2001. "Employee Stock Ownership Plans." In *Handbook of Employee Benefits*, edited by Jerry S. Rosenbloom, 681–740. McGraw-Hill.

Stewart, J. 2002. "Recent Trends in Job Stability and Job Security: Evidence from the March CPS." Working Paper 356. U.S. Bureau of Labor Statistics.

Stock, James H., and David A. Wise. 1990a. "Pensions, the Option Value of Work, and Retirement." *Econometrica* 58 (5): 1151–80.

———. 1990b. "The Pension Inducement to Retire: An Option Value Analysis." In *Issues in the Economics of Aging*, edited by David A. Wise, 205–30. University of Chicago Press.

Sundén, Annika, and Brian J. Surette. 1998. "Gender Differences in the Allocation of Assets in Retirement Savings Plans." *American Economic Review* 88: 207–11.

———. 2000. *Household Borrowing from 401(k) Plans.* Just the Facts on Retirement Issues 1. Chestnut Hill, Mass.: Center for Retirement Research, Boston College.

Thaler, Richard H. 1994a. "Psychology and Savings Policies." *American Economic Review* 84: 186–92.

———. 1994b. "Some Empirical Evidence on Dynamic Inconsistency." Reprint. In *Quasi-Rational Economics*, edited by Richard H. Thaler, 127–36. Russell Sage Foundation.

Turner, John A., and David M. Rajnes. 2002. "Retirement Guarantees in Voluntary Defined Contribution Plans." Working Paper 2002-21. Pension Research Council, University of Pennsylvania.

Tversky, Amos, and Daniel Kahneman. 1974. "Judgment under Uncertainty: Heuristics and Biases." *Science* 185: 1124–31.

Uccello, Cori E. 2000. "401(k) Investment Decisions and Social Security Reform." Working Paper 2000-04. Chestnut Hill, Mass.: Center for Retirement Research, Boston College.

U.S. Bureau of the Census. 1995, 2002. *Statistical Abstract.*

———. Various years. *Current Population Survey.*

U.S. Department of Labor. 1998. *Employee Benefits in Medium and Large Establishments 1995.* Bureau of Labor Statistics Bulletin 2496.

———. 1999. *Employee Benefits in Medium and Large Establishments 1997.* Bureau of Labor Statistics Bulletin 2517.

———. 2001–02. *Abstract of 1998 Form 5500 Annual Reports.* Private Pension Plan Bulletin.

———. 2003. *National Compensation Survey: Employee Benefits in the Private Industry in the United States, 2000.* Bureau of Labor Statistics Bulletin 2555.

U.S. General Accounting Office. 1986. *Employee Stock Ownership Plans: Benefits and Costs of ESOP Tax Incentives for Broadening Stock Ownership.* GAO/PEMD-87-8.

———. 1997. *401(k) Pension Plans: Loan Provisions Enhance Participation but May Affect Income Security for Some.*

———. 1999. *Implications of Private Annuities for Individual Accounts.* GAO/HEHS-99-160.

———. 2001. *Private Pensions: Issues of Coverage and Increasing Contribution Limits for Defined Contribution Plans.* GAO-01-846.

U.S. Internal Revenue Service. 1988–2002. *Data Book.* Publication 55B.

U.S. Social Security Administration. 2002a. *Income of the Aged Chartbook.*

———. 2002b. *The 2002 Annual Report of the Board of Trustees of the Old Age, Survivors and Disability Insurance Trust Funds.*

———. 2003. *The 2003 Annual Report of the Board of Trustees of the Old Age, Survivors and Disability Insurance Trust Funds.*

VanDerhei, Jack. 2002. "The Role of Company Stock in 401(k) Plans." Written statement for the House Education and Work Force Committee Hearing, "Enron and Beyond: Enhancing Worker Retirement Security" (February 13). Washington: Employee Benefit Research Institute.

VanDerhei, Jack, and Craig Copeland. 2001. *The Changing Face of Private Retirement Plans.* EBRI Issue Brief 232. Washington: Employee Benefit Research Institute.

VanDerhei, Jack L., and Kelly A. Olsen. 2001. "Section 401(k) Plans (Cash or Deferred Arrangements) and Thrift Plans." In *The Handbook of Employee Benefits: Design, Funding, and Administration,* edited by Jerry S. Rosenbloom, 496–560. McGraw-Hill.

Vanguard Center for Retirement Research. 2001. "Automatic Enrollment: Vanguard Client Experience." Valley Forge, Pa.

Warshawsky, Mark J. 1995. "Determinants of Pension Plan Formation and Termination." *Benefits Quarterly.* Fourth quarter: 71–80.

Warshawsky, Mark J., and John Ameriks. 2000. "How Prepared Are Americans for Retirement?" In *Forecasting Retirement Needs and Retirement Wealth*, edited by Olivia S. Mitchell, P. Brett Hammond, and Anna M. Rappaport, 33–67. University of Pennsylvania Press for the Pension Research Council.

Watson Wyatt Worldwide. 2002. "Pension Conversions Slow among Fortune 100." *Employee Benefit Review* 57 (1): 47.

Weisbenner, Scott. 1999. "Do Pension Plans with Participant Choice Teach Households to Hold More Equity?" Working Paper 1999-61. Board of Governors of the Federal Reserve System.

Williams, Fred. 1988. "IRS Ruling Hits A&P; Restructuring Led to Partial Termination." *Pensions and Investment Age* (December): 38.

Wolman, William, and Anne Colamosca. 2002. *The Great 401(k) Hoax*. Perseus Printing.

Yaari, Menahem E. 1964. "On the Consumer's Lifetime Allocation Process." *International Economic Review* 5 (3): 304-17.

———. 1965. "Uncertain Lifetime, Life Insurance, and the Theory of the Consumer." *Review of Economic Studies* 32: 137–50.

Yohalem, Martha R. 1977. *Employee Benefit Plans, 1975.* Social Security Bulletin 40.

Index